Poetry and Dialogism

Poetry and Dialogism

Hearing Over

Edited by

Mara Scanlon
University of Mary Washington, USA

and

Chad Engbers
Calvin College, USA

First published 2014 by
PALGRAVE MACMILLAN

Palgrave Macmillan in the UK is an imprint of Macmillan Publishers Limited,
registered in England, company number 785998, of Houndmills, Basingstoke,
Hampshire RG21 6XS.

Palgrave Macmillan in the US is a division of St Martin's Press LLC,
175 Fifth Avenue, New York, NY 10010.

Palgrave Macmillan is the global academic imprint of the above companies
and has companies and representatives throughout the world.

Palgrave® and Macmillan® are registered trademarks in the United States,
the United Kingdom, Europe and other countries.

ISBN 978–1–137–40127–4

This book is printed on paper suitable for recycling and made from fully
managed and sustained forest sources. Logging, pulping and manufacturing
processes are expected to conform to the environmental regulations of the
country of origin.

A catalogue record for this book is available from the British Library.

Library of Congress Cataloging-in-Publication Data
Poetry and dialogism : hearing over / edited by Mara Scanlon, University of
Mary Washington, Fredericksburg, USA ; Chad Engbers, Calvin College,
Grand Rapids, USA.

pages cm

Includes index.
ISBN 978–1–137–40127–4   (hardback)
1. Poetry—History and criticism—Theory, etc.   2. Dialogism (Literary
analysis)   3. Poetics.   4. Literature and morals.   I. Scanlon, Mara, editor.
II. Engbers, Chad, editor.
PN1035.P64 2014
808.1—dc23   2014019772

Typeset by MPS Limited, Chennai, India.

For Christo, Kirby, and Julia

and in memory of John Graham—still, and always,
the superaddressee

mns

For Susanna and Liam

cae

Contents

Acknowledgements

Sincere thanks are due to our attentive support team at Palgrave Macmillan, most expressly Ben Doyle and Sophie Ainscough, and to Dean Richard Finkelstein and Provost Jonathan Levin of the University of Mary Washington for their willingness to provide financial support for some costs of production. The University of Mary Washington also awarded a sabbatical leave that allowed this project to take root. Additionally, the editors gratefully acknowledge Oxford University Press and the *Dalhousie Review* for granting permission to reprint material.

To the Camerons and Scanlons: Is é an teaghlach gach rud. And with gratitude for all those who said *you can but you don't have to*: Mary Rigsby, Gary Richards, Christi Carver, Jennifer Armini, Janet Evans, Kelli Maloy, Amanda Rutstein, Jim Groom, Claudia Emerson, Leslie Martin, Nick Yasinski, and, especially, Jackie Gallagher, Tracy Citeroni, Chris Foss, and Donna Lisker.

Notes on Contributors

Temple Cone is Associate Professor of English at the United States Naval Academy and is the author of three prize-winning books of poetry: *That Singing* (2011), *The Broken Meadow* (2010), and *No Loneliness* (2009). He has published articles on the poets Robinson Jeffers, Ciaran Carson, and Les Murray.

Tom Dolack is currently a Visiting Assistant Professor of Russian at Wheaton College in Norton, MA. He graduated with a Ph.D. in Comparative Literature from the University of Oregon in 2007. His research interests include translation studies, theories of imitation, Renaissance and twentieth-century European poetry, and Russian literature. He is currently working on a book on imitation and the work of the Russian poet Osip Mandelstam.

Chad Engbers is Associate Professor of English at Calvin College in Grand Rapids, MI, where he teaches Renaissance and Russian literature. His scholarship focuses on penitential poetry from early modern England, drawing from the theories of Mikhail Bakhtin, and most recently early modern alchemy. He is currently working on an alchemical reading of John Donne's Holy Sonnets.

Geoffrey Lindsay is Associate Professor of English at the University of Prince Edward Island, where he teaches contemporary poetry and literary theory. His articles on contemporary poets have appeared in *The Yale Review*, *The Sewanee Review*, and *Twentieth Century Literature*. His latest essays are on Anthony Hecht's World War II experiences in Europe and Japan.

Stephen Pierson holds a Ph.D. in Comparative Literature from Purdue University. His dissertation, "A Bakhtinian Reading of a Selection of Poems by Hölderlin and Whitman" (2010), contains a 160-item bibliography on Bakhtinian studies in poetry. A 2013 recipient of the State University of New York (SUNY) Chancellor's Award for Excellence in Scholarship and Creative Activities, Pierson teaches composition and American literature at Onondaga Community College in Syracuse, New York, where he is Professor of English.

Mara Scanlon, Professor of English at the University of Mary Washington, specializes in poetry and poetics, women's literature, ethics and literature, and digital humanities. Selected work includes articles on Robert

Hayden and the dialogic lyric and on Derek Walcott's heteroglossic epic, as well as publications on H.D., Grace Nichols, Claudia Emerson, and Walt Whitman. She was part of the 2008–2010 National Endowment for the Humanities-funded project "Looking for Whitman."

Andrea Witzke Slot is the author of the poetry collection *To Find a New Beauty* (2012) and her creative work appears in such places as *Tupelo Quarterly*, *Spoon River Poetry Review*, *Mezzo Cammin*, *PENA International*, *Verse Daily*, and *Borderlands: Texas Poetry Review*. Her fiction explores the dialogic exchange between prose and poetry while her scholarly work investigates dialogic poetry as a multi-leveled source of social change, including a chapter in the critical collection *Inhabiting "La Patria": Identity, Agency, and "Antoo" in the Work of Julia Alvarez* (2013). Slot teaches at the University of Illinois at Chicago and is both an editor at *Rhino Poetry* and the book review editor at *Fifth Wednesday Journal*.

James D. Sullivan has written extensively on modern and contemporary American poetry, especially in unusual publishing formats. He is the author of *On the Walls and in the Streets: American Poetry Broadsides from the 1960s* (1997). His articles have appeared in *Jacket 2*, *MimeoMimeo*, *African American Review*, *Contemporary Literature*, *Twentieth-Century Literature*, and *Journal of the Midwest Modern Language Association*, as well as in several collections, including *Will Teach for Food: Academic Labor in Crisis* (1997), *White Scholars/African American Texts* (2005), and *Cary Nelson and the Struggle for the University: Poetry, Politics, and the Profession* (2009). He is the co-editor of *Bluffs Literary Magazine*, has a radio show called *Poets' Voices*, and teaches English at Illinois Central College.

Erin Trapp lives in Minneapolis and teaches at the University of Wisconsin–River Falls. She is currently completing a book project entitled *Estranging Lyric*, which explores the problem of European civilian guilt by looking at reconstructions of the lyric subject in postwar poetry. She has published articles on poetics and psychoanalysis in *MLN*, *Postmodern Culture*, and *Cultural Critique*.

William Waters is the author of *Poetry's Touch: On Lyric Address* (2003) and numerous critical articles on related and other subjects; he is completing a study of Rilke's *New Poems*. Fellowships from the National Endowment for the Humanities, the Mellon Foundation, the DAAD, and the Boston University Center for the Humanities have supported his work. He teaches German and Comparative Literature at Boston University, where he is Associate Director of the Center for the Study of Europe and served as the founding chair of the Department of Modern Languages and Comparative Literature.

1

Introduction: Hearing Over

Mara Scanlon

The poet Paul Celan wrote, "The poem wants to reach an Other, it needs this Other, it needs an Over-against. It seeks it out, speaks toward it" (*Selected* 409). Claiming for poems an inherent addressivity—an awareness of the listener or interlocutor, and an anticipation of other voices, minds, or responses—Celan challenges what has become a commonplace contemporary assumption about the genre of poetry (or, more precisely, about the personal lyric, which is often taken as poetry's default form): that it is private, that it is primarily for and about self-reflection and self-expression. But what if Celan's became our new model for reading lyric or, indeed, all poetry? How would we think about the poetic speaker or voice, the forms and traditions of poetry, the personal and sociopolitical purposes of poetry, or the ethics of poetic address and of reading practices? What would this new poetry look like—or is it the poetry we've known all along?

The tradition of poetics that Celan's assertion interrogates is frequently traced back to the powerful influence of the Romantic poets, who turned to and established the lyric as the vehicle for personal expression, theorizing poetry in language that is still frequently invoked—the unmediated "*cri du cœur*," or Wordsworth's "emotion recollected in tranquility."[1] John Stuart Mill's significant and oft-cited theory of poetry, worth reading at some length if only for being what Virginia Jackson has called "the most influentially misread essay in the history of Anglo-American poetics" (9), insists that poetry's central core is personal emotion and that putting such emotion into language will not, or must not, modify or mediate it; but he also insists, importantly, that the reader or listener is not only secondary to the poem but even unwelcome there, a lurking or intrusive presence whose

1

acknowledgement, accommodation, or response actually transforms the utterance itself from poetry to mere "eloquence":

> Poetry and eloquence are both alike the expression or utterance of feeling. But if we may be excused the antithesis, we should say that eloquence is *heard*, poetry is *over*heard. Eloquence supposes an audience; the peculiarity of poetry appears to us to lie in the poet's utter unconsciousness of a listener. Poetry is feeling, confessing itself to itself in moments of solitude, and embodying itself in symbols, which are the nearest possible representations of the feeling in the exact shape in which it exists in the poet's mind. Eloquence is feeling pouring itself out to other minds, courting their sympathy, or endeavoring to influence their belief, or move them to passion or to action.
>
> All poetry is of the nature of soliloquy [. . . N]o trace of consciousness that any eyes are upon us must be visible in the work itself [. . . W]hen he turns around and addresses himself to another person; when the act of utterance is not itself the end, but a means to an end—viz. by the feelings he himself expresses, to work upon the feelings, or upon the belief, or the will, of another—when the expression of his emotions, or of his thoughts tinged by his emotions, is tinged also by that purpose, by that desire of making an impression upon another mind, then it ceases to be poetry, and becomes eloquence. (348–49)

Mill's figure of the poetic reader or listener as an eavesdropper onto what the poet rightfully tries to conceal is affirmed nearly 125 years later by the prominent literary theorist Northrop Frye, who says that the "poet [. . .] turns his back on his listeners" (250), and arguably has been an underlying truism of considerable literary criticism.

This volume's founding assumption is that we must listen again to what poetry is saying, by whom and to whom, not by lurking at keyholes and around corners, but by taking as a given the possibility that poetry may be dialogic and engaged rather than monologic and private, that it may even be heteroglossic in its truest sense, containing different or even clashing discourses without muting them in some singular and finalized "soliloquy."

The direct or indirect addressivity of a poem, and the responsiveness of its real or projected readers or listeners—what William Waters has called "the written word's demand for encounter, for real relationship, presence, even intimacy" ("Answerable" 147)—are only some of the ways that we might conceive of a poem's dialogism, the traces of its awareness of the Other (mind, voice, text, ideology, being, utterance). "Dialogism" is not a term that is employed narrowly; though it may or may not play out in speech acts attributable to separate speakers (what we might more narrowly call dialogue in a play or novel, for example), all understandings of dialogism include the idea of some sort of exchange (of ideas, of words) between two or more identifiably separate beings or articulations.[2] Dialogue may thus be traceable between voices, allusions, or discourses in a text (not simply juxtaposed, but impinging upon or shaping one another to some degree), or in the production or reading practice of the poem (for example, the reader's response to or answerability for it, including possibly the way in which the poem anticipates, demands, or even enacts that response). It may be based less in voice, allusion, or citation than in a fundamental representation of, orientation toward, or response to otherness, as indicated by theorists such as Martin Buber or Emmanuel Levinas, or it may be traced in rhythm, intonation, form, or other poetic devices that encode or signal such otherness or exchange.

But in any of these cases, what is interrogated at its essence is the pervasive, central assumption that poetry is fundamentally one of two things: in lyric poetry, an expression of subjective, personal, isolated experience, a transcendent and self-sufficient *cri du cœur;* or, in epic poetry, a normalizing, impersonal, authoritative treatise or record which, guided by its confident cultural mandate, will not accommodate others' voices and needs. Ironically, of course, these models of lyric and epic poetry are oppositional and create a reductive binary between two primary poetic modes, and yet both are functional, widely accepted, and used to combat the suggestion that poetry may be dialogic. In addition to the strict parameters for lyric poetry established by critics like Mill and Frye, the most notorious naysayer of poetic dialogism, and particularly epic dialogism, is the Russian social, linguistic, and literary theorist Mikhail Mikhailovich Bakhtin, who insists that, although the poet may be aware "as a human being surrounded by living hetero- and polyglossia" of the relationship that exists between discourses, "this relationship could not find a place in the *poetic style* of his work without destroying that style [. . .] and in the process turning the poet into a writer of prose," which echoes Mill's discussion of (lyric) poetry and eloquence very closely ("Discourse" 285). In both cases, to become dialogic is to become something else, something that is ill-defined but is fundamentally not-poetry.

A few thinkers who have most meaningfully examined the possibilities for a truly dialogic poetry may be used to represent some of the established arguments for including the genre in dialogic criticism. To date many have done so by engaging Bakhtin's logic and his wider theories of language and being. David H. Richter, for instance, in his foundational 1990 article "Dialogism and Poetry," reviews Bakhtin's strictures against the genre, which in some texts Bakhtin dismisses as inherently monologic (preferring instead the revolutionary, dialogized, and social genre of the novel) but in others seems to accept. Nevertheless, as I have also noted, literary criticism using Bakhtin has been completely dominated by analysis of prose, turning Bakhtin's own limitations into a working maxim. Drawing on Ralph Radar's methodical and rich 1976 essay, "The Dramatic Monologue and Related Lyric Forms," Richter considers the possible relationships between the poet or self and the speaker in various poetic traditions, weighing for each the extent to which the self may be represented as other, as an objectified or decentralized being in dialogic relation to the reader or other voices/centers of consciousness in the poem. Employing Bakhtin's terminology for language that is dialogized, double-voiced, or resistant, Richter concludes that Bakhtin's own discussion of "poetry" is less authoritative than a "word with a loophole" or a "sidelong glance."

Also endorsing the application of Bakhtinian theory to poetry in his 2002 essay, "Catullus and Bakhtin: The Problems of a Dialogic Lyric," William W. Batstone argues that Bakhtin inherited a definition of the lyric, strongly enforced by Romanticism, that assumes the genre expresses the poet's meaning without mediation, a transparent expression of private emotion by a coherent self (as seen clearly in the Mill quotation above), and this consistently limited his thinking about the lyric. Batstone suggests a fundamental rethinking of this logic based not in the dramatized voices or intertextuality of the lyric but in the theorization of the very self, which for Bakhtin is an entity formed interpersonally and "inhabited by the voices of others." Therefore, the lyric is dialogized in its consciousness, where the self that is assumed to be its core is characterized by an emphasis on "irreducible noncoincidence between the voices which inhabit us and ourselves" (104).[3]

Michael Eskin's work is the deepest theoretical reckoning with dialogism and poetry, and his interest in the ethical underpinnings of this discussion align closely with my own. His monograph, *Ethics and Dialogue in the Works of Levinas, Bakhtin, Mandel'shtam and Celan* (2000), does also contend with Bakhtin's literary theories; reviewing Bakhtin's strong dismissal of rhythm/form as a monologizing force and of poetry as aligned with repressive sociopolitical forces, Eskin provocatively suggests that we can read Bakhtin's utterances on poetry much more positively if we take as our starting point the fact that all language is inherently dialogic[4] and that the Bakhtinian reference to "poetry" indicates writing that submits to authoritative discourses or insulates itself from the social world, rather than a particular genre. Polyphony is possible in certain poetic utterances, though it is necessarily more difficult to achieve than in the novel because it must overcome formal homogenizing forces. But, says Eskin, the result is that poetry is finally more ethical, because the poet is answerable for all aspects of the utterance; poetry "turns a person's indelible existential answerability for his or her acts (including speech acts) into one of its artistically constitutive moments" (388). Importantly and uniquely, Eskin expands the theoretical basis for the field beyond Bakhtin, focusing richly on Levinas, arguably the other primary theorist of dialogism, and including two poets, Osip Mandelstam and Paul Celan, as fundamental philosophers and practitioners. Deeply invested in ethical relations, the four men discussed by Eskin provide models for thinking about dialogism as a fundamental, even pre-linguistic, dynamic or stance of being; an essential way of understanding self–other relations (including those between author and reader); and a manifestation of that way of being or interacting in and between textual or oral utterances, including translation and—or even most fundamentally—poetry. Far from conceiving of dialogism as a separable lens one might apply to poetry and/or poetics, then, Eskin's book discusses them fluidly and at times indissolubly. In addition to its dense philosophical work on these primary figures, Eskin's work shows starkly how limited dialogic literary criticism has been by relying too singularly on Bakhtin, an inadequacy that our volume also redresses.

In addition to these theoretical arguments for analyzing dialogism and poetry, foundational critical work has emerged in the field, work to which the essays in this volume will substantively add as well. For instance, Don Bialostosky has made significant contributions to the dialogic study of Romantic poetry in *Making Tales: The Poetics of Wordsworth's Narrative Experiments* (1984), among other works, and usefully expands our understanding of Bakhtin by drawing deeply on the writings of other theorists in his inner circle of intellectual companions, especially Valentin Voloshinov. Claiming that for these thinkers the very foundation of dialogism is poetic, Bialostosky offers a dialogic reading of the tonal orientation, formal attributes, and social interactions of speaker, hero, and listener in Wordsworth's lyrics. Donald Wesling's book *Bakhtin and the Social Moorings of Poetry* (2003) begins with a chapter in which he helpfully places Bakhtin's genre theory in historical context and ventures a definition of a "poetics of utterance," followed by a series of readings of diverse international poets through that lens. Interested specifically in the clash of social discourses, including its presence in the inner speech of the self, Wesling's book is notable, too, for its sustained discussion of rhythm as a dialogizing function in poetry.[5] Other critical work in dialogism and poetry has been strong but more scattered, with some notable examples being Lynn Shakinovsky's interesting article on the complex "hidden listeners" that dialogize Emily Dickinson's poetry; Catherine Ciepiela's richly developed examination of the tensions between lyric voice and social language in Marina Tsvetaeva's poem "The Pied Piper" and, by extension, other lyrics; and Michael Macovski's discussion of the complex Romantic "I" in terms of "the idea of consubstantial voices" (15) and the agonistic addressee in *Dialogue and Literature*.[6] In essential work that effectively combines dialogism with other critical discourses, such as in "Modernist Bricolage, Postcolonial Hybridity," Jahan Ramazani rethinks the ways in which we have read Euromodernist and postcolonial poetry as necessarily and always adversarial, positing instead two kinds of poetic dialogism: that between literary traditions and cultures, and that within hybrid, polyglot poetry itself, especially that of poets in the developing world who attempt to "break through monologic lyricism" to express a world in which cross-cultural dialogism or hybridity is, more than a literary device, a foundation of experience.

Jacob Blevins's edited collection, *Dialogism and Lyric Self-Fashioning: Bakhtin and the Voices of a Genre* (2008), is a recent volume in the field dedicated to exploring the construction of the lyric voice and subjectivity. Blevins posits, in the introduction to that book, an inherently dialogic construction of selves and all forms of address that can illuminate, for instance, poetic encounters between speakers and addressees, between allusive texts, or between lyrics and the dominant cultural ideologies of their time. This collection is impressive for its historical sweep, considering lyric poems in the Western tradition from ancient Greece through American jazz poetry of the twentieth century. Despite its very specific title, the volume contains several essays that are only marginally engaged with theories of dialogism and not at all with Bakhtin, but that nevertheless do register what we might call agonistic exchanges, addressivity, or intersubjective construction of voice, arguing implicitly for the very existence of poetry that might be called dialogic.

The existing work is substantial and compelling, but there is a basic need for both more comprehensive theorization of dialogism and more critical attention to dialogism in poetry. Therefore, the aim of this volume, which takes as a given the notion that poetry can be dialogic, is not simply to widen the study of dialogism in poetry, but to deepen it as well. For finally, as scholars of poetry and poetics, we too often have been skilled in finding ways to account for the presence of dialogue, whether it manifests as multivocality, communicative utterance, or engagement with the Other, without necessarily troubling assumptions about poetry's fundamental forms and purposes. So critics have talked about intertextuality, ambiguity, fragmentation, and allusion as the controlled choices of an author that somehow come to the poem hermetically sealed, rather than considering how the inclusion of other discourses and words, each with its own history and context, might create dialogue (we have been willing to allow "tension") within the poem or might even subvert the wishes of the poet through the dynamic of the interaction.[7] We have talked about poems of address as apostrophe or as love sonnets, for example, calling the address a trope or tradition, asking to whom the sonnets might be addressed but not what it means to call out the interlocutor in the poem itself (rather than, say, simply hand or send a non-dialogic poem to someone) nor what it does to us as *readers* when the poem is addressed. We have comfortably understood works as dramatic monologues, or as persona poems, or as poems trying to capture colloquial language, permitting narrative and dramatic terms like point-of-view, dramatic irony, and speaker or narrator into our critical vocabularies without thinking of those poems as intentional speech acts.[8]

Why does it matter? The desire to "correct" Bakhtinian shortsightedness or justify the use of his rich theory for the study of poetry has driven much of the scholarship to date, including my own. And in some ways, of course, it does not matter to insist on "dialogic poetry," if the same tendencies and potentialities of poetry are being examined under other terms. But it is reasonable to assume that our reading practices, focal interests, map of literary relationships (including translation and imitation), understanding of formal elements, analysis of dialect and code-switching, and more will *change* if we come to poetry with the assumption that it can be, or even is, dialogic, and that doing so will contribute in a meaningful way to fields like the New Lyric Studies.[9] As much or more so, the intense and fascinating growth of the field of ethics and literature provides, to me, a compelling motive for this work. I have argued elsewhere that those of us who care about poetry must not relinquish its dialogic possibilities because the stakes are too high. Writers on ethics and literature such as Jeffrey T. Nealon, Lawrence Buell, Martha Nussbaum, Wayne Booth, Michael Eskin, Derek Attridge and others have repeatedly proposed models of dialogue and intersubjectivity—both as represented or embodied in the text and, in exemplars of ethical reading and writing practices, as active dialogue between self and textual, imagined, or actual Other, ideas reiterated in the quotation from Celan that opened this chapter.[10] Unless we wish to cede poetry's contribution to—indeed, even its participation in—ethical human encounter, we should consider the potential for and manifestations of dialogism in poetry and, significantly and continually, allow that examination to challenge, reshape, or refine our theories of ethics and dialogism as well, which have rested much too narrowly on novelistic practice.

This volume contributes to that ongoing inquiry. Its essays focus on a diverse array of literatures, theoretical frameworks, and poetic forms, and thereby serve to enrich and complicate our appreciation of the potentials for dialogic poetry. It strives for theoretical rigor and nuance, in a sense not building on prior work so much as endeavoring to build *beneath* it, offering not only additional criticism in a dialogic vein, but also developing the theoretical foundations that underwrite such criticism.

Dialogic theory draws, of course, on the terms, arguments, and limitations of Mikhail Bakhtin as its taproot, probably because Bakhtin himself so deeply engaged literary forms and genres in his theory rather than remaining more abstractly focused on self-other relations or even on oral speech acts. For the most part, the existing critical work on Bakhtin and poetics reads the theorist thoughtfully, and sidesteps the casual appropriation of Bakhtin's sexy and convenient terms (dialogue itself, or the carnivalesque, for example) that characterize too much of the wider literary criticism purporting to be Bakhtinian. Bakhtin is a brilliant, knotty philosopher, whose work rewards dedicated engagement. Nearly all of the essays in this collection at least refer to him, and several provide extended discussions not only of his more famous remarks in *Problems of Dostoevsky's Poetics* and "Discourse in the Novel," but also of earlier works such as "Toward a Philosophy of the Act" and "Author and Hero in Aesthetic Activity." But Bakhtin's somewhat singular dominance also suggests an area for growth in the field; he is not the final word on dialogism, not only because dialogism insistently denies the finality of words, but because the tangled root structure of dialogism *is* a structure only in the most organic sense of that word: it involves several other strands of thought. In addition to Bakhtin, therefore, the essays in this collection draw theoretical grounding from Martin Buber, Leonard Diepeveen, Stuart Hall, Roman Jakobson, Julia Kristeva, Osip Mandelstam, Paul Celan, Chela Sandoval, and others. In short, although this collection attempts to deepen our understanding of

Bakhtin, it also aims to develop our theoretical conception of dialogism in poetry.[11] Too, the volume extends the work of Ramazani and others by considering dialogism in conjunction with models of gender, race, national identity, and other potential sites of exile and marginalization, a combination both regrettably rare and appropriate given dialogism's inherent resistance to distinct authority and finalized or absolute truths.[12]

In keeping with our goal of augmenting the theoretical conversation about poetic dialogism, the earlier essays of this collection focus closely and productively on Bakhtin's philosophy, and the latter branch out from or supplement Bakhtin with other theories, such as those noted above. The essays also cluster into provocative groups. In the first two chapters, Stephen Pierson and Chad Engbers each turn to Bakhtin's early, underexamined writing—and though they find distinct grounds for dialogic poetry, both scholars interestingly work to deconstruct a reductive monologic–dialogic binary, positing instead a concurrent or gradient interpretation. The next two chapters, by Tom Dolack and Geoffrey Lindsay, which are also rooted in Bakhtinian theory but draw deeply on other theorists, speak to dialogic relationships between and within texts and voices, concentrating on imitation, translation, and quotation, including the possible subversiveness of and in such poems. Both William Waters and Temple Cone turn to alternate philosophers (Celan, Mandelstam, Buber) to frame discussions of the "you" and "thou," reflecting on the practice and ethics of addressivity and answerability for poets, poems, and readers, whatever form that connection may take. In arguing conceptually for poetry's resemblance to other situated, social genres in mass media that carry the "quotation marks" of their communicative process, James D. Sullivan's chapter acts as a kind of bridge to the contemporary, more overtly politically engaged poetry that is discussed in the final chapters. Andrea Witzke Slot and Erin Trapp also move well beyond Bakhtin's dialogic paradigm in analyzing the complex interplay of discourses, forms, and words in poetry by a writer of marginalized race or ethnicity; though they deviate on the dialogic poem's possibility for, or interest in, emancipatory or integrative action, Slot and Trapp both also productively rethink an oversimplified poetic speaker. Of course, that rough map provides only a very partial representation of the many ways these fine essays intersect, overlap, or refute one another. Certainly any of the nine chapters might be read autonomously for insight into, say, a specific poet or theorist—but read collectively, they offer a particularly lively and fruitful conversation that posits complex and various foundations, gradations, and practices of poetic dialogism; theorizes a diverse scope and purpose of dialogic poetry, from the most private prayer to engaged political activism; examines subgenres of poetry (lyric, long poem, and epic, psalm to experimental free verse) as well as discourses from the Bible to *Amos 'n' Andy*; and richly contributes as well to the field of ethics and literature.[13] A somewhat fuller overview of individual chapters follows.

Grounded in Bakhtin's early philosophical writings, often neglected in discussions of dialogism, Stephen Pierson suggests that "scholarly consensus on Bakhtin's perspective on poetry—that it is contradictory or misguided—be reconsidered by addressing the question of a dialogic poem in terms of Bakhtin's theory of art and not in terms of his theory of language." Through special attention to the "artistic" utterance and to the Bakhtinian model of author and hero, Pierson describes the processes by which "lyrical utterance" can be expressed monologically: the author's domination over, indeed assimilation of, the hero and depiction of the hero in "limited time and space," and her "assumption of a sympathetic audience" in a way that negates the essential presence of the other. Pierson argues that his poetic exemplar, Walt Whitman's 1855 epic "Song of Myself," "is dialogical in the major ways that every kind of utterance is dialogical—that is, in its change of speaking subjects, finalization of the utterance, expressive intonation, and addressivity." However, artistically it is monologic, as the author fundamentally absorbs the lyrical hero.

Chad Engbers's chapter also roots itself in Bakhtin's early work, especially "Author and Hero in Aesthetic Activity," to supplement a gap in Bakhtin's later works on dialogism and to provide a model for thinking about what Engbers calls "the partially dialogic lyric." He urges us to reframe the question "is this poem dialogic?" as "how dialogic is this poem?" by noting that monologism and dialogism are "not binary categories but graduated ones." Engbers's primary focus on Sir Thomas Wyatt's Penitential Psalms offers a compelling test case, and he closely reads the psalms and their narrative interludes in arguing that the two consciousnesses, David's and the narrator's, cannot merge and still achieve penitence and forgiveness. Though Engbers acknowledges that the voices of Wyatt's sequence do not fit the expectations for dialogism distinguished by *style*, as they are (despite drawing on numerous sources) unified in Wyatt's courtly forms and language, he argues that penitential utterance is inherently dialogic in that it is, by necessity, addressed to a listening other. Engbers challenges the dominance of new historicist readings of Wyatt and enlarges our understanding of Bakhtin's dialogism by delineating how Wyatt's psalms enact Bakhtinian aesthetic activity and confessional self-accounting.

Tom Dolack's chapter argues that, despite our emphasis on originality in poetry since the Romantic era, all poetry should be understood as imitation that falls somewhere along a "spectrum of fidelity" to prior texts. He suggests, then, that poetic translation should not be understood as a fundamentally different task than "original" writing and offers a model of "lyric ventriloquism," in which a translator speaks through, or communicates his own intentions through, a poet's works, creating a dialogic tension in the poetic translation that Dolack, focusing on translation in repressive contexts, also examines as "'Aesopian Language' or speech that attempts to mean more than it says (through ambivalence or allusion) and so evade censorship." Drawing on Jakobson's schematic of the communicative act as well as Bakhtin's linguistic theories of language acquisition and appropriation, Dolack simultaneously counters Bakhtin's resistance to reading poetry as ventriloquism or to seeing the poetic word as socially responsive. Works by Pasternak and Mandelstam provide powerful examples of intentional translations that speak covertly under socio-political duress, and Dolack finishes with an examination of the explicitly dialogic relationship between the French Résistance poet René Char and his translator, the Jewish writer Paul Celan.

Geoffrey Lindsay enriches the concept of dialogism by employing quotation theory, as developed by Leonard Diepeveen, in considering the case of poet Robert Lowell's infamous volume *The Dolphin*, in which the words of his estranged and current wives and his daughter are directly cited, a choice on Lowell's part that raises numerous questions about the ethics of quotation, use of autobiographical material that exceeds one's own self, and work of multiple voices in literature. Moving beyond the critical debate over whether or not names/voices in the poems are simply textual figures or are violations of real women's privacy, Lindsay examines Lowell's text as an example of Bakhtinian polyphony, arguing that "far from having no recourse but silence, the voices of Lizzie, Caroline and Harriet talk back to Lowell's voice: however much Lowell's dominant voice seeks to inscribe his master narrative, we can discern a distinct and alternate narrative through these other voices." As quotation of various voices and discourses in modern and contemporary poetry is so frequent as to be now nearly unexceptional, Lindsay's chapter makes an important case for considering the independent or even subversive quality the citations may retain.

William Waters's essay represents arguably the best current critical work on poetic address, particularly the direct second-person or "you" address. He specifically confronts our discomfort with the notion that the "you" may be the reader herself rather than an identifiable, discrete individual from the poet's own life, noting the "awkward fact" that poetry "enacts [. . .] not so much a stable communicative situation as a chronic hesitation, a faltering, between monologue and dialogue, between 'talking about' and 'talking to'" but embracing the possibility of intimate, rather than coercive, contact. Drawing, like Dolack, on both Mandelstam and Celan, Waters closely analyzes poems by John Keats and Rainer Maria Rilke. Although the traditional view of poetry as the utterance of a single, monologic voice is so often traced back to the Romantic poets, Waters enables us to reconceptualize assumptions about the nature of poetry that we have inherited—often unquestioningly— from the nineteenth century. He submits that the reader is bidden to accept and answer (to) the poem, and thereby situates dialogue both in the poetic address and the reading process. In arguing for the obliga- tory answerability of the reader, Waters is also a significant contributor to the discussion of ethics and literature, including for emerging views of poetry not merely as a conceptual or emotional construct but as an ethical act between human beings.

The chapter by Temple Cone draws on a theorist of dialogism less commonly used in literary studies, religious philosopher Martin Buber. American poet Denise Levertov is known to have drawn on the content of Buber's *Tales of the Hasidim* in her book *The Jacob's Ladder*, but Cone's interest is in tracing first the "thematic significance [. . .] of the dialogi- cal encounter" imagined in Buber's *I and Thou* for Levertov and then, importantly, the way that Levertov's own poetics, through formal details such as her lineation, "enact the dynamic of the I–Thou relation." In close intertextual readings of the writings of poet and philosopher, he asserts too that Levertov "abnegates an expression of experience-focused ego," a depersonalization of the speaking subject which is a challenge to common critical tendencies that reduce the lyric speaker personally or autobiographically; in doing so, Levertov achieves a communal utter- ance that Cone terms "prayerful," and thus further opens the dialogic encounter for the reader herself to engage. Exploring the insistence of both the poet and philosopher on reciprocity and openness to encoun- ters that are human, natural, animal, and divine, Cone's essay proposes an ethical dimension to Levertov's dialogic poetics.

James D. Sullivan's chapter is distinct from the others in the collec- tion in that he focuses more exclusively on a theoretical argument for dialogic poetry and situates that argument in poetry's material, social actuality. Drawing on cultural theorist Stuart Hall's argument that the production, circulation, distribution/consumption, and reproduction of television news occur in a series of "relatively autonomous moments" that each leave "quotation marks" around the product signaling the positions and intentions of all involved, Sullivan contends (contesting lingering claims for poetry as a form of communication that achieves pure transmission) that poetry must be understood also as materially, socially, irrevocably situated and as a practice rather than an abstractable text. This is particularly important, he says, in that poetry, "especially in the lyric mode, continues to create an impression of an unmediated voice, a direct communication between writer and reader," a quality that Bakhtin takes as the decisive marker of the genre. While other contributors to this volume offer definitions or descriptions of dialogic poetry, or of degrees of dialogism in poetry, Sullivan's Bakhtinian-influenced analysis would insist that we understand all poetry as het-eroglot because of its "material cultural practice," the embedded layers of encoded discourse that constitute human communicative activity.

Deeply interested in the role of the "democratized reader" in bringing dialogic poetry to its full potential, Andrea Witzke Slot analyzes what she calls "a double play of ventriloquy" in Harryette Mullen's long poem *Muse & Drudge*, an 81-page work that incorporates imagery, themes, and voices from a vast array of historical, ideological, and cultural contexts—thereby inviting interpretation from a range of readers. Whereas Bakhtin thinks that the subjectivity of a lyric poem makes it monologic, Slot maintains, multiple subjects might inhabit the same poetic space in a way that helps to delimit each subject more clearly through its inter-actions with the others. In fact, subjectivity, along with innovative language, is identified by Slot as a primary impetus for dialogic, and emancipatory, poetry. Slot turns to Chela Sandoval's theories of dif-ferential and oppositional consciousness and to the trope of railroad junctures, which is used by Houston A. Baker to characterize African American literature and the blues. Explicitly extending dialogism's part-nership with race, gender, and cultural studies, Slot closely analyzes the figures, voices, allusions, linguistic codes, and formal devices of Mullen's long poem, arguing that it is "a dynamic means of emancipatory tech-nology," enabling an encounter among voices and readers that may be contentious but is fundamentally ethical.

In the final chapter of the volume, Erin Trapp considers the poetry of Zehra Çirak, a writer of Turkish descent in Germany, and probes Bakhtin's most famous writings on dialogue and dialogism by drawing upon psychoanalytic theory, theories of alterity, and the work of Julia Kristeva, Paul de Man, and others who absorb, extend, and question Bakhtin's seminal ideas. Trapp argues that "Çirak proposes a logic of understanding dialogue not as a process between two individuals," or "two fixed identities," which may be predicated on violence—most specifically the principal model of the European subject and its ethnic other, but by extension interrogating any model that reads poetry fundamentally as the address of an "I" subject to a "you." Rather, it is an "internal dialogue" between an "I" subject and its object or utterance, the "me" that "emerges out of the failure" of dialogic communication. This internal dialogism, which Trapp describes as "a form of searching or desiring that is purposeless," is theorized through the rich psychoanalytic paradigm of creative nonintegration. The question of how and whether Çirak's poetry is dialogic is automatically a political and ethical question about an immigrant's relationship to a national literature and identity, one that Trapp fruitfully scrutinizes with careful attention to Çirak's fertile language.

What is particularly valuable about this volume is that collectively the authors offer rich, complicated, and even contradictory discussion of what dialogism is, how expansively we may define or apply it, and what it looks like when it manifests in poetry. The discourses, forms, and traditions of dialogism and poetics have been, as I have argued here, interacting in ways both explicit and implicit for some years, which has decisively enriched both fields. It is critical to models of dialogism that we interrogate its parameters in this way and think beyond the limitations that may have thwarted its theorists. It is equally essential that we continue to loosen the stranglehold that reductive theories of poetry, or of specific genres such as lyric or epic, have held on readers and practitioners, supporting the intensely valuable conversations generated by movements such as the New Lyric Studies. And for those of us who love poetry and believe in its vitality in a difficult world, it is crucial that we credit its participation in ethical, dialogic exchange.

Notes

1. It is intriguing that despite this legacy, the work of the British Romantic poets has inspired some of the best close examination of dialogic poetry. See in particular Michael Macovski, *Dialogue and Literature*, and Don Bialostosky, *Making Tales*.
2. The terms are obviously slippery and are applied variously. A work like Beth Ellen Roberts's *One Voice and Many: Modern Poets in Dialogue* is really more focused on forms of poetic dialogue attributable to designated speakers, such as the eclogue or ballad, than on theoretical models of dialogism. But William Batstone offers the strong and necessary reminder that even strongly intertextual forms can "serve a fiercely monologic form of authorship" (107).

And, though his focus is in fact on dialogue as speech acts or conversation in the narrower sense, Paul Friedrich claims that all lyrics are dialogical in their attempt to engage a reader, but "little lyric poetry [. . .] contains actual quoted, literal dialogue. The deep structure is always dialogic, whereas the surface structure is only rarely so" (79).

3. Macovski's interesting essay on Lord Byron examines the same phenomenon, arguing that the stylistic juxtaposition of the voices of British contemporaries and rivals in society represents in part the constituent and interrelated parts of Byron's own poetic self. Macovski's work is also worth consulting for his thought-provoking theory of the agonistic addressee.

4. This stance is taken by others in plumbing the complications of Bakhtinian genre theory. See especially Ken Hirschkop, on whom Eskin draws in both texts cited here.

5. Work on poetic form, structure, and/or rhythm as a marker of dialogism is rare but interesting. Friedrich concurs, "The whole question of the subtle interaction between degrees of metricality and degrees of conversationality in lyric poetry remains largely unexplored" (85). And Richter writes, "Bakhtin surely underestimates the degree to which a master of poetic language can use its sonic resources to create the internal dialogue Bakhtin so valued" (20). For more analysis of the dialogizing potential of form and rhythm, see also Bialostosky's *Making Tales*; Eskin; Vered Shemtov; Paul Crumbley; Christopher Callahan; and Mara Scanlon.

6. See also Macovski's edited collection *Dialogue and Critical Discourse*, especially the productive essays by Friedrich and Macovski himself.

7. Possibly more of this work has been done on intensely multivocal or fragmented modernist poetics. Brian Caraher's essay on Ezra Pound, which examines the "social languages" of *Hugh Selwyn Mauberley*, is one example. See also Ian Probstein, who argues for reading allusion and citation in T. S. Eliot as dialogic, though his point is diluted by the less focused insistence that "[i]n essence, Eliot's entire work is a dialogue with humanity" (184 and 199). Leonard Diepeveen's book, *Changing Voices: The Modern Quoting Poem*, is possibly the richest theorization of quotation as a kind of dialogism, the active presence of another voice that he calls its "texture," which includes its "nonparaphrasable meanings" and its history. Diepeveen's interest is in dramatic, rather than lyric, voice in the poem, which encourages attention to multiplicity and interaction and discourages the drive to unify the lyric voice or identify which of the voices in a quoting poem is "real." See also Timothy R. Austin's essay on Shelley, examining the manipulations of direct quotation, which need not bear a factual truth or objectivity.

8. There are a number of critics whose work has laid absolutely essential groundwork here, even if some have not explicitly engaged with theories and theorists of dialogism. Ashton Nichols provides a good model for thinking about dialogism in the dramatic monologue (whose very name would seem to preclude dialogism) and Herbert Tucker's work on the same genre is a strong example of the ways in which the concerns of dialogic theory have been emerging in poetry studies under various names. I would also note here works like Helen Vendler's *Invisible Listeners*; Sharon Cameron's *Lyric Time* and its theory of the choral voice; Virginia Jackson's fascinating study of addressivity, positionality, and genre in *Dickinson's Misery*; or Jonathan

Culler's influential work on apostrophe and Mary Jacobus's use of it in reading *The Prelude*. Though dated by some of the theory it engages, Patricia Parker's introduction to *Lyric Poetry: Beyond New Criticism* asks questions about poetic voice, speaker, and audience that are still important.

9. This term has gained footing with the special section on New Lyric Studies in *PMLA* (January 2008) following Marjorie Perloff's provocative Presidential Address to the MLA in 2006.

10. Nealon, Eskin, and others have marked this as a turn away from the post-structuralist emphasis on textuality over subjectivity.

11. Overall, as this volume looks forward to further research, we might agree that work in poetic dialogism would be enriched by further exploration of these and other figures and most of all of the astounding thinker who both looms over and yet remains largely elusive in dialogic literary criticism, Emmanuel Levinas.

12. There has been a remarkable dearth of women working at the conjunction of the fields of poetic studies and dialogic theory, though naturally we might cite any number of women poets whose work could be usefully examined as dialogic. Some notable exceptions among the literary critics include Heather Dubrow and Lynn Shakinovsky. The concept of dialogism has been used in at least two collections of feminist criticism and theory, but with varying degrees of nuance and depth; see *Feminism, Bakhtin, and the Dialogic*, edited by Dale M. Bauer and Susan Jaret McKinstry, and *A Dialogue of Voices: Feminist Literary Theory and Bakhtin*, edited by Karen Hohne and Helen Wussow.

13. Though Whitman's "Song of Myself" is frequently read as a poem with epic reach, and Mullen's work is arguably the same, the essays deal less explicitly with the questions that might haunt a dialogic *epic*, and more work in this specific field would be welcome. See Scanlon, "'In the Mouths of the Tribe': *Omeros* and the Heteroglossic Nation."

Select bibliography

Attridge, Derek. "Innovation, Literature, Ethics: Relating to the Other." *PMLA* 114.1 (1999): 20–31.

Austin, Timothy R. "Narrative Transmission: Shifting Gears in Shelley's 'Ozymandias.'" *Dialogue and Critical Discourse: Language, Culture, Critical Theory*. Ed. Michael Macovski. New York: Oxford UP, 1997. 29–46.

Bakhtin, Mikhail M. *Art and Answerability: Early Philosophical Essays*. Ed. Michael Holquist and Vadim Liapunov. Trans. Vadim Liapunov. Austin: U of Texas P, 1990.

——. "Discourse in the Novel." *The Dialogic Imagination*. Ed. Michael Holquist. Trans. Caryl Emerson and Michael Holquist. Austin: U of Texas P, 1981. 259–422.

——. "Epic and Novel: Toward a Methodology for the Study of the Novel." *The Dialogic Imagination*. Ed. Michael Holquist. Trans. Caryl Emerson and Michael Holquist. Austin: U of Texas P, 1981. 3–40.

——. "From a Prehistory of Novelistic Discourse." *The Dialogic Imagination*. Ed. Michael Holquist. Trans. Caryl Emerson and Michael Holquist. Austin: U of Texas P, 1981. 41–83.

——. *Problems of Dostoevsky's Poetics.* Ed. and trans. Caryl Emerson. Minneapolis: U of Minnesota P, 1984.

——. *Speech Genres and Other Late Essays.* Ed. Caryl Emerson and Michael Holquist. Trans. Vern W. McGee. Austin: U of Texas P, 1986.

——. *Toward a Philosophy of the Act.* Ed. Vadim Liapunov and Michael Holquist. Trans. and notes by Vadim Liapunov. Austin: U of Texas P, 1993.

Batstone, William W. "Catullus and Bakhtin: The Problems of a Dialogic Lyric." *Bakhtin and the Classics.* Ed. R. Bracht Branham. Evanston, IL: Northwestern UP, 2002. 99–136.

Bauer, Dale M. and Susan Jaret McKinstry, eds. *Feminism, Bakhtin, and the Dialogic.* Buffalo: State U of New York P, 1991.

Bialostosky, Don H. "Architectonics, Rhetoric, and Poetics in the Bakhtin School's Early Phenomenological and Social Texts." *Rhetoric Society Quarterly* 36 (2006): 355–76.

——. *Making Tales: The Poetics of Wordsworth's Narrative Experiments.* Chicago: U of Chicago P, 1984.

Blevins, Jacob, ed. *Dialogism and Lyric Self-Fashioning: Bakhtin and the Voices of a Genre.* Selinsgrove: Susquehanna UP, 2008.

Booth, Wayne. *The Company We Keep: An Ethics of Reading.* Berkeley: U of California P, 1988.

Buber, Martin. *I and Thou.* 2nd ed. Trans. Ronald Gregor Smith. New York: Scribner, 1987.

Buell, Lawrence. "Introduction: In Pursuit of Ethics." *PMLA* 114.1 (1999): 7–19.

Callahan, Christopher. "Subjective Identity and Collective Conscience in the Songs of Colin Muset." *Dialogism and Lyric Self-Fashioning: Bakhtin and the Voices of a Genre.* Ed. Jacob Blevins. Selinsgrove: Susquehanna UP, 2008. 97–112.

Cameron, Sharon. *Lyric Time: Dickinson and the Limits of Genre.* Baltimore: Johns Hopkins UP, 1979.

Caraher, Brian G. "Reading Pound with Bakhtin: Sculpting the Social Languages of *Hugh Selwyn Mauberley*'s 'Mere Surface.'" *Modern Language Quarterly: A Journal of Literary History* 49.1 (March 1988): 38–64.

Celan, Paul. *Selected Poems and Prose of Paul Celan.* Trans. John Felstinek. New York: W. W. Norton and Company, 2001.

Ciepiela, Catherine. "Taking Monologism Seriously: Bakhtin and Tsvetaeva's 'The Pied Piper.'" *Slavic Review* 53.4 (Winter 1994): 1010–24.

Crumbley, Paul. "Dickinson's Dashes and the Limits of Discourse." *Emily Dickinson Journal* 1.2 (1992): 8–29.

Culler, Jonathan. "Changes in the Study of the Lyric." *Lyric Poetry: Beyond New Criticism.* Eds. Chaviva Hošek and Patricia Parker. Ithaca, NY: Cornell UP, 1985. 38–54.

Davidson, Michael. "Discourse in Poetry: Bakhtin and the Extensions of the Dialogical." *Code of Signals: Recent Writings in Poetics.* Ed. Michael Palmer. Berkeley, CA: North Atlantic Books, 1983. 143–50.

Diepeveen, Leonard. *Changing Voices: The Modern Quoting Poem.* Ann Arbor: U of Michigan P, 1993.

Dubrow, Heather. "The Domain of Echo: Lyric Audiences." *The Challenges of Orpheus: Lyric Poetry and Early Modern England.* Baltimore: Johns Hopkins UP, 2008. 54–105.

Eskin, Michael. "Bakhtin on Poetry." *Poetics Today* 21.2 (2000): 379–91.

——. *Ethics and Dialogue in the Works of Levinas, Bakhtin, Mandel'shtam, and Celan.* New York: Oxford UP, 2000.

Friedrich, Paul. "Dialogue in Lyric Narrative." *Dialogue and Critical Discourse: Language, Culture, Critical Theory.* Ed. Michael Macovski. New York: Oxford UP, 1997. 79–98.

Frye, Northrop. *Anatomy of Criticism.* Princeton, NJ: Princeton UP, 1957.

Hirschkop, Ken. "A Response to the Forum on Mikhail Bakhtin." *Bakhtin: Essays and Dialogues on his Work.* Ed. Gary Saul Morson. Chicago: The U of Chicago P, 1981. 73–80.

——. and David Shepherd, eds. *Bakhtin and Cultural Theory.* 2nd ed. Manchester: Manchester UP, 2002.

Hohne, Karen and Helen Wussow, eds. *A Dialogue of Voices: Feminist Literary Theory and Bakhtin.* Minneapolis: U of Minnesota P, 1994.

Holquist, Michael. *Dialogism: Bakhtin and his World.* London and New York: Routledge, 1990.

Hošek, Chaviva, and Patricia Parker, eds. *Lyric Poetry: Beyond New Criticism.* Ithaca, NY: Cornell UP, 1985.

Jackson, Virginia. *Dickinson's Misery: A Theory of Lyric Reading.* Princeton, NJ: Princeton UP, 2005.

Jacobus, Mary. "Apostrophe and Lyric Voice in *The Prelude.*" *Lyric Poetry: Beyond New Criticism.* Eds. Chaviva Hošek and Patricia Parker. Ithaca, NY: Cornell UP, 1985. 167–81.

Levinas, Emmanuel. *Alterity and Transcendence.* Trans. Michael B. Smith. New York: Columbia UP, 2001.

——. *Entre Nous: Thinking of the Other.* Trans. Michael B. Smith and Barbara Harshay. New York: Columbia UP, 2000.

——. *Humanism of the Other.* Trans. Nidra Poller. Champagne-Urbana, IL: U of Illinois P, 2005.

Macovski, Michael. *Dialogue and Literature: Apostrophe, Auditors, and the Collapse of Romantic Discourse.* New York: Oxford UP, 1994.

——. ed. *Dialogue and Critical Discourse: Language, Culture, Critical Theory.* New York: Oxford UP, 1997.

Mandelstam, Osip. *The Complete Critical Prose.* Ed. Jane Gary Harris. New York: Ardis Publishing, 1997.

Mill, John Stuart. *Essays on Poetry.* Ed. F. Parvin Sharpless. Columbia, SC: U of South Carolina P, 1976.

Nealon, Jeffrey T. "The Ethics of Dialogue: Bakhtin and Levinas." *College English* 59.2 (1997): 129–48.

Nichols, Ashton. "Dialogism in the Dramatic Monologue: Suppressed Voices in Browning." *VIJ: Victorians Institute Journal* 18 (1990): 29–51.

Nussbaum, Martha C. *Love's Knowledge: Essays on Philosophy and Literature.* New York: Oxford UP, 1990.

Parker, Patricia. Introduction. *Lyric Poetry: Beyond New Criticism.* Ed. Chaviva Hošek and Patricia Parker. Ithaca, NY: Cornell UP, 1985. 11–28.

Pechey, Graham. "Not the Novel: Bakhtin, Poetry, Truth, God." *Bakhtin and Cultural Theory.* Manchester and New York: Manchester UP, 2001. 62–84.

Perloff, Marjorie. "Presidential Address 2006: It Must Change." *PMLA: Publications of the Modern Language Association of America* 122.3 (May 2007): 652–62.

Pierson, Stephen. "A Bibliographic Note and Bibliography on Bakhtinian Studies in Poetry." *Social Science Research Network.* Web. March 2012.

Probstein, Ian. "*The Waste Land* as a Human Drama Revealed by Eliot's Dialogic Imagination." *Dialogism and Lyric Self-Fashioning: Bakhtin and the Voices of a Genre*. Ed. Jacob Blevins. Selinsgrove: Susquehanna UP, 2008. 180–203.

Radar, Ralph W. "The Dramatic Monologue and Related Forms." *Critical Inquiry* 3.1 (Autumn 1976): 131–51.

Ramazani, Jahan. "Modernist Bricolage, Postcolonial Hybridity." *Modernism/Modernity* 13.3 (September 2006): 445–63.

——. *Poetry and its Others: News, Prayer, Song, and the Dialogue of Genres*. Chicago: U of Chicago P, 2013.

Richter, David H. "Dialogism and Poetry." *Studies in the Literary Imagination* XXIII.1 (Spring 1990): 9–27.

Robbins, Jill. *Altered Reading: Levinas and Literature*. Chicago: U of Chicago P, 1999.

Roberts, Beth Ellen. *One Voice and Many: Modern Poets in Dialogue*. Newark: U of Delaware P, 2006.

Scanlon, Mara. "Ethics and the Lyric: Form, Dialogue, Answerability." *College Literature* 34.1 (Winter 2007): 1–22.

——. "'In the Mouths of the Tribe': *Omeros* and the Heteroglossic Nation." *Bucknell Review* XLIII.2 (2000, Special issue on Bakhtin and the Nation): 101–17.

Shakinovsky, Lynn. "Hidden Listeners: Dialogism in Emily Dickinson." *Discours Social/Social Discourse* 3.1–2 (1990): 199–215.

Shapiro, Marianne and Michael Shapiro. "Dialogism and the Lyric Addressee." *University of Toronto Quarterly* 61.3 (Spring 1992): 392–413.

Shemtov, Vered. "Metrical Hybridization: Prosodic Ambiguities as a Form of Social Dialogue." *Poetics Today* 22.1 (Spring 2001): 65–87.

Tucker, Herbert. "Dramatic Monologue and the Overhearing of Lyric." *Lyric Poetry: Beyond New Criticism*. Ed. Chaviva Hošek and Patricia Parker. Ithaca, NY: Cornell UP, 1985. 226–43.

Vendler, Helen. *Invisible Listeners: Lyric Intimacy in Herbert, Whitman, and Ashbery*. Princeton, NJ: Princeton UP, 2005.

Waters, William. "Answerable Aesthetics: Reading 'You' in Rilke." *Comparative Literature* 48:2 (1996 Spring): 128–49.

——. *Poetry's Touch: On Lyric Address*. Ithaca, NY: Cornell UP, 2003.

Wesling, Donald. *Bakhtin and the Social Moorings of Poetry*. Lewisburg, PA: Bucknell UP, 2003.

2
Dialogism and Monologism in "Song of Myself"

Stephen Pierson

For Howard Mancing

"Dialogic relations are always present, even among profoundly monologic speech works."
(Bakhtin, "The Problem of the Text" 110)

Bakhtin's critique of poetry as a monologic speech genre has not fared well over the last forty years.[1] Most commentators have found that it contradicts Bakhtin's own ideas about the dialogic nature of discourse, language, or the utterance. The general contention is that if discourse, language, or the utterance contains degrees and kinds of otherness (that is, if they are intrinsically dialogical), then poetry is dialogical, inasmuch as it can be analyzed as discourse, language, or utterance. Additionally, some critics have pointed to Bakhtin's dialogic reading of Pushkin's Romantic lyric "Parting" as evidence of a contradiction between Bakhtin's theory and practice, while other commentators have proffered dialogic analyses of poetry as a reconsideration of Bakhtin's perspective on poetry. Even more telling are the recent essays in Jacob Blevins' anthology *Dialogism and Lyric Self-Fashioning: Bakhtin and the Voices of a Genre*, which ignore Bakhtin's monologic assessment of poetry. Blevins himself provides a rationale for this omission: "Bakhtin's notion of dialogism is an important, thoughtful understanding of the dynamic nature of language, both inside and outside of literary discourse, but Bakhtin simply miscalculated the dialogic potential of poetry" (16).[2]

I wish to trouble this mainstream criticism by arguing, as my epigraph suggests, that Bakhtin's thinking about dialogism and poetry[3] allows for reading poetry dialogically and monologically at the same time:

20

dialogically as utterance, and monologically as a work of verbal art. In other words, I wish to demonstrate that, while Bakhtin finds all utterances dialogical insofar as they are shaped by otherness, he does not find all utterances *artistically* dialogical. This artistic (*tvorcheskii*) quality depends partly on the degree to which the author remains outside the hero of the utterance with respect to space, time, and value. (The hero in question is the character(s), theme, or language of the utterance.) Walt Whitman's "Song of Myself" will serve as my exemplar, for though it is hybridized and novelized in certain respects, it is decidedly monological in the way its author merges with, rather than diverges from, the hero of the poem.[4]

This interpretation holds out several advantages to students of literature. In addition to allowing for a new kind of Bakhtinian reading of poetry (i.e., simultaneously as dialogic utterance and monologic work), it reminds us that Bakhtin distinguishes his dialogic theory of language from his dialogic theory of art. Though both derive from Bakhtin's ontology and theory of cognition, Bakhtin applies the concept of dialogism to language and literature differently. This difference has been largely ignored in the scholarship, the bulk of which rejects Bakhtin's critique of poetry on the basis of his theory of language. However, it should be rejected or confirmed on the basis of Bakhtin's theory of art. Not surprisingly, the commentary mainly ignores Bakhtin's early philosophical writing, particularly *Toward a Philosophy of the Act* and "Author and Hero in Aesthetic Activity." Yet these treatises reveal the philosophical underpinnings of an "aesthetics of verbal creation" that is better known as the dialogic imagination. Indeed, "Author and Hero" is not only Bakhtin's longest theoretical statement on literature. It also contains his longest passage on lyric poetry as a genre (167–72), a passage that is almost entirely ignored in the scholarship. Thus, my interpretation holds out the possibility of recuperating the importance of Bakhtin's early philosophical treatises to his ideas about literature in general and the question of a dialogic poem in particular. To understand how an utterance, such as a poem, can be dialogical as an utterance and monological as a work of art, a discussion of the dialogic nature of language, followed by Bakhtin's theory of verbal art, is in order.

In what way is an utterance like "Song of Myself" intrinsically dialogical, and how does Bakhtin's claim about dialogism in language constitute a theory of language, as opposed to a theory of verbal art?[5] Bakhtin addresses the first question in his influential "The Problem of Speech Genres," where he argues that every actual use of language, written or spoken, short or long, is dialogical in the ways that it is determined by human agency, especially the beholder of the utterance, "for whom the utterance is constructed" (94). Bakhtin asserts that his predecessors in the philosophy of language (i.e., Karl Vossler, Wilhelm von Humboldt, and Ferdinand de Saussure) have ignored or underestimated "the role of the *other* in the process of speech communication" (70, Bakhtin's emphasis), but that in order to obtain a comprehensive account of meaning in language, otherness in language must be considered. Such an account will include not only linguistic meanings (i.e., lexical, grammatical, and syntactical) but also those translinguistic meanings that join themselves to language in actual language use. Bakhtin calls these translinguistic meanings "dialogical echoes" (99), "dialogic overtones" (71, note c), and "dialogic reverberations" (94)—characterizations that indicate the importance of aurality in Bakhtin's philosophy of language and that are similar to the phrase "dialogic relations" in my epigraph.

The concept of the utterance is essential to this dialogic theory of language, for it is a *"real unit* of speech communication" as opposed to some language unit abstracted from use (71, Bakhtin's emphasis). Moreover, in the "constitutive" features that define the utterance, as opposed to language units, one can perceive the dialogic of language use. For example, whereas language units are "absolutely neutral" with respect to an "expressive aspect" (84), an utterance does have such expression (85) owing to the context of the utterance: who is speaking, to whom, for what reason, and under what circumstance? One of Bakhtin's examples is the phrase "the sea," considered as language, compared with the same phrase in the utterance "'The Sea! The Sea!' (exclaimed by 10,000 Greeks in Xenophon)" (85).

The dialogic of language use can also be heard in the two related features of the utterance—"the change of speaking subjects" and "the *finalization* of the utterance" (76, Bakhtin's emphasis). Each feature, respectively, has to do with the beholder's perception that a user of language has begun and completed an utterance, an actual and whole use of language. In the change of speaking subjects, the beholder of the utterance not only recognizes that a new utterance has begun but also that it stands in relation to other utterances. As Bakhtin notes, no user of language is "the biblical Adam" expressing a point of view on a given topic for the first time (93). In the finalization of the utterance, the beholder perceives that the completion of the utterance is a sign, a "silent *dixi*" ("I have spoken"), and that it is now the beholder's turn to respond, however actively or passively, to the utterance (72). An analogy would be the way the viewer of a film senses the ending when the music subsides or the camera draws back from its object. Thus, the beginning and ending of utterance mark it off as "a link in the chain of speech communication" (91) and give the utterance the quality of someone's utterances in a dialogue, which Bakhtin considers the prototypical utterance (72).

An utterance is also dialogical in its "addressivity"—that is, as "the quality of [the utterance's] being directed to someone" (95). This feature is not to be confused with lexical, grammatical, or syntactic means of formal address, for addressivity has to do with the type of addressee conceptualized by the speaker or writer and perceived by the beholder of the utterance. Types of addressee range from one's colleagues in everyday dialogue to literary specialists, such as the readers of this essay. Addressivity is also apparent in the language agent's anticipation of the beholder's response: "I parry objections that I foresee, I make all kinds of provisions, and so forth" (95). Besides, an utterance reveals a consideration of the beholder's knowledge and expectations because these "will determine his [*sic*] active responsive understanding of my utterance" (95–6). Such considerations determine the writer or speaker's choice of diction, genre, and style of speech (96). Still another type of addressivity is the addressee's social position, which shapes the style of the utterance. Familiar and intimate styles, for example, regard the addressee as an equal in society, and this attitude gives rise to a certain frankness in speech (97). Bakhtin holds that a theory of language that aims to include genre and style must take into account not only language units but also "the speaker's attitude toward the *other* and his utterances (existing or anticipated)" (97, Bakhtin's emphasis).

The foregoing overview of Bakhtin's theory of language demonstrates that Bakhtin considers dialogism a fact of language use, just as he does polyglossia and heteroglossia. However, although he finds dialogism in every utterance, Bakhtin does not find every kind utterance artistically dialogical. That is to say, Bakhtin does not consider every utterance to represent the dialogic nature of cognition and communication. Put differently, some utterances do not represent other utterances.

That Bakhtin finds certain genres more artistic than others is evident throughout his oeuvre.[6] For example, the term "artistic" (*tvorcheskii*) in Bakhtin's writing is translated as "artistic" or "creative." Moreover, the term *tvorchestvo*, which also appears in Bakhtin's writing, is translated as "art" or "creation," as it commonly is in Russian. However, whereas *tvorchestvo* can also denote something like our loan word "oeuvre," the adjective *tvorcheskii* always denotes something like the English "crea-tive" or "artistic," though always in the loftiest sense of the term.

Furthermore, the sense of the artistic or creative quality in literature is evident in a number of passages in Bakhtin's essays and monographs. For example, in "The Problem of the Text," where he describes a dia-logic theory of language, Bakhtin wonders how "*even the pure lyricist*" cannot recognize that she, like any user of language, is directing her language toward others and their voices (110; my emphasis). Bakhtin also asks whether a "single-voiced word" is "naïve and unsuitable for authentic creativity," and answers that a "truly creative voice" depends on the representation of a second voice in the discourse. This can be accomplished by the writer's ability to use language while remaining outside it, in an indirect style of speech (110). To be sure, Bakhtin finds every utterance "more or less creative" in the way it constitutes some degree of "assimilation . . . of others' words (and not the words of language)" (89). However, such creativity is unintentional, and in "Discourse in the Novel," Bakhtin notes that in poetry "the natural dialogization of the word is not put to artistic use. . . . " (284). In *Problems of Dostoevsky's Poetics* (the original title was *The Problems of Dostoevsky's Art*), Bakhtin argues that what makes Dostoevsky a very great artist is that he undertook "a new artistic task" by not merging his own consciousness with those of his characters (8–9). These passages demonstrate that the concept of an artistic utterance is important to Bakhtin's theory of literature, that it has to do with representing other-ness, and that an utterance is artistically dialogic insofar as it represents the dialogic of understanding and language.

In fact, Bakhtin lays the foundation for this theory of art in *Toward a Philosophy of the Act* and "Author and Hero." There Bakhtin develops the aesthetic ramifications of his social ontology into a theory of litera-ture in which the poem, among other genres, including prose genres, is thought to have a lesser capacity for representing the dialogic of cogni-tion and language. A brief overview of this neglected part of Bakhtin's writing will bear out this point and pave the way for its application to Whitman's poetry.

In *Toward a Philosophy of the Act*, Bakhtin argues that human beings *experience* the world as unique human beings owing to their unique posi-tion in space and time—unique because no one else occupies another person's place in being, and because one's existence is non-repeatable (40–3). What is more, the non-coincidence of self and other in life—which makes for a unique existence and answerable cognition—results in every human being's having a surplus of perception and knowing vis-à-vis another human being. Bakhtin finds "[t]his ever-present excess" ("Author" 22–3) of perception and cognition "aesthetically productive" (10). For example, whereas the self can see parts of its own body (parts of arms and legs, for example), it can see the whole "outward express-edness" of the other in social interaction—i.e., the other's body, body language, countenance, and situation of the body in space, including the horizon behind and background of the body. Thus, "two different worlds are reflected in the pupils" of self and other when they "gaze at each other," and, though this difference could be considerably reduced by assuming similar positions in space, a complete reduction would entail their merging into the same person (23). One's non-coincidence with the other prevents this, however: "This ever-present *excess* of my seeing, knowing, and possessing in relation to any other human being is founded in the uniqueness and irreplaceability of my place in the world. For only I—the one and only I—occupy in a given set of cir-cumstances this particular place at this particular time; all other human beings are situated outside me" (22–3).

Bakhtin substantiates his claim about the aesthetically generative character of self and other in a variety of ways. A primary example is where he argues that whereas one cannot even imagine one's "outward image" in one's own dreams or fantasies, one can imagine the exterior of another person "with remarkable clarity and completeness—down to expressions of surprise, delight, fright, love, or fear on their faces" (28–9). Additionally, Bakhtin maintains that even a mirror is unable to provide the dialogic aesthetic of self and other in life. To begin with, the image is a mere reflection of the self and not another person (32). Besides, this image encompasses only a part of what in life is a whole body, and even this part is on the surface of the mirror and not in actual space. Furthermore, one cannot approach one's own image "from the outside." The result is some vague, unnatural, and dubious other, despite one's best efforts to vivify this image by attitudinizing a bit in front of the mirror. The image thus remains one that no one has ever actually experienced in life, one that lacks dialogic power of self and other in life (32). Indeed, Bakhtin grounds a general aesthetic theory in the dialogic of the self–other relationship:

> If there is only one unitary and unique participant, there can be no *aesthetic* event. An absolute consciousness, a conscious that has noth-ing transgredient to itself, nothing situated outside itself and capable of delimiting it from outside—such a conscious cannot be "aestheti-cized"; one can commune in it, but it cannot be seen as a *whole* that

is capable of being consummated. An aesthetic event can take place only when there are [at least] two participants present; it presupposes [at least] two noncoinciding consciousnesses. (22)

Furthermore, Bakhtin develops this aesthetic theory into a theory of verbal art, one that is related to but different from his theory of language, and one that explains why he finds the poem to have less capacity than the novel to represent the dialogic of life and language.

Bakhtin describes this theory in "Lyrical Hero and Author," a subsection in "Author and Hero in Aesthetic Activity" (167–72), and he illustrates it with a reading of "Parting" (*Toward* 65–75; "Author" 211–21). In Bakhtin's theory and practice, self and other in life become the author and hero of the written utterance, and exploiting one's outsideness in life becomes the writer's strategy for achieving a dialogic imagination in writing, specifically by remaining outside the hero of the utterance with respect to place, time, and value.

Bakhtin argues that in a lyrical utterance, author and hero merge, almost completely, and this merging contributes to the monologic character of the work. This monologism stems from two "constitutive moments" of the lyric, one of which is the hero's lack of "spatial expressedness" (168). That is to say, the lyrical hero cannot really be seen or heard because she does not appear to be in real space. She lacks a horizon and background, and there is virtually no image of her body or countenance. She seems more spirit than body, more infinite than finite—an image valorized by Romantic writers but denigrated by Bakhtin as inartistic. Additionally, the lyrical hero lacks a substantial story and, thus, a *Bildung* of inner life or soul. What is presented is an "episode" in the life of a hero rather than a whole life (168).

The second monologic attribute of the lyrical utterance is the author's assumption of a sympathetic audience, much like a member of a chorus. This "choral support" makes the lyric sound authoritative (169). Bakhtin holds that the lyrical state of mind ("what sings in me") is not a natural emotion but an artificial one, no matter how immediate it may feel (169). Its artificiality consists of its simulation of compassionate listeners who sanction the existence of the speaker. In this regard, the lyric poem is like the music that once accompanied it, for in both music and lyric the creator of the medium aims to be the author of his own "inner life," despite that inner life's being a function of social interaction (170). By presenting one's "own naturalness as a value," the lyrical utterance strives to overcome the creative nature of the dialogic aesthetics of lived life, aesthetics that stem from the non-coincidence of self and other and the resultant surplus of seeing and knowing that every human being possesses with regard to another human being (170–1).

Such an utterance can take place only in an "atmosphere of trust, love, and possible choral support" (172), Bakhtin asserts. The lyricist uses these cognitive faculties to organize the representation of herself to her audience. However, unlike in life, where one's presentation is understood through actual, dynamic social interaction in space and time, in the lyrical utterance the presentation of the self is largely self-sufficient and divested of objective features and relations, focusing instead on the inner life of the speaker who surrounds herself in a warm, sultry, and even passionate atmosphere. In short, as with the lyrical author's decision to depict the hero in limited space and time, the lyrical author's deployment of an atmosphere of warmth, confidence, and love strengthens the position of the author over the hero, who is weak, dependent, and a mere reflection of the author's life and mind. In a lyric, the dialogic aesthetic of self and other in life is negligible because of the predominance of the author over the hero: "one more step—and the lyrical work is on the verge of becoming a pure, objectless form of the possible cherishing of a possible hero (for only the hero can be the bearer of a content, i.e., of the prosaic value-context)" (172).

Like the passages on confession and biographical writing ("Author" 156–62), the ones on lyric poetry reveal a conception of this genre as monological owing to its close author–hero relationship. Put differently, the lyric's monologic author–hero relationship violates the non-coincidence principle. Indeed, the lyrical utterance attempts to obviate that principle by simulating the presence of a loving audience. Moreover, instead of exploiting the aesthetic potential of remaining outside the hero, the lyric writer assimilates the hero, so much so that it is hard to think of lyrical author and lyrical speaker as separate entities. Moreover, Bakhtin's identification of the merged author–hero relationship in prose genres, as well as in lyric poetry, suggests that the monologic character of any kind of utterance, as a work of art, depends in some degree on the proximity of author to hero with respect to time, place, and value. It also suggests that a monologic work of art fails to recognize the aesthetic value of otherness in life that can contribute to the highest aims of art. Even so, any kind of utterance, no matter how monologic in its author–hero relationship, remains dialogic as an utterance, as my reading of "Song of Myself" will show.

To be sure, Whitman's poem is dialogic in the major ways that every kind of utterance is dialogical—that is, in its change of speaking subjects, finalization of the utterance, expressive intonation, and addressivity. When Whitman begins Song of Myself with "I celebrate myself,"[7] a new utterance has begun in a way that absolutely marks it off from all other utterances, including the untitled preface to *Leaves of Grass* that precedes it, and the eleven untitled poems that follow it. Moreover, with this change of speaking subjects, the reader recognizes the utterance's relationship to other utterances, especially like-utterances, such as poems (i.e., utterances, usually metrical, arranged in lines rather than continuous sentences) that treat the self (a common topic in Greco-Roman and Romantic lyric poetry). The more savvy reader (then and now) recognizes the epideictic style of the poem and way the American content of the poem reflects a quest for an American identity in literature (a goal of many writers in 1855, prompted by Emerson's call for such a writer). As the reader reads through many lines of verse, she also becomes aware of the poem's relationship to other long poems that treat the self, such as *The Prelude, Childe Harold,* and *The Bridge,* to name a few. Thus, while the change of speaking subjects in Whitman's poem demarcates a new utterance, it also reveals certain kinds of otherness made possible by the use of language, including other complex cultural utterances, however distant ("Speech Genres" 93).

"Song of Myself" is also dialogic in its finalization, which sets the stage for the reader's responsive understanding, however active or passive:

> The last scud of day holds back for me,
> It flings my likeness after the rest and true as any on the
>   shadowed wilds,
> It coaxes me to the vapor and the dusk.
> I depart as air . . . . I shake my white locks at the runaway sun,
> I effuse my flesh in eddies and drift it in lacy jags.
> I bequeath myself to the dirt to grow from the grass I love,
> If you want me again look for me under your bootsoles.
>
> You will hardly know who I am or what I mean,
> But I shall be good health to you nevertheless,
> And filter and fibre your blood.
>
> Failing to fetch me at first keep encouraged,
> Missing me one place search another,
> I stop some where waiting for you[.]

(55–6)

Here the finalization of the poem—the sheer fact of its actual completion—is sufficient and necessary for it to be a dialogic marker of the poem, inasmuch as this ending now makes possible the reader's responsive understanding to the whole utterance. However, the imagery and metaphors of the passage ("last scud of day," "shadowed wilds," "vapor and the dusk," "runaway sun") facilitate the reader's perception of the utterance's completion. Additionally, the image of leaving oneself to the earth ("I bequeath myself to the dirt"), along with the image of the speaker's stopping and waiting, heightens the reader's expectation of closure. What is more, Whitman's raising the question of his poem's meaning, alongside verbs of fetching, missing, searching, finding, and waiting, all point to his own realization that the ending of his poem will mark the beginning of the reader's responsive understanding. Such are the "dialogic overtones" in "Song of Myself," overtones that remind the reader that every utterance, even a complex one, is "like a rejoinder in a dialogue" (76).

The dialogic of the utterance is also evident in the expressive intonation of "Song of Myself." Every word in the poem, and many of its phrases and clauses, has appeared in other utterances before and after 1855. Yet the unique composition of these words in an actual utterance at a particular moment in time imparts to the whole utterance an evaluative tone for the first time. The tone is mainly confident, much like the atmosphere of trust that Bakhtin finds characteristic of lyric poetry. The first two lines set this tone: "I CELEBRATE myself / And what I assume you shall assume . . ." (13). In the following line, Whitman even provides a scientific reason for having this trust: "For every atom belonging to me as good belongs to you." This self-confidence in his speech and his readers' understanding pervades the poem, even in parts that make the poem a hybrid, such as its epic catalogs:

> Off on the lakes the pikefisher watches and waits by
>   the hole in the frozen surface,
> The stumps stand thick round the clearing, the squatter
>   strikes deep with his axe,
> The flatboatmen make fast toward dusk near the
>   cottonwood or pekantrees,
> The coon-seekers go now through the regions
>   of the Red river, or through those drained by
>   the Tennessee, or through those of the Arkansas,
> The torches shine in the dark that hangs on the
>   Chattahoochee or Altamahaw;

> Patriarchs sit at supper with sons and grandsons and
>   great grandsons around them,
> In walls of adobe, in canvass tents, rest hunters and
>   trappers after their day's sport.

(23)

The opening stanza and the catalog, though different modes of writing, are identical in their tone of self-assurance. In both, the reader perceives the speaker's confidence in the importance of what is being said and contemplated. Moreover, the tone remains consistent throughout the catalog (and other catalogs) despite the variety of items, creatures, and social ranks. A tone of supreme confidence is especially evident in Whitman's oracular assertion that he simultaneously attracts and is attracted to everything in the catalog: "And these one and all tend inward to me, and I tend outward to them, / And such as it is be of these more or less I am" (23). This sureness of purpose can also be heard in the poem's integrated narratives, such as this legend:

> The runaway slave came to my house and stopped outside,
> I heard his motions crackling the twigs of the woodpile,
> Through the swung half-door of the kitchen I saw him
>   limpsey and weak,
> And went where he sat on a log, and led him in and assured him,
> And brought water and filled a tub for his sweated body
>   and bruised feet,
> And gave him a room that entered from my own, and
>   gave him some coarse clean clothes.

(19)

The anaphora emphasizes the speaker's self-assurance and imparts an oratorical quality to the passage, much in keeping with its epideictic style. Whitman's self-confidence is also apparent in the purely lyrical passages of the poem: "A few light kisses . . . a few embraces . . . a reaching around of arms, / The play of shine and shade on the trees as the supple boughs wag, / The delight alone or in the rush of the streets, or along the fields and hillsides, / The feeling of health . . . the full-noon trill . . . the song of me rising from bed and meeting the sun" (13).

"Song of Myself" is also dialogical in its addressivity, particularly the type of audience it evokes. Because the goal of the 1855 *Leaves of Grass*, as stated in the opening paragraph of the untitled preface, is to break new ground in Western poetry, the reader can discern that the type of addressee in "Song of Myself" is "a differentiated collective of specialists in some particular area of cultural communication" ("Speech Genres" 95). This is perceivable in the several literary devices (anaphora, imagery, metaphor) and types of writing (catalog, lyric, narrative) Whitman deploys to present his bona fides to his principal audience, the literati.

Another type of addressivity can be seen and heard in the way Whitman anticipates his reader's response to his utterance. Below are four such passages, followed by commentary:

(1) You are also asking me questions, and I hear you;
I answer that I cannot answer . . . you must find out for yourself.

(52)

(2) Have you reckoned a thousand acres much? Have you
reckoned the Earth much?
Have you practiced so long to learn to read?
Have you felt so proud to get at the meaning of poems?

(14)

(3) I do not despise you priests;
My faith is the greatest of faiths and the least of faiths.

(48)

(4) The sky up there . . . yet here or next door or across the way?
The saints and sages in history . . . but you yourself?

(48)

In the first passage, we hear Whitman anticipating what readers might think of him and his verse, of the goals and meaning of his writing, and of its lack of meter, unusual length, frank sexuality, shifting topics, or any other likely thought that might arise from reading "Song of Myself." In the second passage, Whitman is heard anticipating—if not challenging—his reader's estimation of the value of reading poetry compared with landed wealth, as well as his reader's own skill in reading and understanding poetry. In the third passage, Whitman anticipates what the religious establishment might think of his ideas, and, ironically, offers them assurance in the way of a paradox. And in the fourth passage, Whitman can be heard anticipating ordinary citizens' lack of self-confidence in their potential for spiritual satisfaction.

Thus, like all utterances, Whitman's poem possesses the four major dialogic attributes of the utterance, attributes that define an utterance and that are a function of the role of the other in language use. At the same time, it is a work that Bakhtin would find artistically monological in its merged author–hero relationship. Put differently, Bakhtin would find "Song of Myself" inartistic in its merged author–hero relationship, which he would attribute to Whitman's inability or unwillingness to recognize the aesthetically creative nature of the non-coincidence of self and other in life.

This monologic art, to begin with, is evident in the lyrical hero's lack of "spatial expressedness" ("Author" 168), a lack that prevents the reader from perceiving the hero in space and time. For instance, we see at the outset of the poem that he has, in romantic fashion, decided to leave civilization for "the woods and become undisguised and naked" (13). Additionally, we read in an early passage that the hero is bearded, while at the end of the poem we see that that hero has white hair. The hero also appears unkempt and licentious, goes by the name "Walt Whitman" (just as the author does), and has a democratic sensibility and average modesty: "Walt Whitman, an American, one of the roughs, a kosmos, / Disorderly fleshy and sensual . . . eating drinking and breeding, / No sentimentalist . . . no stander above men and women or apart from them . . . no more modest than immodest" (29). Yet, notwithstanding the other 1,300 lines of the poem, the reader is left with a vague image of the hero. We cannot see his countenance, have no good idea where he speaks from or what is behind him, and learn little about his social development. Truly, he seems to be more spirit than body, contrary to Whitman's own rejection of this binary opposition. Bakhtin, however, notes that the infinity of the lyrical hero is monological and typical of Romantic literature ("Author" 168). Unlike one's encounter with others in daily intercourse, where one experiences a surplus of perception and cognition with respect to another human being, the reader's encounter with the lyrical hero leaves the reader with an incomplete picture of the hero's external image and life. What image the reader does have suggests that he resembles the picture of the poet himself on the frontispiece (a reproduction of an engraving taken in 1854). This picture shows Whitman, from head to knee, facing the viewer directly. His right arm is akimbo, he wears a slouch hat and workman's clothes, and his countenance is cocky but inviting. All together, it is an image of self-confidence. However, even if the reader were to equate author with speaker, the image of this person would still be indefinite, for he is rarely seen in actual space, with a horizon and background behind him, and he shows no development over time. The narrative of the hero's caring for the fugitive slave is an exception. Indeed, after 1,336 lines of verse, his life shows no development out of a plot, and no time has elapsed. Time is commensurate with the reading of the poem. Clearly, the merging of author and hero in "Song of Myself" is almost complete. The reader might sense some aesthetic distance between the two in the way of a persona. Yet even this is questionable, given the realistic image of Whitman on the frontispiece and his identification of the hero half way through the poem as himself. Thus, "Song of Myself" illustrates Bakhtin's argument that one way a lyric poem overcomes the dialogic aesthetic of self and other in life is by providing the reader with a minimal image of the lyrical hero in space and time and a maximal image of the author.

"Song of Myself" also exhibits the second characteristic of a monologic author–hero relationship: a "possible choral support" ("Author" 170). This is Bakhtin's metaphor for the way in which the lyric voice is imbued with a sense of sympathetic listeners. This self-assurance, as noted above, is heard throughout the poem, and constitutes the poem's particular expression as an utterance. However, the dialogic of life is not the dialogic of art, and representing one's own self-confidence does not count as art in Bakhtin's theory of literature. Indeed, the simulation of like-minded readers comes at the expense of the hero's life. Almost any line in the poem can supply an example of this lyrical quality, though a particularly strong example occurs where Whitman speaks of his relationship to geologic time:

Cycles ferried my cradle, rowing and rowing like cheerful
   boatmen;
For room to me stars kept aside in their own rings,
They sent influences to look after what was to hold me.

Before I was born out of my mother generations guided me,
My embryo has never been torpid . . . nothing could overlay it;
For it the nebula cohered to an orb . . . the long slow strata
   piled to rest it on . . . vast vegetables gave it sustenance,

Monstrous sauroids transported it in their mouths and
   deposited it with care.

All forces have been steadily employed to complete and
  delight me,
Now I stand on this spot with my soul.

(50)

These lines are spoken as though every person listening is in complete
agreement with them. This concord is heard in the speaker's presentation of the argument as scientific fact; in the emphatic repetition of the
subject-verb syntax of every clause; and in the absolute conviction of
the negatives "never" and "nothing." The perception of a sympathetic
audience is also evident in what is not heard: doubt, misgivings, or
equivocation. This is not a lyrical utterance on the verge of disintegration, to which the lyric is susceptible ("Author" 171–2). In fact, although
few of Whitman's contemporaries would share his atheistic cosmology,
he speaks of it as though his views are unanimous. A choral support of
trust is especially strong where Whitman speaks of love: "I swear I will
never mention love or death inside a house, / And I swear I never will
translate myself at all, only to him or her who privately stays with me
in the open air" (53). The intonation of such lines have become fodder
for parodies of Whitman's verse, yet they are spoken by Whitman with
the utmost gravity, sincerity, and self-possessedness. The choral support is absolute in lines such as these: "I hear the sound of the human
voice . . . a sound I love" (31). As Bakhtin notes, such verse could
not sustain its tone if "solitariness of sound is in principle excluded"
("Author" 170). In fact, by using a voice that projects an atmosphere
of affection and self-confidence, Whitman objectifies himself in a way
that Bakhtin contends is monological and typical of the lyric genre. In
doing so, a lyrical hero in "Song of Myself" is barely perceptible, for the
inner life of the person speaking has become the life of a character who
has been completely assimilated by the author. Instead of exploiting his
ontological privilege of being outside the hero, Whitman has chosen to
speak for and through him, as though self and other could be one and
the same person, as though an "[a]esthetic event" could occur where
there is only one consciousness, with nothing "transgredient" to it in
time, space, or value ("Author" 22).

A comparison with "Parting" will further substantiate my claim about
the monologic character of the author–hero relationship in "Song of
Myself." Whereas this poem has "two active persons in the poem" (the
lyrical hero and Pushkin's lover Amalia Riznich), and two aesthetic

subjects outside the poem (the author and reader), "Song of Myself" has an author and reader (like every utterance), but only one active person in the poem, the author, who largely assimilates the lyrical hero to his own position (*Toward* 66). While there are a few moments in the poem that appear to foreground more than one hero in the poem, we see (unlike in "Parting") no difference with respect to the "emotional-volitional tone" (*Toward* 67) of the two heroes:

> I mind how we lay in June, such a transparent summer morning;
> You settled your head athwart my hips and gently turned
>   over upon me,
> And parted the shirt from my bosom-bone, and plunged your
>   tongue to my barestript heart,
> And reached till you felt my beard, and reached till you
>   held my feet.
>
> Swiftly arose and spread around me the peace and joy and
>   knowledge that pass all the art and argument of the earth.
>
> (15)

The language in this passage does not vary according to spatial, temporal or evaluative difference of the two heroes. Every word and phrase is heard in the evaluative context of the author; not even the lyrical hero's voice (the "I" of the passage) can be heard. The two heroes might as well be one, for the lyrical hero himself cannot be seen or heard in any substantive way because of the predominance of the author. Even when a narrative moment in the poem appears to reveal two centers of value, as in the narrative of the slave's visit to Whitman's house, the language of the poem remains within the evaluative tone of the author:

> And [I] remember perfectly well his revolving eyes and his
>   awkwardness,
> And remember putting plasters on the galls of his neck and
>   ankles;
> He staid with me a week before he was recuperated and
>   passed north,
> I had him sit next me at table . . . my firelock leaned in
>   the corner.
>
> (19)

Unlike in "Parting," where the lyrical heroes' real difference—their being unique persons, with unique backgrounds and experiences, confronting each other in space and time—results in corresponding tonal differences, Whitman's narrative, like the whole work, is monological, in that everything that is heard is given in the evaluative tone of the author, who has integrated the lyrical hero into his own inward expression. Thus, the potential dialogic of the two heroes in the passage above, whose lives and experiences are drastically different and who now confront one another under difficult circumstance (it was a felony to harbor fugitive slaves in 1855), cannot be heard. "[M]y house" is heard in the evaluative context of the author, for example. It is Whitman's house to both heroes. Similarly, the escaping slave's "revolving eyes and his awkwardness" are perceived from Whitman's perspective. Even the significant closure of the narrative—"my firelock leaned in the corner"—suggests that it was not needed as far as Whitman is concerned. In short, there is one value-center, not two, in the poem, the lyrical hero, but even this value-center presents himself to the reader as scarcely indistinguishable from the author. Thus, unlike Pushkin's poem and Dostoevsky's fiction, Whitman's poem is inartistic insofar as it lacks a "plurality of independent and unmerged voices and consciousnesses" (*Problems* 6). This lack is a consequence of Whitman's relinquishing his "privilege of being outside the hero to the fullest extent" ("Author" 167) and choosing instead to merge with his lyrical hero and even reader ("And what I shall assume, you shall assume"). Evidently, Whitman—a poet who saw himself in a tradition of the shaman, bard, and poet-prophet—ignores or rejects the dialogic aesthetic of lived life as a source of artistic inspiration. In brief, "Song of Myself" exhibits a monologic author–hero relationship, for it is merged in such a degree that it is difficult to see and hear anything but the vestige of a lyrical hero.

The preceding argument, along with the above exposition of Bakhtin's distinction between dialogism in language and literature, demonstrates that Bakhtin's writing allows for reading the same poem as dialogic utterance and monologic work of art. Consequently, it also challenges the consensus that Bakhtin's critique of poetry[8] as a monologic speech genre is contradictory or misguided. This may be the most significant implication of all, for, as Catherine Ciepiela has noted, one reason Bakhtin's theory of poetry has been rejected is because it is valid: poetry truly is an authoritative discourse that belongs to the centripetal forces in the life and language and literature (1013); and for those who love poetry, including this writer, the thought of its being on the wrong side of history is difficult to contemplate.

Notes

1. For a bibliography on Bakhtinian studies in poetry, see my 160-item bibliography in Appendix A of my dissertation (2010). It contains items not yet included in The Bakhtin Centre's Analytical Database out of Sheffield University. For brief surveys of the literature, see Ciepiela, Eskin, Niazi, and Scanlon.
2. For minority opinions on Bakhtin's theory of poetry, see Batstone, Ciepiela, Eskin, Niazi, Phillips, and Pierson.
3. The question of the disputed works in Bakhtin scholarship does not concern us here, for I am using only non-disputed works.
4. The notion that Bakhtin draws a distinction between an utterance and an artistic utterance has been touched upon in the scholarship, though I seem to be the first to have elaborated on it. See Batstone, Richter, and Pierson. My position follows Batstone, though differs from his in that whereas he considers the utterance-work distinction useless, I find it a rich vein of Bakhtinian thought that sheds light on the concept of dialogism, on its differentiated application to literature and language differently, and on the innovative approach to poetry offered here: reading it simultaneously dialogically and monologically.
5. Bakhtin's dialogic theory of language follows logically from his dialogic theory of cognition, which is set forth in *Toward a Philosophy of the Act* and "Author and Hero in Aesthetic Activity." Otherness is essential to the formation of both understanding and language, and one can infer from Bakhtin's writing that an utterance is a form of thought, a "performed action," to use one of his terms for a type of cognition. For a discussion of Bakhtin's dialogic theory of human understanding, see my dissertation (57–107).
6. I ignore Russian, and I am indebted to the Bakhtin scholar Sergeiy Sandler for my information on Bakhtin's terms "artistic" and "art".
7. All quoted passages from "Song of Myself," as well as the page numbers given in parenthetical citations, refer to the first (1855) edition of *Leaves of Grass*, as it appears in the authoritative Walt Whitman Archive, ed. Ed Folsom and Kenneth M. Price. (http://www.whitmanarchive.org/published/LG/1855/images/index.html).
8. Bakhtin notes that Western poetry becomes radically dialogized by the twentieth century (*Problems* 200), yet this point is ignored by many commentators, especially those who proffer dialogic readings of twentieth-century poems as a reconsideration of Bakhtin's critique of poetry as monological.

Works cited

Bakhtin, M. M. "Author and Hero in Aesthetic Activity." *Art and Answerability: Early Philosophical Essays by M. M. Bakhtin.* Ed. Michael Holquist and Vadim Liapunov. Trans. Vadim Liapunov. Austin: U of Texas P, 1990. 4–256.

——. "The Problem of Speech Genres." *Speech Genres and Other Late Essays.* Ed. Caryl Emerson and Michael Holquist. Trans. Vernon W. McGee. Austin: U of Texas P, 1986. 60–102.

——. "The Problem of the Text in Linguistics, Philology, and the Human Sciences: An Experiment in Philosophical Analysis." *Speech Genres and Other Late Essays.*

Ed. Caryl Emerson and Michael Holquist. Trans. Vernon W. McGee. Austin: U of Texas P, 1986. 103–31.

——. *Problems of Dostoevsky's Poetics* (1963). Ed. and trans. Caryl Emerson. Minneapolis: U of Minnesota P, 1984.

——. *Toward a Philosophy of the Act.* Trans. Vadim Liapunov. Ed. Vadim Liapunov and Michael Holquist. Austin: U of Texas P, 1993.

Batstone, William W. "Catullus and Bakhtin: The Problems of a Dialogic Lyric." *Bakhtin and the Classics.* Ed. R. Bracht Branham. Evanston, IL: Northwestern UP, 2002. 99–136.

Blevins, Jacob, ed. *Dialogism and Lyric Self-Fashioning: Bakhtin and the Voices of a Genre.* Selinsgrove, PA: Susquehanna UP, 2008.

Ciepiela, Catherine. "Taking Monologism Seriously: Bakhtin and Tsvetaeva's 'The Pied Piper.'" *Slavic Review* 53.4 (1994): 1010–24.

Eskin, Michael. "Bakhtin on Poetry." *Poetics Today* 21.2 (2000): 379–91.

Niazi, Mohammed. "Encountering the Other in the General Text: An Approach to Intertext through the Poetry of German Sensibility." *Comparative Literature*: 52.2 (2000): 97–118.

Phillippy, Patricia Berrahou. *Love's Remedies: Recantation and Renaissance Lyric Poetry.* Cranberry, NJ: Associated U P, 1995.

Phillips, Dana. "Whitman and Genre: The Dialogic in 'Song of Myself.'" *Bloom's Modern Critical Interpretations: Walt Whitman's "Song of Myself."* Ed. Harold Bloom. Philadelphia: Chelsea House, 2003. 195–221.

Pierson, Stephen. *A Bakhtinian Reading of a Selection of Poems by Hölderlin and Whitman.* Diss. Purdue U, 2010.

Richter, David. "Dialogism and Poetry." *Studies in the Literary Imagination* 23.1 (1990): 9–20.

Sandler, Sergeiy. "'Artistic' and 'Art' in Bakhtin's Oeuvre." Email to Stephen Pierson. 5 November 2013.

Scanlon, Mara. "Ethics and the Lyric: Form, Dialogue, Answerability." *College Literature* 34.1 (2007): 1–22.

Whitman, Walt. "Song of Myself." *Leaves of Grass*, 1855 ed. *The Walt Whitman Archive.* Ed. Ed Folsom and Kenneth M. Price. Web.

3

Aesthetic Activity in Sir Thomas Wyatt's Penitential Psalms

Chad Engbers

> O wad some Power the giftie gie us
> To see oursels as ithers see us!
> It wad frae mony a blunder free us,
> An' foolish notion . . .
>
> (Robert Burns, "To a Louse")

Can a poem be dialogic? If we are to follow Mikhail M. Bakhtin's remarks in "Discourse in the Novel"—his most mature exposition of dialogism—we would likely answer "no." In that essay, Bakhtin repeatedly insists that, although all language is shaped by the voices of others, prose novels integrate those other voices, while in poetry such voices are "artificially extinguished" (284). In a novel, we encounter the voices of many personalities and social classes, and each group speaks differently. Dialogism, as Bakhtin explains it, is primarily evident in stylistic features such as the "hybrid construction": a single word, phrase, or sentence that clearly "contains mixed within it two utterances, two speech manners, two styles" (304ff.). In a poem, according to Bakhtin, the voice of the poet is the only authoritative voice. All of the words in a poem have had to pass through the heteroglossia of the poet's own world, of course, but in the poem itself "the records of the passage remain in the slag of the creative process, which is then cleared away (as scaffolding is cleared away once construction is finished), so that the finished work may rise as unitary speech [. . .]" (331). Other voices may even linger in a poem, as when an author makes an allusion to an earlier work, but in such cases the other voices are clearly subordinated to the point of view of the poet—in effect losing their genuine "otherness."

It is this otherness—or, to use Bakhtin's term, this outsideness (*vnenakhodimost'*)—that is the principal requirement for dialogism, whether or not it is expressed in hybrid constructions or other stylistic features. One way to move beyond Bakhtin's own bias toward the novel is to explore literary manifestations of outsideness that are different from the stylistic features on which Bakhtin focuses.

William Batstone, for instance, explains that a dialogic poem is possible as long as it is founded upon a dialogic understanding of self, "a divided self, a self which is intersected by embodied discourses and may speak now with one voice, now with another" (104–5). In a novel, multiple voices become embodied in multiple characters, and the fabric of the novel is thus woven out of several discrete consciousnesses and language styles. For a lyric poem to be dialogic, it must present a self that is internally divided, a single consciousness that contains within itself the kinds of different views and voices that might populate a novel—admittedly a tall order for a short poem. Outsideness is still present in this kind of lyric; it is simply that—to speak somewhat paradoxically—outsideness occurs within a single self.[1] The dialogic self, Batstone explains, is not a finished product but an emerging project, incomplete and unfinalized. A poem which presents such a self will include "inevitable slippage between the authoring and authored self" (105). Batstone observes that not every lyric poem can achieve this effect, which arises more organically from the formal complexity of a novel. We might say that a dialogic poem surpasses the natural potential of its form; a dialogic novel simply fulfills it.

Batstone offers as examples several lyric poems by Catullus, in which the poet's self emerges as an uncertain amalgamation of his views about himself and others' views about him.[2] Although Batstone acknowledges that the lyric is not as organically dialogic as the novel, and that many lyric poems are not dialogic at all (106), his primary contention is that dialogism is not—as Bakhtin held—limited to particular genres. As the study of Catullus demonstrates, dialogism is at root more phenomenological than stylistic or even generic: it is a matter of multiple perspectives that are outside one another, whatever the literary form in which those perspectives are presented.

Even Batstone's groundbreaking essay, however, leaves open a considerable gap between the exceptionally dialogic poems of Catullus and the strictly monologic poems that Bakhtin seems to have in mind throughout "Discourse in the Novel." What about poems that fall short of the dialogic requirements set forth by Bakhtin and Batstone, but which nevertheless show more dialogism than others? Dialogue and monologue are, after all, not binary categories but graduated ones: works of literature are dialogic to varying degrees. The appropriate

question is therefore not "is this poem dialogic?" but rather, "how dialogic is this poem?" Bakhtin himself spends little time on the middle
ground between dialogue and monologue. Although he occasionally
acknowledges that "the phenomenon of internal dialogization is present to a greater or lesser extent in all realms of the life of the word," he
tends to locate these degrees primarily in various kinds of prose fiction,
not in lyric poetry ("Discourse" 284).

This essay argues that poetry can indeed be dialogic, even in the
Bakhtinian sense of that word, as long as we are willing to follow
Batstone and others in understanding dialogism in ways deeper than
style, and if we are willing to acknowledge varying degrees of dialogism. One way to do this is to move back in Bakhtin's own thinking on
dialogism to its roots in his earliest writings, which are more concerned
with phenomenology and ethics than with literary genre or style. In
this essay, I use Bakhtin's early piece "Author and Hero in Aesthetic
Activity" to discuss the dialogic qualities of a sequence of poems that
might at first seem utterly undialogic—Sir Thomas Wyatt's Penitential
Psalms. Not only is dialogism a suitable and even necessary paradigm
for understanding these poems, but these poems can help us to refine
Bakhtin's idea of dialogism.

1.   Wyatt and David in aesthetic activity

Sir Thomas Wyatt's *Certain Psalms*, probably written in 1541, is an
English rendition of seven biblical psalms—6, 32, 38, 51, 102, 130, and
143—collectively known as the Penitential Psalms. By the time of the
English Renaissance, it was commonplace to read the seven psalms as
King David's repentance for what Anne Lake Prescott has felicitously
called "the Bathsheba affair" (149): David lusts after Bathsheba, sends
her husband Uriah into the front lines of battle, and is finally accused
by the prophet Nathan for the dual crimes of adultery and murder.[3]
Wyatt retells all of these events in a verse prologue before the first
psalm (Psalm 6). At the end of the prologue, David retreats to an isolated cave to repent, and the seven psalms thus represent his cries for
forgiveness. Between each of the psalms, Wyatt provides further narrative segments that explain what David is feeling and doing between
his penitential songs.[4]

In terms of style, Wyatt's psalms could scarcely be called dialogic.
There are few, if any, hybrid constructions. It is true that the voices of
David and the narrator at least seem to be fully outside one another: the
narrator is limited to the interludes, David to the psalms; the narrator

speaks in *ottava rima*, David in *terza rima*. It is perfectly clear when each person is speaking.

The real reason why hybrid constructions do not appear in the sequence, however, is not that the voices are so distinct, but that they are altogether too unified stylistically. Aside from the separate verse forms, the voices are nearly indistinguishable. Both speak in Wyatt's own courtly tones, given to formal flourishes, rhetorical amplification, and extended comparisons. Similarly, Wyatt's style seamlessly integrates a whole host of voices from his source material, beginning with the original psalms in Hebrew (a language which Wyatt could almost certainly not read), but also including a long line of commentators and translators culminating in Pietro Aretino, whose Italian version of the psalms was clearly Wyatt's model.[5] None of these voices is evident as distinct entities in Wyatt's finished version. To use Bakhtin's metaphor, all of these previous voices enter Lethe and forget their previous meanings before entering Wyatt's psalms ("Discourse" 297).

To choose just one example, in one place David concludes that outward deeds do not constitute repentance itself but are merely "the sign or fruit alone" of true contrition (line 655). H. A. Mason suggests that Wyatt is borrowing from William Tyndale's prologue to the book of Romans: "Even so are all other good works outward *signs* and outward *fruit* of faith and of the spirit; which justify not a man but that a man is justified already before God inwardly in the heart, through faith and through the spirit purchased by Christ's blood" (Tyndale 216, emphasis added; Mason 189). Tyndale's own words, as it happens, are already a translation and adaptation of Martin Luther's prologue to Romans: "So all good works are only external *signs* which follow out of faith, like good *fruit*, they demonstrate that a person is already inwardly righteous before God" (Luther 374, emphasis added). The general theological idea here, and the specific phrase "sign or fruit," seem to show Wyatt integrating a short tradition of Reformation voices with the voice of Aretino—an Italian Catholic whose version does not include this distinctly Protestant parsing of good works. The differences between the psalmist, Tyndale, Luther, Aretino, and Wyatt are all but erased, however, in Wyatt's rendition. One can read the entire sequence without once being jarred by a voice that seems different or slightly out of place. The jar comes only when one consults the footnotes of a scholarly edition and realizes the vast array of other voices neatly concealed beneath Wyatt's unified courtly style. In this respect, the sequence seems to clearly illustrate some of Bakhtin's own assertions about poetic discourse: "Poetry also sees its own language surrounded

by other languages, surrounded by literary and extra-literary heteroglossia. But poetry, striving for maximal purity, works in its own language
as if that language were unitary, the only language, as if there were no
heteroglossia outside it" ("Discourse" 399, emphasis in original). From
a stylistic point of view, then, the outsideness of David and the narrator are somewhat artificial. Both really speak in Wyatt's voice, and
Wyatt's voice speaks as if it were the *only* voice. This is true, however,
only stylistically.

Wyatt's psalm sequence is at least partially dialogic because the two
perspectives of David and the narrator, despite their stylistic unity, are
dramatically different phenomenologically—both in what they perceive
and in how they perceive it. A good example of their difference occurs
in Psalm 32 and in the narrative interlude following it. In the psalm,
David praises God for having heard his prayer, releasing him from sin:

> Such Joy as he that scapes his enemy's ward
> With loosed bonds hath in his liberty,
> Such Joy, my Joy, thou hast to me prepared.

> (lines 265–7)[6]

In the following interlude, Wyatt picks up the word "Joy" and embeds
it in a dramatic scene as a shaft of sunshine enters the cave and gleams
off David's harp:

> This while a beam that bright sun forth sends,
> That sun the which was never cloud could hide,
> Pierceth the cave and on the harp descends,
> Whose glancing light the cords did overglide,
> And such luster upon the harp extends
> As light of lamp upon the gold clean tried:
> The turn whereof into his eyes did start,
> Surprised with Joy by penance of the heart.

> (309–16)

Both David and the narrator perceive David's joy, but David attributes
the joy to God ("Such Joy [. . .] thou hast to me prepared"), while the
narrator attributes it to David's penance ("Surprised with Joy by penance of the heart"). This difference between these two perspectives,
small though it may seem, is crucial to the sincerity of David's repentance. If David believed that it was his own penance that gave him joy,
he could scarcely be repentant.

At the heart of most penitential poetry is this rhetorical crux: a truly devout penitent cannot recognize her penitence as devout. A sincerely repenting sinner must be wholly in the moment, focused entirely on his own guilt before God. True contrition is therefore distinctly unpoetic. To become *poesis*, a made thing, the penitence must be considered objectively, from a third-person point of view. For a penitent to do this, to consider the holiness of his own contrition, is to run the risk of pride. In another part of the sequence, the narrator describes David as a "marble image of singular reverence" (line 306). If it were David perceiving himself as a marble image, he would immediately lose his singular reverence. Self-admiration and true contrition are completely antithetical. How, then, can sincere repentance be turned into poetry? One way—Wyatt's way—is to employ an outside narrator, a virtuous voyeur who can report the scene on the penitent's behalf, thereby protecting the penitent from the moral dangers of self-perception. So in the sunlit scene quoted above, the narrator's word "Joy" echoes its early use by David, but fulfills that word by adding to it, from the outside, the value of David's repentance. The narrator's perspective of David is, in fact, analogous to the shaft of light: it shines in upon David from outside the cave of David's own self-perception, infusing David with value that he cannot give himself.

This relationship between the narrator and David is, in fact, exactly the kind of relationship that is the central focus of Bakhtin's first major work, "Author and Hero in Aesthetic Activity." There are countless things about me—such as the color of my eyes, the expression on my face, or even my posture—which I am unable to see completely without reference to a point outside myself. Another person, however, can see them at a glance. Outsideness is key: it is precisely because the other is outside my experience that she can discern my environment.[7] In other words, the difference between these two perspectives is precisely the difference between the first-person and third-person points of view. David, doubled over on the floor of the cave, sees only dust. He cannot see his own crumpled body in its entirety or the sun breaking through the clouds outside the cave. Only a third-person observer, such as the narrator, can see all of this. David can perceive the joy of grace from God; the narrator complements this joy with the joy of David's own penance. Bakhtin describes the difference between these first- and third-person perspectives with the term "excess."[8] The word is perhaps misleading with its strong connotations of quantity. The perspectives of the *I* and *other* differ not only in degree (that is, in the amount of information), but in kind. For Bakhtin the inherent difference between me and an other does not necessarily alienate us. On the contrary, our outsideness is precisely what makes our interactions productive. What the narrator does by perceiving David, and thereby granting him a wholeness that he himself could not achieve, is what Bakhtin calls aesthetic activity.

Aesthetic activity occurs in two stages. The first is what Bakhtin calls a "projection." When I attempt to understand another human being, I must first come as close as possible to seeing the world as that human being sees it—I must approximate his horizon by projecting myself into his position. Bakhtin is disappointingly vague on the logistics of this maneuver: "How this projection of myself into him is possible and in what form [. . .] we shall not consider here" (25). More important to Bakhtin is the second stage, in which I return to my vantage point outside the person's horizon and combine the results of my projection with my own perspective of the person's context. This is, of course, exactly what an author does for a hero in a work of literature:

> The author not only sees and knows everything seen and known by the hero individually and by all the heroes collectively, but he also sees and knows *more* than they do; moreover, he sees and knows something that is in principle inaccessible to them. And it is precisely in this invariably determinate and stable *excess* that we find all those moments that bring about the consummation of the whole. (12, emphasis in original)

Such aesthetic activity is the basic element of relationships between authors and heroes (in art) and between others and individuals (in life). Because this essay is taking up the matter of penitential poetry, it is worth noting that aesthetic activity is also an essential component of repentance, where forgiveness is the particular form of aesthetic wholeness bestowed on the penitent *I*. Bakhtin makes this connection explicit:

> Similar to the aesthetic relationship of the author to the hero, or of form to the hero and his life, are such relationships as the following: the relationship of an unmotivated valuation to the object of such valuation [. . .]; the relationship of a confirmative acceptance to the one accepted and confirmed; the relationship of a gift to a need; of an act of freely granted forgiveness to a transgression; of an act of grace to a sinner. (90)

Theological references of this kind—frequently references to the theology of penitence in particular—appear so persistently throughout "Author and Hero" that they do begin to feel like an abiding concern for Bakhtin, perhaps one which he suppressed given the realities of Stalinist censorship. Graham Pechey has described Bakhtin's early thought as "a theologically inflected aesthetics—or an aesthetically inflected theology" (47).[9]

It is not my intention in this essay to argue for an explicitly theological reading of Bakhtin. His paradigm of aesthetic activity suits Wyatt's psalms—and penitential poetry in general—even if his theological language is understood as mere metaphor. At the same time, however, Bakhtin's theologically inflected aesthetic model offers obvious advantages to poetry that is itself overtly theological. One senses that Wyatt's psalms and Bakhtin's "Author and Hero," distant though they are in focus, milieu, and rhetorical purpose, are in many ways exploring the same questions.

Even aside from this theological congruity, Wyatt's psalms are well-suited to Bakhtin's early writings because, while most literature *constitutes* aesthetic activity, this sequence is also *about* aesthetic activity.[10] Wyatt makes the act of authorship visible by including the narrator. Wyatt himself could have offered David the benefits of aesthetic activity simply by translating the psalms without interludes, silently aestheticizing David from behind the scenes. By including the narrator, however, he presents both author and hero as characters, thereby dramatizing aesthetic activity itself. This formal choice is entirely appropriate to a sequence of penitential psalms. The central theme of the poems, a sinful soul receiving an act of grace, is perfectly aligned with its form: a hero receiving the aesthetic activity of an author (or narrator). The narrator cannot, of course, offer David wholeness in the theological sense. He does, however, offer him the phenomenological equivalent of that wholeness, and he can do so only because he enjoys that principle ingredient of dialogism: outsideness.

2.   David's confessional self-accounting

"Author and Hero in Aesthetic Activity" is an essay not only on literary dynamics, but on dynamics that occur among people in real life, and the kind of wholeness we offer one another through aesthetic activity rarely lasts. In the most provocative portions of "Author and Hero," Bakhtin discusses several variations on, and deviations from, aesthetic activity. The most important of these deviations is what Bakhtin calls "confessional self-accounting." Early in the essay, Bakhtin describes what happens when "the hero takes possession of the author" (17). The author accomplishes the first task of aesthetic activity but not the second: she projects herself into the hero's consciousness but fails to return to a position outside the hero. The hero's point of view becomes authoritative, and without any excess perspective from the author, this point of view will always remain incomplete. In effect, there is no distinct author and no distinct hero, only a single author/ hero. "Confessional self-accounting" is one mode of discourse that can emerge from this fusion.

In a confessional self-accounting the author/hero offers an account *of* herself *to* herself. One single consciousness attempts to act not only as author and hero, but also as audience, all at the same time. Confessional self-accounting therefore differs from confession to a priest: there is no other present for this particular form of self-accounting. "A pure, axiologically solitary relationship to myself," Bakhtin writes, "this is what constitutes the ultimate limit toward which confessional self-accounting strives [. . .]" (142). A confessional self-accounting gives all authority to the hero—there is no outside other with whom to share it. The author/hero of a confessional self-accounting wants the wholeness of aesthetic activity, but he does not want it to come from an other.

In fact, confessional self-accounting, by definition, aggressively resists the other. Such discourse does not simply preclude aesthetic activity; in its purest form, self-accounting actively negates any interaction with the other. It is not merely non-aesthetic; it is anti-aesthetic. The best example of confessional self-accounting (although Bakhtin does not mention it as such in "Author and Hero") is probably Dostoevsky's *Notes From Underground*, wherein the Underground Man repeatedly—in fact, obsessively—overcomes various aesthetic definitions of himself from an imaginary audience: "But do you not perhaps think, gentlemen, that I am now repenting of something before you, that I am asking your forgiveness for something? . . . I'm sure you think so. . . . However, I assure you that it is all the same to me even if you do . . . " (6–7; ellipses in original). In *Problems of Dostoevsky's Poetics*, Bakhtin refers to these lines—and others near them—as examples of intensely dialogic discourse (228). Earlier in that book, he observes that the Underground Man enjoys nothing from the outsideness of others:

There is literally nothing we can say about the hero of "Notes from Underground" that he does not already know himself. [. . .] What the Underground Man thinks about most of all is what others think or might think about him; he tries to keep one step ahead of every other consciousness, every other thought about him, every other point of view about him. [. . .] The hero from underground eavesdrops on every word someone says about him, he looks at himself, as it were, in all the mirrors of other people's consciousness, he knows all the possible refractions in those mirrors. (52–3)[11]

King David, singing his songs in a subterranean cave, is another self-loathing soul producing notes from underground. The aesthetic work of the narrator, however, gives him a wholeness—even holiness—which Dostoevsky cruelly withholds from his unnamed hero. The Underground Man offers an instructive foil to Wyatt's David: he suggests the positive power of aesthetic activity by embodying its absence.

In one moment of Wyatt's sequence, however, David lapses into something close to a confessional self-accounting. It occurs in the narrative interlude following Psalm 102, so the narrator is still present—in fact, we witness the episode only in the narrator's words—but David briefly begins to perform the narratorial role for himself. He listens to his own voice, and he likes what he hears. In the preceding song, Psalm 102, David has lamented his own wretched condition, but he has also contemplated the transcendent goodness and mercy of God. In the narrative interlude following the psalm, David is comforted by these thoughts of grace:

> When David had perceived in his breast
> The sprite of God returned that was exiled,
> Because he knew he hath alone expressed
> These great things that greater sprite compiled,
> As shawm or pipe lets out the sound impressed,
> By music's art forged tofore and filed,
> I say when David had perceived this
> The sprite of comfort in him revived is.
>
> (632–9)

In other words, David is comforted when he considers the artfulness of his own song. He is aware that the "great things" have come from a "greater sprite" than his own—the spirit of God newly returned to his breast—but as the stanza progresses, his mind seems to turn from the greatness of the things to the craftsmanship with which they have been expressed. Lines 636 and 637 are rich in aesthetic imagery, blending metaphors of music and metallurgy to explain the beauty and strength of the song that David has made. The spirit of God may be the breath, but David is the shawm, and it is the shawm that crafts great music out of silent air.

In the following stanza, David continues to ponder his own role in bringing about his newly discovered comfort: he attributes mercy to his own penance. He acknowledges to himself that God has sometimes lent the gift of prophesy to evil people and even to animals, but he interprets his own situation as one of well-earned forgiveness:

> But our David judgeth in his intent
> Himself by penance clean out of this case [i.e., of wicked
>   men and animals],
> Whereby he hath remission of offence,
> And ginneth to allow his pain and penitence.
>
> (644–7)

In these lines, David begins to act as his own narrator. He judges his own intentions and deems them good. He finds joy in his own penance—as only the narrator could do earlier. He sees *himself* as an image of singular reverence. The narrator's outsideness in this segment effectively disappears: there is very little that the narrator can say of David that David is not already saying of himself.

His power trip, however, is a short one. In the third stanza of the interlude, he realizes the error of thinking that his own actions have effected any grace. Frustrated with himself, he

> takes all outward deed in vain
> To bear the name of rightful penitence,
> Which is alone the heart returned again
> And sore contrite that doth his fault bemoan,
> And outward deed the sign or fruit alone.
>
> (651–5)

In other words, David leaves the evaluation of his outward deeds to the outside narrator, returning his consciousness to the business of his inner life and effectively redrawing the boundary across which aesthetic activity occurs.

In short, aesthetic activity can be highly unstable—especially in real life. Aesthetic wholeness is quickly subsumed into our ongoing consciousness of ourselves, yet the inability of this self-consciousness to complete itself perpetually drives us to seek aesthetic interaction with others. Aesthetic activity is thus one moment in the complex phenomenological event of lived life. In life, aesthetic activity frequently turns into self-accounting simply because of the passage of time. Early in "Author and Hero," Bakhtin explains that we constantly attempt to form images of ourselves from the viewpoints of hypothetical others, but that these images can *only* be hypothetical because we always experience them as *I*, not as an *other*. Such images "are rendered completely immanent to our own consciousness, are translated, as it were, into its language" (16). Even if, in fulfillment of Robert Burns's wish, some Power would give us the gift to see ourselves as wholly as others see us, Bakhtin explains, the vision would not last:

> Our consciousness would take that whole into account and would surmount it as just one of the moments in its own unity. [. . .] The last word, that is, would still belong to our own consciousness rather than to the consciousness of another, and our own consciousness would never say to itself the word that would consummate it. After looking at ourselves through the eyes of another, we always return— in life—into ourselves again. (16–17)

David's vacillating relationship to the narrator is completely lifelike. David moves in and out of aesthetic activity—at times becoming highly aestheticized (as when he is described as a "marble image of singular reverence"), at times lapsing into confessional self-accounting (as when he judges and acquits himself on the strength of his penance).

In fact, the changing ways in which David relates to himself and to his narrator are reminiscent of Bakhtin's own description of the dialogic word:

> The word, directed toward its object, enters a dialogically agitated and tension-filled environment of alien words, value judgments and accents, weaves in and out of complex interrelationships, merges with some, recoils from others, intersects with yet a third group: and all this may crucially shape discourse, may leave a trace in all its semantic layers, may complicate its expression and influence its entire stylistic profile. ("Discourse" 276)

The kind of activity that Bakhtin describes here exists between David and the narrator despite the fact that their mutual outsideness has not crucially shaped the stylistic profile of Wyatt's psalms. The poems would admittedly be *more* dialogic if the voices of Wyatt and the narrator were distinct enough stylistically to allow for hybrid constructions and double-voiced discourse. But the principle aspect of dialogism—outsideness—is abundant and productive in the psalms. Like all penitential poetry, these poems are built out of the interaction of two distinct consciousnesses, which appear in the poem not as discrete languages *per se*, but rather as different modes of perception. Both modes are necessary. Without David's psalms, the narrator's interludes would have no real point, and penitence would be conveyed through general abstractions; without the narrator's interludes, we might too easily take David at his word when he describes himself as nothing more than a wretched sinner. The narrator's perception of David tends to result in aesthetic activity; David's perception of himself tends to result in confessional self-accounting and prayer. These two forms of perception—and their attendant forms of discourse—tend to follow from one another in a loosely dialogic way.

3. How dialogic are Wyatt's psalms?

The advantages of a dialogic paradigm are quickly apparent when one considers, for example, new historicist studies of Wyatt's psalms. Stephen Greenblatt analyzes these psalms in the first chapter of his landmark *Renaissance Self-Fashioning from More to Shakespeare*. In essence, Greenblatt's reading of the psalms amounts to a reductive version of aesthetic activity. Wyatt is cast as the hero, and "power"—in all its many faces and forms—plays the role of dominating author. It is a reductive reading because Greenblatt assumes that the authority of the other is absolute; he cannot conceive of any authority in Wyatt's voice that is independent of the other. "Wyatt" is nothing more than a product of his environment. Where traditional criticism of Wyatt has emphasized his inwardness and individuality, Greenblatt sees Wyatt himself as a cultural artifact:

> I would suggest that there is no privileged sphere of individuality in Wyatt, set off from linguistic convention, from social pressure, from the shaping force of religious and political power. Wyatt may complain about the abuses of the court, he may declare his independence from a corrupting sexual or political entanglement, but he always does so from within a context governed by the essential values of domination and submission, the values of a system of power that has an absolute monarch as head of both church and state. For all his impulse to negate, Wyatt cannot fashion himself in opposition to power and the conventions power deploys; on the contrary, those conventions are precisely what constitute Wyatt's self-fashioning. (120)

Bakhtin might call such analysis "impoverishing," because it reduces multiple voices to one. As Alexandra Halasz has observed, Greenblatt makes no real distinction between God and Henry VIII, the two strong authority figures under whom Sir Thomas Wyatt served (325).[12] Wyatt's voice, in Greenblatt's reading, is ultimately nothing more than the voices of these authorities speaking through him.

Greenblatt makes a similar assumption when explaining the rhetorical work of the psalms upon the reader. "The penitential psalms," he says,

> must be experienced as expressions of the reader's own conscious-ness: the distance between reader and text is effaced and the poems absorbed into the reader's inner life, which is in turn the legitimate object of both secular and religious power. And if this conception seems to exalt the reader (or the translator), such exaltation is sharply tempered by the fact that here the reader is virtually created by the text he absorbs. (119–20)

If this view seems extreme—how can the distance between reader and text actually be effaced?—it should be noted that Greenblatt is in good and very old company on this point. A treatise by the early church father Athanasius, reprinted with psalters throughout the sixteenth century, makes a surprisingly similar assertion for the rhetorical power of the psalms:

> But whosoever take this booke in his hand, he reputeth & thinketh all the wordes he readeth (except the wordes of prophecy) to be as his very owne wordes spoken in his owne person, yea and who soever do but here them reade, he is so affected to them, as he were the very man that read them, or first spake them, and so is disposed to warde them wordes of the verses, when they bee uttered, as they were properlye his owne onelye wordes, first by him conceyved and pronounced. (Parker sig.C1v)

Outsideness is erased; my own words become effaced by the words of the other.

Bakhtin offers a paradigm better suited to the phenomenological complexity of penitential literature in general—and Wyatt's psalms in particular. Wyatt, after all, has not merely become a robot reciting the psalms as if he had thought them up; he adds his own words and accents to them. Even if Bakhtin allowed for the possibility of two conscious-nesses to merge as completely as Athanasius and Greenblatt suggest, he would point out that such an event would be completely undesirable. Outsideness is a necessary condition of aesthetic and ethical activity, and Bakhtin would likely claim that the psalms become meaningful only when we return from our projections into them, understanding them as part of the lives we live outside the psalms. Projection is useful, but it is the return into our own beings that makes our interactions with an other productive. Discussing a possible projection into a suffering man, Bakhtin remarks that

> my projection of myself into him must be followed by a return into myself, a return to my own place outside the suffering person, for only from this place can the material derived from my projecting myself into the other be rendered meaningful ethically, cognitively, aesthetically. If this return into myself did not actually take place, the pathological phenomenon of experiencing another's suffering as one's own would result—an infection with another's suffering, and nothing more. ("Author and Hero" 26)[13]

These remarks offer better descriptions of our own interaction with David than do the assertions of Greenblatt and Athanasius. We might sympathize with David, but his experience does not efface our own. We do not become kings in caves; we are (in all likelihood) not confessing to adultery and murder. We are authors to David's hero; others to his *I*. By retaining our otherness, we have the power to admire him.

As we work our way through the psalms, we find the narrator responding to David's desperation with sympathy and admiration; we find David's psalms restlessly moving beyond what aesthetic activity the narrator might offer him in the interludes. Such is the course of true repentance, which—like the course of true love—never did run smooth. E. M. W. Tillyard once complained that Wyatt's psalms are "penitential not merely in matter, but to those whose task it is to read them" (48). There is probably more truth in this statement than Tillyard himself realized. As we follow David's progress through the sequence, we experience a close representation of the phenomenology of repentance: the desperation of contrition, the comfort of forgiveness and grace, the return to anxious repentance. What makes the experience of this sequence so lifelike is the interaction of multiple consciousnesses.

Clearly there are dynamics at work in Wyatt's psalms—both within the text itself and between the text and the reader—that are best explained by some notion of dialogism. To reach an appropriately supple understanding of dialogism, however, I suggest that we must carefully read "Author and Hero in Aesthetic Activity" and "Discourse in the Novel" in conjunction with one another. A careful reading of the earlier essay will see it not as a primitive precursor to dialogism, a staunch endorsement of closure and finalization, but as an exposition of multiple forms of activity between authors and heroes. A careful reading of "Discourse in the Novel" will take into account the gap between the monologic form of lyric that Bakhtin seems to have in mind while speaking of poetry and the strict stylistic form of dialogic discourse that he claims for the novel. In this gap sit Wyatt's psalms, and Bakhtin's writings, taken together, offer us the best way to explain their dialogic richness.

Notes

1. Although this essay is concerned only with literary phenomena, it should be noted that the notion of a dialogic self has gained some traction in psychological circles. For recent studies, see Jones and Morioka.
2. Bakhtin himself does acknowledge a similarly complex self in the satires of Horace and Varro ("Discourse" 371n.1).
3. The biblical version of the story is found in 2 Samuel 11–12. Clare Costley King'oo's monograph *Miserere Mei* provides a thorough account of the place of the seven Penitential Psalms in the culture of medieval and early modern England.
4. Wyatt models his psalms very closely on *I Sette Salmi de la Penitentia di David*, an Italian version of the Penitential Psalms published by Pietro Aretino (Venice, 1534). Aretino writes in prose, not verse, but formal arrangement of first-person psalms and third-person narrative interludes was his idea before it was Wyatt's, and much of what this essay says about Wyatt could also be said of Aretino.
5. Wyatt seems to have worked with several versions of the Psalms: the Vulgate, another Latin translation by Ulrich Zwingli (included in the Campensis paraphrase), the English psalter of George Joye, and Miles Coverdale's translation in the 1535 English Bible. A succinct, but thorough, summary of Wyatt's sources has been provided by R. A. Rebholz in his edition of *The Complete Poems* (452–4).
6. All quotations from Wyatt's psalms have been taken from the modernized version in *The Complete English Poems*, edited by R. A. Rebholz. The Muir/Thomson edition offers the poems in original spelling.
7. As Craig Brandist has noted, Bakhtin's notion of outsideness is clearly and deeply rooted in the philosophy of Max Scheler (44ff.). Brian Poole's article "From Phenomenology to Dialogue" describes several aspects of aesthetic activity, including outsideness, that come from Scheler, as well as from the Marburg philosopher Nicolai Hartmann. Outsideness is one concept that remained important to Bakhtin throughout his career. He develops it in the twenties in "Author and Hero," his first major essay, and is still applying the idea in his 1970 letter to *Novy Mir*: "In order to understand, it is immensely important for the person who understands to be *located outside* the object of his or her creative understanding" ("Response" 7, emphasis added).

8. Bakhtin's Russian word, *izbytok*, suggests abundance, but not the indulgence or wastefulness that "excess" sometimes connotes in English.

9. Pechey seems to be echoing Sergey Bocharov, who spoke personally with Bakhtin in 1974, and who has called "Author and Hero" an essay "which one could call Bakhtin's theology in the form of aesthetics or his aesthetics resolved in theological terms" (1018). The volume containing Pechey's essay, Felch and Contino's *Bakhtin and Religion: A Feeling for Faith*, contains compelling investigations of Bakhtin's religious commitments throughout his career.

10. For this reason, Wyatt's psalms offer an even better illustration of Bakhtin's ideas than Pushkin's "Parting," the poem which Bakhtin himself explicates near the end of "Author and Hero."

11. Here and throughout the Dostoevsky book, Bakhtin's descriptions of *Notes from Underground* are strongly reminiscent of his descriptions of confessional self-accounting in "Author and Hero." He also observes that Dostoevsky's working title for *Notes from Underground* was "Confession" (227).

12. Halasz's own view of the psalms, however, is also impoverished. In her deconstructive reading, the narrator offers words of repentance in place of David's own psalms. In doing so, the narrator "suggest[s] the inadequacy of David's penitence" and "begins to dislodge David from the penitential position" (331). Halasz, like Greenblatt, seems unwilling to imagine more than one truly authoritative discourse at work in any piece of literature. She can only see the narrator and David in competition, not cooperation.

13. As Poole has demonstrated, Bakhtin's idea here—and specifically the language of infection—comes directly from Max Scheler's writings on empathy (see Poole 114ff.).

Works cited

Aretino, Pietro. *Paraphrase vpon the seaven pen[i]tentiall psalmes of [t]he kingly prophet tra[n]slated out of Italian by I.H.* Douai: G. Pinchon, 1635. STC 19910.5 British Library.

Bakhtin, Mikhail M. "Author and Hero in Aesthetic Activity." *Art and Answerability: Early Philosophical Essays by M. M. Bakhtin.* Ed. Michael Holquist and Vadim Liapunov. Trans. Vadim Liapunov. Austin: U of Texas P, 1990. 4–256.

———. "Discourse in the Novel." *The Dialogic Imagination: Four Essays by M. M. Bakhtin.* Ed. Michael Holquist. Trans. Caryl Emerson and Michael Holquist. 259–422.

———. *Problems of Dostoevsky's Poetics.* Ed. and trans. Caryl Emerson. Minneapolis: U of Minnesota P, 1984.

———. "Response to a Question from *Novy Mir.*" *Speech Genres and Other Late Essays.* Ed. Caryl Emerson and Michael Holquist. Trans. Vern W. McGee. Austin: U of Texas P, 1986. 1–7.

Batstone, William W. "Catullus and Bakhtin: The Problems of a Dialogic Lyric." *Bakhtin and the Classics.* Ed. R. Bracht Branham. Evanston, IL: Northwestern UP, 2002. 99–136.

Bocharov, Sergey. "Conversations with Bakhtin." Trans. Stephen Blackwell. *PMLA* 109 (1994): 1009–24.

Brandist, Craig. *The Bakhtin Circle: Philosophy, Culture, and Politics*. London: Pluto Press, 2002.

Dostoevsky, Fyodor. *Notes From Underground*. Trans. Richard Pevear and Larissa Volokhonsky. New York: Alfred A. Knopf, 1993.

Emerson, Caryl. "Building a Responsive Self in a Post-Relativistic World: The Contribution of Mikhail Bakhtin." *The Self: Beyond the Postmodern Crisis*. Ed. Paul C. Vitch and Susan M. Felch. Wilmington, DE: ISI Books, 2006. 25–41.

Felch, Susan M., and Paul J. Contino, eds. *Bakhtin and Religion: A Feeling for Faith*. Evanston, IL: Northwestern UP, 2001.

Greenblatt, Stephen. "Power, Sexuality, and Inwardness in Wyatt's Poetry." *Renaissance Self-Fashioning from More to Shakespeare*. Chicago: U of Chicago P, 1980. 115–56.

Halasz, Alexandra. "Wyatt's David." *Texas Studies in Literature and Language* 30:3 (Fall 1998): 320–44.

Jones, Raya A., and Masayoshi Morioka, eds. *Jungian and Dialogical Self Perspectives*. London: Palgrave, 2011.

King'oo, Clare Costley. *Miserere Mei: The Penitential Psalms in Late Medieval and Early Modern England*. Notre Dame, IN: Notre Dame UP, 2012.

Leatherbarrow, W. J. "Introduction." *Crime and Punishment*. Trans. Richard Pevear and Larissa Volokhonsky. New York: Alfred A. Knopf, 1993. xi–xxvi.

Luther, Martin. "Preface to the Epistle of St. Paul to the Romans." *Luther's Works*. Ed. E. Theodore Bachmann. Philadelphia: Muhlenberg Press, 1960. Vol. 35. 365–80.

Mason, H. A. *Editing Wyatt*. Cambridge, UK: *Cambridge Quarterly*, 1972.

Morson, Gary Saul, and Caryl Emerson. *Mikhail Bakhtin: Creation of a Prosaics*. Stanford: Standford UP, 1990.

Parker, Matthew. *The whole Psalter translated into English metre, which contayneth an hundreth and fifty Psalmes*. London: John Daye, 1567. STC 2729. Cambridge University Library.

Pechey, Graham. "Philosophy and Theology in 'Aesthetic Activity.'" *Bakhtin and Religion: A Feeling for Faith*. Ed. Susan M. Felch and Paul J. Contino. Evanston, IL: Northwestern UP, 2001. 47–62.

Poole, Brian. "From Phenomenology to Dialogue: Max Scheler's Phenomenological Tradition and Mikhail Bakhtin's Development from 'Toward a Philosophy of the Act' to his Study of Dostoevsky." *Bakhtin and Cultural Theory*. Ed. Ken Hirschkop and David Shepherd. Manchester: Manchester UP, 2002. 109–35.

Prescott, Anne Lake. "King David as a 'Right Poet': Sidney and the Psalmist." *English Literary Renaissance* 19 (1989): 131–51.

Tillyard, E. M. W. *The Poetry of Sir Thomas Wyatt: A Selection and a Study*. London: Chatto & Windus, 1949.

Tyndale, William. "The Prologue to the Romans." *Tyndale's New Testament*. Ed. David Daniell. New Haven: Yale UP, 1989. 207–24.

Wyatt, Thomas. *Certayne psalmes chosen out of the psalter of Dauid, commonlye called the .vii. penytentiall psalmes, drawen into englyshe meter by Sir Thomas Wyat knyght, wherunto is added a prolage of [the] auctore before euery psalme, very pleasau[n]t [and] profettable to the godly reader*. London, 1549. STC 2726. Cambridge University Library.

——. *Collected Poems of Sir Thomas Wyatt*. Ed. Kenneth Muir and Patricia Thomson. Liverpool: Liverpool UP, 1969.

——. *Sir Thomas Wyatt: The Complete Poems*. Ed. R. A. Rebholz. New Haven: Yale UP, 1981.

4
Lyric Ventriloquism and the Dialogic Translations of Pasternak, Mandelstam and Celan

Tom Dolack

For what has been said is just repetition,
What has been said has been said.
(*The Complaints of Khakheperre-sonb*, 19th century BC[1])

Imitation, translation, and dialogism

The Egyptian lament quoted as my epigraph jumps to the heart of one of the central issues of literary history: the use of other people's words as a source—the source—of literary production. If everything was already "just repetition" four thousand years ago, how can the modern poet possibly hope to create something new? The answer has been the same since Antiquity: the original use of other people's words, or in a word: imitation. I use imitation here in a broad sense that covers its historical usages including lexical and stylistic appropriation; rewriting and retelling; translation; and various forms of intertextuality. Imitation was recognized for much of the history of literary theory as a central aspect of art. It was central to both Greek and Roman poetics[2] as expounded by Horace,[3] Cicero,[4] Seneca[5] and Quintilian,[6] among others. This *imitatio* was revived by Petrarch and the Renaissance Humanists who used imitation first of the Classical models, and later of contemporary figures, chief among them Petrarch himself, as their means of reviving their respective national traditions.[7] The Romans' and humanists' faith in imitation, which

57

progresses through the Neoclassical, stems from the Aristotelian tradition of mimesis that views imitation as a natural and basic human faculty underlying all culture (a belief shared by contemporary anthropology[8]). Beginning with the Romantics, and continuing to this day, imitation becomes something to be hidden—whence Harold Bloom's "anxiety of influence," which is another way of viewing a specific type of imitation, specifically the kind that pretends not to be. This anxiety is related to a similar angst about artistic imitation that dates back to Plato where the poet is to be distrusted, if not entirely exiled from the Republic, because his imitations are too removed from Higher Reality (605 b–c).

Looking at imitation from a historical perspective, it is my contention that imitation is no less central to poetic production today than it was in Antiquity. Viewing all poetry as a form of imitation can provide a new lens with which to view the lyric and intertextual relationships within poetry. It also allows us to unite the study of poetic translation and "original" poetry since both are located within the same spectrum, although at different ends of it. Having made this move, I will discuss a particular aspect of poetic translation, what I call "lyric ventriloquism," or the ability to speak through another poet's words through translation, in an attempt to elucidate an aspect of the dialogic nature of poetic translation.

The most prominent contemporary theorist of the type of repetition and use of other people's words discussed here is Mikhail Bakhtin, who claims in "Discourse in the Novel":

> The word in language is half someone else's. It becomes "one's own" only when the speaker populates it with his own intention, his own accent, when he appropriates the word, adapting it to his own semantic and expressive intention. Prior to this moment of appropriation, the word does not exist in a neutral and impersonal language [. . .], but rather it exists in other people's mouths, in other people's contexts, serving other people's intentions: it is from there that one must take the word, and make it one's own. (293–4)

According to Bakhtin, novelistic discourse is founded on such a form of ventriloquism[9] where an author can only signify by appropriating the words of others, by speaking through another's language. In turn the appropriated words assume meaning by their relation with their origin and so enter into a form of dialogue or duet. Such use of others' words is, broadly speaking, a form of imitation.

Contrary to virtually all of the tradition of looking at imitation, Bakhtin excludes poetry from this process. Bakhtin's reasoning is that the language of a poetic text is isolated from all other language, it is "unitary"; "the poet strips the word of others' intentions" (297) and so can use other poets' words, but cannot speak *through* them as is the case in non-poetic language. The word in novelistic discourse is not cut off from history and society, while the word in poetry does not say what it means, but rather *is* what it means and so gains signification through form and even the diachronic associations within poetic language, but lacks the broader overtones that invade other forms of discourse.[10]

On one level there is nothing to argue with here, since for most readers form is the distinguishing feature of poetry (viz. Roman Jakobson's axis of selection v. axis of combination), but on other, at times more important, levels this approach bypasses a type of polyglossia or dialogue that is fundamental to much of the lyric tradition just as it is to the novel. Bakhtin comes close to admitting as much at times, for instance when he states that "language may remember only its life in poetic contexts (in such contexts, however, even concrete reminiscences are possible)" (297), which is to admit the presence of multiple voices, but still wall them off from true polyvocal discourse. This same move can be seen later when he states that "[p]oetry also sees its own language surrounded by other languages, surrounded by literary and extra-literary heteroglossia. But poetry, striving for maximal purity, works in its own language, *as if* that language were unitary, the only language, as if there were no heteroglossia outside it" (399, emphasis in original). It is this "as if" that I wish to take issue with in approaching lyric as a whole and not simply limiting it to its linguistic and formal unity.[11]

In examining the question of the dialogic nature of the lyric, I wish to take a slightly different approach and begin with a discussion of imitation. For my purposes here I use "imitation" in a broad sense that includes emulation (the attempt to achieve the same end or produce the same effect using different verbal or formal means) and translation (Jakobson's "translation proper," the transfer of denotative meaning from one language to another). Imitation can be viewed as a spectrum of fidelity to a model or set of models. On one end is Walter Benjamin and Vladimir Nabokov's ideal of translation, the interlinear, word-by-word translation—most successfully exemplified by interlinear versions of holy texts—and on the other is the adaptation or the poem "in the style of" or "after" a certain author, the use of a source text merely as a starting point for an original poem—most notoriously exemplified by Robert Lowell in his *Imitations*. Each position on this spectrum will indicate a slightly different relationship with a given source text, but all indicate some degree of intertextual relationship with the words of another author, and so also indicate a specific opportunity for interacting with those same words and of speaking *through* them.

Translation may seem at first an odd locus to examine the dialogic nature of the lyric; it might be presumed that poetic translation is a perfect example of Bakhtin's claim for the unitary nature of the poem. A translation, as the term is commonly used, is meant to replace or occlude the original text for those who do not have access to the original language, and doubtless there are times—instruction manuals, legal documents, many forms of professional correspondence and scientific publications—when the translation can wholly replace its source. To some extent, this is what Bakhtin says happens to speech as it is "carried over" or appropriated from one poet to another: as a text enters into its afterlife through the process of poetic translation, the word is immersed in Lethe and assumes entirely its role in the new poem. An analysis of the praxis of poetic translation reveals, however, that poetic language in translation is not so forgetful, and can in fact "remember" contexts other than the poetic. This is, indeed, one of the main bridges between poetic translation and imitation: both enable a form of polyglossia, both through the multivalence of the text—the way the source text relates to the target text—and through the way in which both a translation and an imitation permit, even require, the poet to speak through the words of another poet. I refer to this ability to speak through the words of another poet through translation or imitation and reach outward to areas where poetry, tradition, and history overlap as "lyric ventriloquism." It is through this ventriloquism that poet-translators gain their voice, and it is through this same ventriloquism that poet-imitators gain additional voices. The poetic text, whether a translation or not, is an etiological device that speaks through and interprets its sources at the same time that its sources permit and set the conditions for interpretation. In this sense, lyric ventriloquism is closely related to Bakhtin's sense of parody—"[t]hus every parody is an intentional dialogized hybrid. Within it, languages and styles actively and mutually illuminate one another" (76)—and can therefore be studied in Bakhtinian terms.

Pasternak and literary ventriloquism

It is well understood that during the Soviet period poets translated certain authors and certain texts as a means of surreptitiously commenting on Soviet life and the censorship that stopped many of them from publishing their own "original" works. The critic Efim Etkind caused the destruction of an entire print run of *Masters of Poetic Translation* (1968) and greatly contributed to his eventual exile from the USSR[12] by publishing the following comment in his introduction to an anthology of poetic translation: "[d]eprived of the possibility of expressing themselves to the full in original writing, Russian poets [. . .] used the language of Goethe, Shakespeare, Orbeliani or Hugo to talk to the reader" (cited in Etkind, *Notes* 32). Translation thus became a form of "Aesopian Language" or speech that attempts to mean more than it says (through ambivalence or allusion) and so evade censorship of one sort or another.[13]

One of the most famous examples of this phenomenon is Boris Pasternak who, in the face of increasing difficulty in publishing his work, was forced to rely increasingly on translation as a means of supporting himself. He eventually translated poets such as Byron, Keats, Verlaine, Rilke and Goethe, and about a half dozen plays of Shakespeare.[14] Osip Mandelstam once remarked to him in the presence of Anna Akhmatova that "[y]our complete works will consist of twelve volumes of translations and a single volume of your own verse"[15] (39), a comment that reveals both the necessity for translation as well as the deep-seeded ambiguity about it, although it brushes over the opportunities of the practice.[16]

The translator's selection of which text or texts to translate can be important on several different levels, including the language and period translated from, the author selected, the specific texts (which poems, or collections, if not the complete works) chosen and the style in which they are translated. Pasternak's choice of source texts (when it was his choice) is a case in point. In Pasternak's oeuvre, his translations of several of Shakespeare's sonnets stand out. Of the 154 original sonnets, Pasternak selected three to translate; this selection in itself becomes a means of signification, a way of speaking merely through his choice of poems. Isolating specific themes and images out of the many offered by Shakespeare's collection allows Pasternak a way of saying "this is what I think is important or germane for the present." The author can speak through this form of selection even before any transformations are made to the text that parade as the words of the original author. His translation of sonnet 66 (published in 1940) is a particularly good example of the use of Aesopian language.[17] Shakespeare's original begins with the exclamation "Tired with all these, for restful death I cry," followed by a litany of grievances about contemporary society. In translating these lines Pasternak has the subterfuge of claiming that he is merely following Shakespeare's lead and so his translation decries solely the social ills of Elizabethan England—an argument easily shoehorned into Soviet diatribes against the bourgeois mores of past/foreign cultures—and he can maintain the ventriloquist's excuse: "I'm not saying it, it's the dummy."

But a translation, like any speech act, gains its meaning not only by the denotative meaning of its words, but by its interactions with a given milieu and an understood history. This is why the *Don Quixote* of Borges' Pierre Menard can be "almost infinitely richer" (94), even though it is verbally identical with its source text. This can be understood in terms of Jakobson's schematic of the six factors required for a communicative act to take place (66):

	CONTEXT	
ADDRESSER	MESSAGE	ADDRESSEE
	CONTACT	
	CODE	

During translation, each of these factors undergoes some change. The addressee of a translation necessarily changes since a translation is directed to speakers of a different language and often a different time and culture. The addresser of the text becomes not just the original author but an amalgam of the author and the translator. The code must certainly change in order for translation (or rather "translation proper," as Jakobson puts it) to take place. The means of contact is certainly different barring the rare instance where a source text is published simultaneously with its translation. The issue of the message is perhaps the most fraught because definitions of the term "translation" itself often rest on it. By some definitions, if the message is altered the transformation ceases to be translation and enters fully into the realm of original composition, while others would say that some alteration to the message is inherent not only in translation, but in the act of decoding any communication.

Context is the subtlest issue of all of these factors. Simply taking a specific set of words and transferring them to a new milieu will affect their meaning and possibly even their referent. When Pasternak translates Shakespeare's line "Tired with all these, for restful death I cry" (513) as "Измучась всем, я умереть хочу [Being tired out by everything, I want to die]" (314) these words rest not just in Shakespeare's mouth, but in Pasternak's. This gives him the ability to speak through the English poet as through a ventriloquist's dummy and consequently the ability to apply the Elizabethan's comment to Stalinist Russia, while at the same time maintaining the subterfuge that "I'm only the translator." Thus it becomes possible to comment, if in an indirect manner, on the unbearable conditions in the Soviet Union, giving a freedom to the Soviet poet which would otherwise be impossible.

The translator also does not need to be completely restricted by the words of his source, but can change the translation in ways that allow him or her to place new words and new meanings in the source's mouth. For instance in sonnet 66, Pasternak can express things more emphatically than the original, as when he further emphasizes his pessimism by translating "Tired with all these, from these would I be gone" (513), as "Измучась всем, не стал бы жить и дня [Being tired out by everything, it wouldn't be worth living even a day]" (314). While it would be difficult to imagine being able to publish the idea that it is not worth living a day in Soviet Russia, it can be done through the voice of Shakespeare.

But Aesopian language has its restrictions and not everything could be passed through censors under the guise of translation. In translating the ninth line of the sonnet, "And art made tongue-tied by authority" (513), Pasternak shows a bit of circumspection in rendering it as "И вспомнит, что мысли заткнут рот [And remember that thoughts will stopper the mouth]" (314). The direct allusion to censorship, even if nominally referring to sixteenth-century England, would have been a red flag and greatly reduced its chances of being published. Instead, the direct exercise of authority over art is reduced to an act self-censorship, mirroring the way that Pasternak's own thoughts must plug his mouth and pen. But all is not lost regarding Shakespeare's attack on censorship. Anyone familiar with the original poem (or another, more literal translation) can understand the subtext and can read the original as another layer of the palimpsest.

A sign that the authorities were aware, at least at times, of the power of Aesopian language can be seen in the fact that Pasternak's translation of sonnet 74 was not published until 1975, fifteen years after the poet's death. The trouble with the sonnet for the Soviet censors and, we can imagine, Pasternak's attraction to it can be seen in the opening quatrain, which Pasternak renders as:

Но успокойся. В дни, когда в острог
Навек я смертью буду взят под стражу
Одна живая память этих строк
Еще переживет мою пропажу.

(314)

But be calm. In the days when to the stockade
I will be taken into custody forever by death
Only the living memory of these lines
Will still endure my loss.

Despite attributing his disappearance to death instead of "fell arrest,"[18] it would not be difficult for any reader during the height of Stalin's purges to make the leap from Shakespeare's "fell arrest" and Pasternak's "taken into custody forever" and "my loss" to the political arrests rampant at the time. This subtext is only strengthened by the poet's appeal to immortality in his verse, the lyric equivalent of "writing for the drawer" or Bulgakov's "manuscripts don't burn." Although the words are supposed to belong to Shakespeare, due to the context Pasternak is able to ventriloquate through the Bard's poem;[19] Shakespeare can comment on the Soviet Union.

The translation is thus able to speak with at least two voices, Shakespeare's original, and Pasternak the translator's. We can add to this a third, Pasternak the poet's, which dictates what can be read between the lines and could not be said explicitly. Ignoring either of the separate levels, or the relationship of the two together, is to fail to understand the text as a whole. The polyphonic nature of the text is inherent to its success as both translation and as "original" composition.

Mandelstam, Petrarch and the revival of humanism

Pasternak was not the only one to use translation in this polyphonic way. Far from it. Another of the greatest uses of the political application of translation, though far less understood as such,[20] is Osip Mandelstam's translations of Petrarch's sonnets 311, 301, 164 and 319— in that order—dating from December of 1933 and January of 1934, just months before his first arrest and during a period when he was unable to publish his own "original" poetry. Mandelstam uses his translation of a foreign sonnet to express a pessimism about contemporary life that otherwise would have been unpublishable; it gives him, as for Pasternak, a voice where he was otherwise denied one.

The opening quatrain of Petrarch's #319 reads:

> I dì miei più leggier' che nesun cervo,
> Fuggîr come ombra, et non vider più bene
> Ch'un batter d'occhio, et poche hore serene,
> Ch'amare et dolci ne la mente servo.

> (159)

> My days more nimbly than any hind,
> Have fled like a shadow and have not seen a more blessing
> Than the wink of an eye, and few serene hours,
> That bitter and sweet I retain in my mind.

Mandelstam translates this as:

Промчались дни мои, как бы оленей
Косящий бег. Срок счастья был короче,
Чем взмах ресницы. Из последней мочи
Я в горсть зажал лишь пепел наслаждений.

(362)

My days rushed past like
The crooked run of deer. The term of my happiness was shorter
Than the blink of an eye. With my last strength
I grasped in my fist only the ash of enjoyment.

Writing shortly before his arrest for authoring the anti-Stalin poem "Мы живем под собою не чуя страны [We live not feeling the earth beneath us]"—composed at the same time as this translation—the poem is transformed from the bucolic and amorous musings of Petrarch the love poet to the bitter reflection of Mandelstam the dissident. This shift is particularly evident in the shift from the present of "I retain in mind" to the barren past of "I grasped in my fist only the ash of enjoyment."

Again, context is responsible for this deictic shift in the meaning of Petrarch's words. The word here is "half someone else's," Petrarch's words become Mandelstam's through translation, and since words gain meaning through their context, the text changes through this act of transference even before the intentional changes on the part of the translator. Context here includes many aspects of the conditions of the text's reception. Most obvious is of course the change from Renaissance Italy to Soviet Russia. Also operative, though, is the shift from Petrarch's *Canzoniere*, a collection of 366 sonnets keyed to the liturgical calendar and devoted to Petrarch's beloved Laura, who dies midway through the collection. In its original setting, #319 clearly refers to Laura's death and Petrarch's sorrow at her loss. Extracted from this setting, the reference to Laura is not clear and this opens up a productive ambiguity in the text. This can be seen in the first tercet of the sonnet. Petrarch's text clearly alludes to his beloved's death:

Ma la forma miglior, che vive anchora,
Et vivrà sempre, su ne l'alto cielo,
Di sue bellezze ognor più m'innamora;

But the best form, which lives still,
And always will live, up in high heaven,
Can, with every hour, charm me more with her beauties;

Mandelstam's version still refers to a deep loss, but loses much of its religious overtones:

Но то, что в ней едва существовало,
Днесь, вырвавшись наверх, в очаг лазури,
Пленять и ранить может, как бывало.

(363)

But that which barely existed in her,
Now, having escaped upward into the hearth of azure,
Can take prisoner and wound like it used to.

Not coming as part of a sequence with a clearly defined antecedent, but as four sonnets arranged independently, it is not as clear what the antecedent of "her" [or "it"] is in the Russian poems. If we are to read it as Petrarch's words transposed to Soviet soil, there is little difficulty: "she" is Laura. But, if the words are to be taken as Mandelstam's (and there is plenty of textual evidence that we should do so, including a consistent toning down of the amatory elements of the poem (Semenko, Поэтикиа 127; Nadezhda Mandelstam 239), there is much more room for interpretation; a powerful ambiguity emerges, leaving room for the reader to decide exactly what it is that has "torn upward." In light of the other three translations, which use the image of a nightingale as a stand-in for the poet, what is lost can be read in terms of a tradition that has been lost in the wake of the Bolshevik Revolution, and therefore echoes the same type of loss felt by the Renaissance humanists, first among them Petrarch, for the Classical heritage. It is therefore not surprising that Mandelstam would resort to imitation (in the guise of translation) to recuperate this loss, just as Petrarch himself did.

On a more fundamental level, this sense of lost tradition is the motivating factor of the sequence of translations. Petrarch would have been important to Mandelstam not only as the great love poet, but also as the exemplar of Renaissance humanism, the movement dedicated to the revival of Classical knowledge through philology, especially imitation of past models. Humanism is also often credited with placing the human individual at the center of the intellectual world. It is this idea that is closer to the modern use of the word, including Mandelstam's own use of the term. In an essay written about a decade before his Petrarch translations, "Humanism and the Present," Mandelstam places humanism in opposition to forces that subsume the individual to society as a whole. While not mentioning the Soviet Union explicitly, it is clear that Mandelstam has post-Revolutionary transformations and the steady eroding of individual freedom in mind: "Nevertheless, there is also another form of social architecture whose scale and measure is man. It does not use man to build, it builds for man. Its grandeur is constructed not on the insignificance of individuality but on the highest form of expediency, in accord with its needs" (181). Thus, in translating the most well-known of humanists, Mandelstam is appropriating a set of ethical, moral, and cultural values from the past, at least as he viewed them.[21]

This humanism returns us to the practice of *imitatio* or heuristic imitation. Poets such as Petrarch, Garcilaso de la Vega, Joachim Du Bellay, and Thomas Wyatt used imitation of select Classical and, later, contemporary models as a means of reviving their respective literary traditions, contributing to the beginning of the Renaissance in each country. Mandelstam's translations are engaged in the same process of importation and can be viewed as a form of imitation.

Celan, Char, and humanism in action

As a final example of the dialogic nature of poetic translation, one taken from post-World War II German poetry, I submit Paul Celan's version of René Char's *Feuillets d'Hypnos* [*Leaves of Hypnos*].[22] Char's collection of poetry was composed during his activity in the French Résistance during the German occupation of France, a fact Celan makes clear in the subtitle to his translation (absent from the original), *Aufzeichnungen aus dem Maquis* [*Notebooks from the Maquis*], alluding to the armed guerilla groups of southern France that fought against the Nazi occupiers. As a man who lost both of his parents in the Holocaust and who was himself forced into a labor camp in southern Romania for close to two years, Celan had a special relationship with Char, who actively fought the forces that killed his family and nearly eradicated his tradition. In addition, Char was an important figure in French letters following the war because, unlike so many other intellectuals, he did not capitulate with the Vichy government or flee the country, and so held a certain moral authority (La Charité 77). In translating Char's text, Celan performs a similar type of ethical appropriation to Mandelstam.[23] Celan himself alludes to the moral values Char represents for him when he writes to his wife, "One day we will only see beings such as Char" (*Correspondance* 63).

For Celan, this ethical emulation was not just a form of wishful think-ing, but took the form of translation and imitation. In an unsent letter to Char, Celan writes:

> Beware of those who ape you, René Char. (I know well of what I speak, alas.) In their nullity they consider you a source of images to be added up in order to create a semblance for themselves: they do not *reflect* you, they darken you. [. . .] You see, I have always tried to *understand* you, to *respond* to you, to take your work like one takes a hand; and it was, of course, *my* hand that took *yours*, there it was certain not to miss the encounter. (*Selections* 183–4; emphasis in original)

This image of shaking hands recalls one of the most important images from Celan's critical prose: the poem as a *Flaschenpost* or message in a bottle sent to the reader in posterity: "A poem, as a manifesta-tion of language and thus essentially dialogue, can be a message in a bottle, sent out in the—not always greatly hopeful—belief that somewhere and sometime it could wash up on land, on heartland perhaps. Poems in this sense, too, are under way: they are making toward something" (*Selected Poems and Prose* 396). Celan appropri-ates this idea from Mandelstam, who writes in "О собеседнике [On the Addressee]", "without dialogue, lyric poetry cannot exist. [. . .] [P]oetry as a whole is always directed toward a more or less distant, unknown addressee, in whose existence the poet does not doubt, not doubting in himself" (*Critical Prose* 72, 73). For both poets, poetry is inherently dialogic, except Celan adds a new element to Mandelstam's formulation. Mandelstam's emphasis is on the sending of the message to its future reader, while Celan turns poetry into a dialogic process containing both an act of reception and an act of transmission.

In Celan's oeuvre translation can be seen as the act of reception, the picking up of the message in a bottle, and his "original" poetry as the sending out of a message to a new reader in posterity. Both are dialogic, and both are necessary for the continuing of tradition's conversation, but each places the poet in a different relationship with his interlocutor. We see in Celan's letter his reaching out to Char, his picking up of that "message in a bottle," his extending of the hand to the past, to the other: "[T]he poem wants to reach an Other, it needs this Other, it needs an Over-against. It seeks it out, speaks toward it. For the poem making toward an Other, each thing, each human being is a form of this Other" (*Selected Poems and Prose* 409). In translating Char (or any other of the many poets he translated) Celan is placing himself as that Other, as the man who picks up the message in a bottle that washes up on the sands of time. This act of reception and of completed dialogue is the necessary first step before new poetry, new messages can be created and sent off into time. Celan received a tribute to this very act of delayed reception from Char himself, who inscribed a copy of Celan's translation of *Leaves* with "À Paul Celan, à qui je pensais [To Paul Celan, the one I was thinking of]" (qtd. in Felstiner 137). Char's comment, retroactively addressing his collection to Celan, can be seen as the extending of a hand to establish human contact; the translation is where the two poets meet. The second stage of this poetic confluence is Celan's production of original verse, his extension of the hand to his own readers in posterity. Thus the establishing of a dialogue through translation is only the first step to further dialogue.

A full examination of Celan's translation of Char is beyond the scope of the present work, but one place in particular points both to Char's underlying purpose in writing the volume and to Celan's in translating it. Char concludes his prefatory note to the volume with the following paragraph: "Ces notes marquent la résistance d'un humanisme conscient de ses devoirs, discret sur ses vertus, désirant réserver *l'inaccessible* champ libre à la fantaisie de ses soleils, et décidé à payer le *prix* pour cela. [These notes mark the resistance of a humanism aware of its duties, discreet about its virtues, wanting to set aside the *inaccessible* free field for the fantasy of its suns, and decided to pay the *price* for it]" (173; emphasis in original). What are we to make of this "resistance of a humanism aware of its duties"? It is clear from the use of the word "résistance" and its connection with the French Résistance (this is further supported by several passages from the collection itself) that this duty is to stand against oppression and the threat of Nazi occupation. *Leaves of Hypnos* is Char's lyric memoir of his activities fighting against the German occupation, and would grant Char a preeminent moral authority in post-World War II French letters. In appropriating Char's text and speaking through it by means of translation, Celan speaks through this moral position; the victim of Nazi atrocities is able to offer resistance to the forces that nearly destroyed Celan's "tribe" or "branch." While Char uses the term humanism in its modern sense that privileges the ethical implications of the term, man as autonomous agent (as used by Althusser or Sartre, for example), Celan—much like Mandelstam in his translation of Petrarch—is engaged in a humanism that combines this modern sense with the original Renaissance emphasis on philology and man as the measure of all things.

The dialogic element, which is so important for Celan, can be found in Char as well, and is linked with the hope necessary for the human condition. In 178 Char writes about his copy of Georges de la Tour's "Job et sa femme [Job and his Wife]," which depicts a woman standing over a thin old man, holding a candle and wearing a large red dress that dominates the canvas, almost pushing the woman's face out of the picture: "Depuis deux ans, pas un réfractaire qui n'ait, passant la porte, brûlé ses yeux aux preuves de cette chandelle. [. . .] Les mots qui tombent de cette terrestre silhouette d'ange rouge sont des mots essentiels, des mots qui portent immédiatement secours. [. . .] Le Verbe de la femme donne naissance à l'inespéré mieux que n'importe quelle aurore. [For two years, not one rebel, upon entering through the door, hasn't burned his eyes on the proofs of that tallow candle. [. . .] The words that fall from this red angel's terrestrial silhouette are essential words, words that immediately bring aid. [. . .] The woman's Word gives birth to the unhoped-for better than any daybreak]" (218). Even the battle-hardened *maquisards* are touched by the painting. Just as the woman-angel's words bring aid and succor to the old man, the painting brings hope, no matter how "unhoped for," to the Résistance fighters.

The poem ends with "Reconnaissance à Georges de La Tour qui maîtrisa les ténèbres hitlériennes avec un dialogue d'êtres humains [Gratitude to Georges de la Tour who mastered the Hitler shades with a dialogue of human beings]" (218). The dialogue refers not only to the exchange between Job and his wife with its bestowal of quasi-divine wisdom and hope, but to the connection established between Char and those who saw the painting. It is this connection between human beings that overcomes the dehumanizing effects of the "Hitler shades." Celan is himself engaged in his own form of dialogue with Char, a dialogue that is completed after the defeat of the Nazis. This is why he can refer to the occupation as the "Hitlernacht [Hitler night]" (531) instead of "Hitler shades." Night is a much broader state of darkness, but also invariably makes way for the dawn. The candle of the woman's speech, the tongue of flame—a tongue required for dialogue—appears to shine that much brighter at night than in the shade.

This is a different example of ventriloquism at work. This appropriation can only be operative if both voices are present, if the word belongs to both Char and Celan, allowing the one to speak and to produce meaning through the words of the other. Examples such as the translations examined here help demonstrate how poetic language can, while maintaining certain hermetic elements, retain a dialogue with the outside world and be *co*existent with it, how lyric discourse, like novelistic discourse, is inherently situated and contextualized.

Translation, especially poetic translation, is dialogic in nature,[24] and it, along with its cultural role, will not be fully understood until it is read dialogically, that is as a collection of voices, each of which allows the existence of the other's voice in so far as the one speaks through the other. Consequently it is impossible to distinguish in any consistent, a priori way between poetic translation and imitation, and due to its dialogic nature, translation is more productively studied as a form of (polyvocal) imitation. All texts, all discourse—including poetic discourse—is imitative and multi-voiced, though some texts foreground the appropriated voice more, while others are more centered on the appropriating voice. Ultimately what will be interesting for those who study the lyric as imitation is not whether it is multi-voiced or not, but how the voices relate and the ends to which such duets and choruses have been put.

Appendix: poems cited

Shakespeare #66

> Tired with all these, for restful death I cry:
> As to behold desert a beggar born,
> And needy nothing trimmed in jollity,
> And purest faith unhappily forsworn,
> And guilded honour shamefully misplaced,
> And maiden virtue rudely strumpeted,
> And right perfection wrongfully disgraced,
> And strength by limping sway disablèd,
> And art made tongue-tied by authority,
> And folly (doctor-like) controlling skill,
> And simple truth miscalled simplicity,
> And captive good attending captain ill.
>   Tired with all these, from these would I be gone,
>   Save that to die I leave my love alone.

Pasternak's translation of #66

> Измучась всем, я умереть хочу.
> Тоска смотреть, как мается бедняк,
> И как шутя живется богачу,
> И доверять, и попадать впросак,

И наблюдать, как наглость лезет в свет,
И честь девичья катится ко дну,
И знать, что ходу совершенствам нет,
И видеть мощь у немощи в плену
И вспоминать, что мысли заткнут рот,
И разум сносит глупости хулу,
И прямодушье простотой слывет,
И доброта прислуживает злу.
Измучась всем, не стал бы жить и дня,
Да другу будет трудно без меня.

Literal translation of Pasternak's translation of Shakespeare #66

Being tired out by everything, I want to die.
It is an anguish to watch the poor man toil
And the rich man get on as if joking,
And confide and put one's foot in it,
And observe impudence crawling into the world
And maidenly honor rolling to the bottom
And know that this is no path to perfection
And see power as captive feebleness
And remember that thoughts will stopper the mouth
And reason takes down the criticism of stupidity
And straightforwardness has the reputation of simpleness
And goodness tends upon evil.
Being tired out by everything, it's not worth living even a day,
But it will be hard for my [male] friend without me.

Shakespeare #74

But be contented when that fell arrest
Without all bail shall carry me away;
My life hath in this line some interest,
Which for memorial still with thee shall stay.
When thou reviewest this, thou dost review
The very part was consecrate to thee.
The earth can have but earth, which is his due;
My spirit is thine, the better part of me.
So then thou hast but lost the dregs of life,
The prey of worms, my body being dead,
The coward conquest of a wretch's knife,

Too base of thee to be remembered.
The worth of that, is that which it contains,
And that is this, and this with thee remains.

Pasternak's translation of Shakespeare #74

Но успокойся. В дни, когда в острог
Навек я смертью буду взят под стражу,
Одна живая память этих строк
Еще переживет мою пропажу.
И ты увидишь, их перечитав,
Что было лучшею моей частицей.
Вернется в землю мой земной состав,
Мой дух к тебе, как прежде, обратится.
И ты поймешь, что только прах исчез,
Не стоящий нисколько сожаленья,
То, что отнять бы мог головорез,
добыча ограбленья, жертва тленья.
А ценно было только то одно,
Что и теперь тебе посвящено.

Literal translation of Pasternak's translation of Shakespeare #74

But be calm. In the days when to the stockade
I will be taken into custody forever by death
Only the lively memory of these lines
Will still endure my loss.
And you will find, having read them
What was my best part.
My earthly component will return to earth
My soul will address you, as before
And you will understand that only ashes disappeared,
Not being worth any pity,
That which could take away the cutthroat,
The spoils of brigandry, the sacrifice of decay.
And what was valuable was only
What is now sacred for you.

Petrarch #319

I dì miei più leggier' che nesun cervo
Fuggîr come ombra, et non vider più bene

Ch'un batter d'occhio, et poche hore serene,
Ch'amare et dolci ne la mente servo.
    Misero mondo, instabile et protervo,
Del tutto è cieco chi 'n te pon sua spene:
Ché 'n te mi fu 'l cor tolto, et or sel tene
Tal ch'è già terra, et non giunge osso a nervo.
    Ma la forma miglior, che vive anchora,
Et vivrà sempre, su ne l'alto cielo,
Di sue bellezze ognor più m'innamora;
    Et vo, sol in pensar, cangiando il pelo,
Qual ella è oggi, e 'n qual parte dimora,
Qual a vedere il suo leggiadro velo.

Literal translation of Petrarch #319

    My days more nimbly than any hind,
Have fled like a shadow and have not seen more blessing
Than the wink of an eye, and few serene hours,
That bitter and sweet I retain in my mind.
    Miserable world, unstable and haughty,
he is blind to everything who puts his hopes on you:
because in you my heart was taken, and now holds it
such a one who is still earth and does not join bone to sinew.
    But the best form, which lives still,
and always will live, up in high heaven,
now can still charm me with her beauties;
    and I go, thinking, while my hair changes [color],
of what she is like today, and in what parts she dwells,
what it is like to see her graceful veil.

Mandelstam's translation of Petarch #319

Промчались дни мои, как бы оленей
Косящий бег. Срок счастья был короче,
Чем взмах ресницы. Из последней мочи
Я в горсть зажал лишь пепел наслаждений.

По милости надменных обольщений
Ночует сердце в склепе скромной ночи,
К земле бескостной жмется. Средоточий
Знакомых ищет, сладостных сплетений.

Но то, что в ней едва существовало,
Днесь, вырвавшись наверх, в очаг лазури,
Пленять и ранить может, как бывало.

И я догадываюсь, брови хмуря:
Как хороша? к какой толпе пристала?
Как там клубится легких складок буря?

Literal translation of Mandelstam's translation of Petrarch #319

My days rushed past like
The crooked run of deer. The term of my happiness was shorter
Than the blink of an eye. With my last strength
I grasped in my fist just the ash of enjoyment.

By the kindness of haughty delusions
[My] heart spends the night in the crypt of dark night,
Is pressed against the boneless earth, it searches for
Partitions, acquaintances—sweet interweavings.

But that which barely existed in her,
Now, having torn upward into the hearth of azure,
Can take prisoner and wound like it did.

And I guess, wrinkling [my] brow,
How good [looking], and to which crowd [she] belonged,
How there the storm of light folds whirls.

Notes

1. Translated by Miriam Lichtheim. Cited in Deutscher 96.
2. See Russell and Sörbom.
3. See the *Ars poetica*, especially pages 11 and 17.
4. See *De Oratore* II.XXII.
5. See particularly letter LXXXIV.
6. See the *Institutio oratoria*, pages 85–9.
7. See Thomas Greene's *The Light in Troy*.
8. For an introduction see Richerson and Boyd.
9. Bakhtin uses the term himself: "[t]he author does not speak in a given language [. . .] but he speaks, as it were, *through* language, a language [. . .] that he merely ventriloquates" (299). It has been argued that Bakhtin used

his own form of ventriloquism by publishing some of his works under the names of friends (Valentin Voloshinov and Pavel Medvedev) who were more congenial to the Stalinist regime (Clark and Holquist 146–70). While this account has been disputed (Morson and Emerson 101–19), it does appear that there was certainly some ventriloquism, even if it was on more of a personal than a textual level.

10. On Bakhtin and poetry see Eskin 114–25.
11. I do not wish to insinuate here that Bakhtin was necessarily a weak reader of poetry. He certainly had an appreciation for Russian poetry as evidenced by his lectures on the history of Russian literature as well as his later essays. See Emerson on Bakhtin's more complicated relationship with the lyric.
12. His support for the dissident authors Joseph Brodsky and Alexander Solzhenitsyn was the other major factor.
13. See Lev Losev's *On the Beneficence of Censorship: Aesopian Language in Modern Russian Literature* as well as Thomas Venclova's "The Game of the Soviet Censor." See also Brian James Baer's "Literary Translation and the Construction of a Soviet Intelligentsia" where he makes the connection with Pasternak's translations of Shakespeare's plays.
14. On Pasternak's translations of Shakespeare's plays, see Anna Kay France's *Boris Pasternak's Translations of Shakespeare*.
15. Translations are mine unless another translator of the source text is listed in the Works Cited.
16. An omission made at times even by scholars of translation, such as when Maurice Friedberg, in his *Literary Translation in Russia: A Cultural History,* states that:

> A number of important poets and prose writers who for political reasons were denied the opportunity to publish original work were 'mercifully' allowed to translate to earn their livelihoods. Such men and women must not be compared to those important Russian authors of the past who, for whatever personal reason, *chose* to do some translating work or even devoted most of their energies to it, like Vasily Zhukovsky. No, these Soviet translators were engaged in literary forced labor of sorts. Theirs was *translation under duress.* (114, emphasis in original)

While certainly true, this ignores the artistic opportunities translation provided, given the circumstances. (For a subtler approach, see Baer.) Part of my argument is that Soviet translators should, in at least part of their output, be favorably compared to the likes of Zhukovsky.
17. Complete texts of the originals and the translations for my discussion of both Pasternak and Mandelstam can be found at the end of the paper.
18. Shakespeare clearly intends the legal sense of the word as the sonnet is shot through with references to criminality, an important subtext for Pasternak.
19. A process necessary for producing individual meaning in Bakhtin. As Michael Holquist paraphrases him: "I can appropriate meaning to my own purposes only by ventriloquating others" ("Politics" 169).
20. The scholarship on Mandelstam and translation tends to focus on the texts either purely as translations (and not as original works) or within the context of Mandelstam's work as a whole. See Mureddu; Semenko,

"Мандельштам – переводчик Петрарки" and *Поэтика позднего Мандельштама* 68–96; Venclova, "Вячеслав Иванов И Осип Мандельштам;" Ilyushin; Baines 70–1; and Cazzola.

21. See Dolack for a fuller discussion in relation to sonnet 311.
22. The German version is titled simply *Hypnos* and was originally published in *Neue Rundschau* in 1958.
23. Celan in fact translated Mandelstam beginning about the same time as his translations of Char. Mandelstam also appears, directly or indirectly, in more than a few of his original poems (most prominently in "Es ist alles anders [It is all different]," but also in "Mandorla," "Nachmittag mit Zirkus und Zitadelle [Afternoon with Circus and Citadel]," and "In Eins [In One]," just to name a few). His name had added significance for Celan as "Mandelstamm" in German means "almond branch," an image associated with the Jewish people. Celan also believed at the time that Mandelstam died at the hands of the Germans in the early days of the war, and not at the hands of the Soviets in a camp in Siberia (Ivanović 342–7). See, inter alia, Eskin, Olschner, Terras and Weimar, and Broda.
24. A point made by other scholars including Daniel Pinti and Léon Robel in more narrowly focused arguments.

Works cited

Akhmatova, Anna. *Собрание сочинений в шести томах*. Vol. 5. Moscow: Ellis Lak, 1998–2002.

Baer, Brian James. "Literary Translation and the Construction of a Soviet Intelligentsia." *The Massachusetts Review* 47.3 (2006): 537–60.

Baines, Jennifer. *Mandelstam: The Later Poetry*. New York: Cambridge UP, 1976.

Bakhtin, M. M. "Discourse in the Novel." *The Dialogic Imagination: Four Essays by M. M. Bakhtin*. Ed. Michael Holquist. Trans. Caryl Emerson and Michael Holquist. Austin: U of Texas P, 1981. 259–422.

——. "From the Prehistory of Novelistic Discourse." *The Dialogic Imagination: Four Essays by M.M. Bakhtin*. Ed. Michael Holquist. Trans. Caryl Emerson and Michael Holquist. Austin: U of Texas P, 1981. 41–83.

Bloom, Harold. *The Anxiety of Influence: A Theory of Poetry*. New York: Oxford UP, 1997.

Borges, Jorge Luis. "Pierre Menard, Author of the Quixote." *Collected Fictions*. Trans. Andrew Hurley. New York: Viking, 1998. 88–95.

Broda, Martine. *Dans La Main De Personne: Essai Sur Paul Celan*. Paris: Les Éditions du Cerf, 1986.

Cazzola, Piero. "Osip Mandel'štam, traduttore russo del Petrarca." Centre d'études franco-italiennes. *Dynamique d'une Expansion Culturelle: Pétrarque En Europe, XIVe–XXe Siècle: Actes Du XXVIe Congrès International Du CEFI, Turin Et Chambéry, 11–15 Décembre 1995: À La Mémoire De Franco Simone*. Paris: Champion, 2001. 401–13.

Celan, Paul. *Correspondance (1951–1970): Avec un choix de letters de Paul Celan à son fils Eric. Éditée et commentée par Bertrand Badiou avec le concours d'Eric Celan*. Vol. 1. Paris: Seuil, 2001.

——. *Gesammelte Werke in fünf Bänden*. Vol. 4. Frankfurt: Suhrkamp, 1986.

——. *Paul Celan: Selections*. Ed. and trans. by Pierre Joris. Berkeley: U of California P, 2005.

——. *Selected Poems and Prose of Paul Celan*. Trans. John Felstiner. New York: W. W. Norton, 2001.

Char, René. *Œuvres completes*. Paris: Gallimard, 1983.

Cicero. *De Oratore. Book I–II, with an English translation by E.W. Sutton*. Cambridge, MA: Harvard UP, 1988.

Clark, Katerina, and Michael Holquist. *Mikhail Bakhtin*. Cambridge, MA: Harvard UP, 1984.

Deutscher, Guy. *The Unfolding of Language: An Evolutionary Tour of Mankind's Greatest Invention*. New York: Metropolitan Books, 2005.

Dolack, Tom. "Mandelstam's Petrarch Translations and His Humanist Archaeology." *Annali d'Italianistica* 26 (2008): 187–201.

Emerson, Caryl. "Prosaics and the Problem of Form." *The Slavic and East European Journal* 41.1 (1997): 16–39.

Eskin, Michael. *Ethics and Dialogue in the Works of Levinas, Bakhtin, Mandel'shtam, and Celan*. New York: Oxford UP, 2000.

Etkind, Efim. *Notes of a Non-Conspirator*. Trans. Peter France. New York: Oxford UP, 1978.

——. "Поэтический перевод в истории русской литературы" *Мастера русского стихотворного перевода*. Vol. 1. Ed. Efim Ètkind. Leningrad: Sovetskii pisatel', 1968. 5–72.

Felstiner, John. *Paul Celan: Poet, Survivor, Jew*. New Haven, CT: Yale UP, 1995.

France, Anna Kay. *Boris Pasternak's Translations of Shakespeare*. Berkeley: U of California P, 1978.

Friedberg, Maurice. *Literary Translation in Russia: A Cultural History*. University Park, PA: Pennsylvania State UP, 1997.

Greene, Thomas M. *The Light in Troy: Imitation and Discovery in Renaissance Poetry*. New Haven, CT: Yale UP, 1982.

Holquist, Michael. *Dialogism: Bakhtin and his World*. New York: Routledge, 2002.

——. "The Politics of Representation." *Allegory and Representation*. Ed. Stephen Jay Greenblatt. Baltimore, MD: Johns Hopkins UP, 1981. 163–83.

Horace. *Ars Poetica*. Trans. Leon Golden. In *Horace for Students of Literature: The "Ars Poetica" and its Tradition*. Ed. O. B. Hardison, Jr. and Leon Golden. Miami: UP of Florida, 1995.

Ilyushin, A. A. "Данте и Петрарка в интерпретациях Мандельштама." *Жизнь и творчество О. Э. Мандельштама: Воспоминания; Материалы к биографии*. Voronezh: Izdatelstvo Voronezhskogo universiteta, 1990.

Ivanović, Christine. "»Da sah ich dich, Mandelstamm«." *»Fremde Nähe«: Celan als Übersetzer*. Marbach am Neckar, Germany: Deutsche Schillergesellschaft, 1997. 337–54.

Jakobson, Roman. "Linguistics and Poetics." *Language in Literature*. Ed. Krystyna Pomorska and Stephen Rudy. Cambridge, MA: Harvard UP, 1987. 62–94.

La Charité, Virginia A. *The Poetics and the Poetry of René Char*. Chapel Hill: U of North Carolina P, 1968.

Losev, Lev. *On the Beneficence of Censorship: Aesopian Language in Modern Russian Literature*. Munich: O. Sagner in Kommission, 1984.

Mandelstam, Nadezhda. *Hope Against Hope: A Memoir*. Trans. Max Hayward. New York: Atheneum, 1970.

Mandelstam, Osip. *Собрание сочинений в четырех томах.* Vol. 1. Moscow: Terra, 1991.

——. "Humanism and the Present." *The Complete Critical Prose and Letters.* Ed. Jane Gary Harris. Trans. Jane Gary Harris and Constance Link. Ann Arbor: Ardis, 1979. 181–3.

Morson, Gary Saul, and Caryl Emerson. *Mikhail Bakhtin: Creation of a Prosaics.* Stanford, CA: Stanford UP, 1990.

Mureddu, Donata. "Mandel'štam and Petrarch." *Scando-Slavica* 26 (1980): 53–84.

Olschner, Leonard. "Poetic Mutations of Silence: At the Nexus of Paul Celan and Osip Mandelstam." *Wordtraces: Readings of Paul Celan.* Ed. Aris Fioretos. Baltimore: The Johns Hopkins UP, 1994. 369–85.

Pasternak, Boris. *Собрание Сочинений в пяти томах.* Vol. 2. Moscow: Khudozhestvennaia literatura, 1989.

Petrarca, Francesco. *Opere.* Florence: Sansoni, 1975.

Pinti, Daniel J. "Dialogism, Heteroglossia, and Late Medieval Translation." *Bakhtin and Medieval Voices.* Gainesville: UP of Florida, 1995. 109–21.

Plato. *The Republic of Plato. Translated with Notes and an Interpretive Essay by Allan Bloom.* New York: Basic Books, 1991.

Quintilian. *The Institutio oratoria of Quintilian with an English Translation by H. E. Butler.* New York: G. P. Putnam's Sons, 1922.

Richerson, Peter J. and Robert Boyd. *Not by Genes Alone: How Culture Transformed Human Evolution.* Chicago: U of Chicago P, 2005.

Robel, Léon. "Bakhtine et la traduction." *Mélanges offerts à Jean Peytard, I & II.* Annales Littéraires de l'Université de Besançon: 502 & 503. Paris: Belles Lettres, 1993. 641–8.

Russell, D. A. "De Imitione." In *Creative Imitation in Latin Literature.* Ed. David West and Tony Woodman. New York: Cambridge UP, 1979.

Semenko, I. "Мандельштам – переводчик Петрарки." *Voprosy literatury* 14, no. 10 (1970): 153–69.

——. *Поэтика позднего Мандельштама: От черновых редакций к окончательному тексту.* Rome: Carucci, 1986.

Seneca. *Ad Lucilium epistulae morales with an English Translation by Richard M. Gummere.* Cambridge, MA: Harvard UP, 1962.

Shakespeare, William. *The Complete Sonnets and Poems.* New York: Oxford UP, 2002.

Sörbom, Göran. "The Classical Concept of Mimesis." *A Companion to Art Theory.* Ed. Paul Smith and Carolyn Wilde. Malden, MA: Blackwell, 2002.

Terras, Victor and Karl S. Weimar. "Mandelstam and Celan: A Postscript." *Germano-Slavica: A Canadian Journal of Germanic and Slavic Comparative Studies.* 2 (1978): 353–70.

Venclova, Thomas. "Вячеслав Иванов и Осип Мандельштам – переводчики Петрарки (на примере сонета CCCXI)." *Собеседники на пиру. Статьи о русской литературе.* Vilnius: Baltos Lankos, 1997. 168–83.

——. "The Game of the Soviet Censor." *The New York Review of Books,* 1983, 31 March: 34–5.

5

Robert Lowell's "common novel plot": Names, Naming, and Polyphony in *The Dolphin*

Geoffrey Lindsay

Even before its publication in 1973, Robert Lowell's *The Dolphin* was a controversial collection, and it has continued to be a focus of debate. The book's subject matter is not the issue, since it is, as Lowell himself notes, "the common novel plot" of "one man, two women" (*Dolphin* 48). Essentially, the poems record Lowell's difficult transition from one marriage to another, from marriage to Elizabeth Hardwick (called "Lizzie" in the poems) to Caroline Blackwood. The criticism, which, as the Ian Hamilton and Paul Mariani biographies reveal, enveloped friend and foe alike, polarized around two related issues. The first entailed the use of names of actual people (Caroline, Lizzie, and daughter Harriet). Not only were Lowell's, Hardwick's, and Blackwood's friends and acquaintances to be privy to this marital drama, the wider reading audience was now to be allowed a window into the houses and bedrooms of the unofficial Poet Laureate.

In an era before reality television such exhibitionism seemed a gross violation of an individual's right to privacy. To other readers, the fact that Lowell would quote (apparently verbatim or with minor changes) from private conversations and letters between the two women and himself without their prior knowledge or approval was an even more grievous violation of artistic and moral integrity. An anguished Elizabeth Bishop wrote Lowell after reading the poems in manuscript and asked, "[B]ut these letters—aren't you violating a trust? IF you were given permission—IF you hadn't changed them . . . etc. *But art just isn't worth that much.* [. . .] It is not being 'gentle' to use personal, tragic, anguished letters that way—it's cruel" (qtd. in Hamilton 423).

This essay originally appeared in *The Dalhousie Review* 75 (Winter 1996): 351–68; it is reprinted here by permission of *The Dalhousie Review*.

Stanley Kunitz called some passages "too ugly, for being too cruel, too intimately cruel" (qtd. in Hamilton 422), while W. H. Auden threatened to refuse to speak to Lowell (Hamilton 425). After *The Dolphin* was published, along with *For Lizzie and Harriet* and *History* in 1973, Adrienne Rich, once a friend of Lowell's, would write the following:

> Finally, what does one say about a poet who, having left his wife and daughter for another marriage, then titles a book with their names, and goes on to appropriate his ex-wife's letters written under the stress and pain of desertion, into a book of poems nominally addressed to the new wife? [. . .] The inclusion of the letter poems stands as one of the most vindictive and mean-spirited acts in the history of poetry, one for which I can think of no precedent: and the same unproportioned ego that was capable of this act is damagingly at work in all three of Lowell's books. (qtd. in Hamilton 433)

Later criticism tends to focus less on the personal elements and more on the artistic merits of the volume. Steven Gould Axelrod and Vereen Bell, for instance, largely treat "Lizzie" and "Caroline" as textual characters with origins in the extratextual. "Lowell's marital affairs are more pretext (pre-text) than text," Axelrod writes, "the real text is his mind in the act of grasping at the bare events and turning back upon itself, converting them and itself to fiction" (215). Bell says that "the Lowell who writes poems has, because of the way they are written, the same fictional status as his two other fictional characters. It is forgivable that we do not always see this distinction between writer and maker, but not to see it is to miss the point" (203). Implicit in this approach is the New Critical notion that the poet and the speaker of the poem are never one and the same; thus the poet's literary creations and his or her models are similarly distinct, despite Lowell's use of his models' actual words. Because of the framing convention of art, we can discuss "Lizzie" without worrying about Elizabeth Hardwick, at least from these critics' and Lowell's perspective. In a letter written before *The Dolphin* was published, Lowell writes of changes he has made to the manuscript:

> The terrible thing isn't the mixing of fact and fiction, but the wife pleading with her husband to return—this backed by "documents." [. . .]
> Now the book must still be painful to Lizzie, and won't satisfy Elizabeth [Bishop]. As Caroline says, it can't be otherwise with the book's donnee. However, even fairly small changes make Lizzie less a documented presence. A distinct, even idiosyncratic voice isn't the

same as someone, almost fixed as non-fictional evidence, that you could call on the phone. She dims slightly and Caroline and I somewhat lengthen. (qtd. in Hamilton 426)

Lowell's third-person depiction of "the wife" and "her husband" and his defensive distinction between an "idiosyncratic" voice and someone "that you could call on the phone" demonstrate the separation, however narrow, Lowell saw between his life and art; hence his justification for publishing *The Dolphin*. As much as he drew on his life for his material, Lowell seems to have had few real misgivings about his method:

> Conscience incurable
> convinces me I am not writing my life;
> life never assures which part of ourself is life.
> Ours was never a book, though sparks of it
> spotted the page with superficial burns:
> the fiction I colored with first-hand evidence,
> letters and talk I marketed as fiction—
>
> (*Dolphin* 59)

But despite the changes in manuscript and Lowell's confidence, readers continue to express a lingering unease with Lowell's methods. John A. Ward, in an article entitled "'Not Avoiding Injury': Robert Lowell," asks, "[D]oes he [Lowell] affirm or violate the integrity of his former and current loves by treating them in detail and by name in his verse?" (138). Whereas in the earlier confessional volumes, *Life Studies* and *For the Union Dead*, Lowell had "managed to describe [his marriage] in detail without naming," the names used in *The Dolphin* are an unwarranted invasion of privacy, a sign that Lowell's ability to believe in what he was doing was failing. Ward's comment is insightful:

[W]hen Lowell names in *The Dolphin* he shows us that he has lost confidence in the subtle, intimate, trusting pull of the beloved to help him out of mania into life and writing; the old intimacy and implication are gone, replaced by a sometimes coarse candour. The familiar shape of affirmation in the sequence of poems is still there, but it is wholly unconvincing. Lowell goes beyond the boundaries of the confidentiality and transformation so carefully established in *Life Studies* and *For the Union Dead* and uses names because the authenticity of erotic and loving experience is beginning to escape him, or has become too fragile or ironic to capture in verse. (140)

I think this is a just and subtle reading of *The Dolphin*, but I would argue that Lowell's attempt at transformation fails in other ways, as well, ways that are of less interest to Ward and which have to do with Lowell's quoting from and naming of Elizabeth Hardwick. First, one more comment by Ward: "Elizabeth Hardwick, Harriet Lowell, and Caroline Blackwood must have felt exposed and knew that their experience and remarks were forever to be part of a public record, a record that sometimes abused them and left them no recourse but silence" (140).

It is this last point that I wish to consider in reading *The Dolphin* as a polyphonic poem. Drawing upon research in quotation theory, I will argue that far from having no recourse but silence, the voices of Lizzie, Caroline, and Harriet talk back to Lowell's voice: however much Lowell's dominant voice seeks to inscribe his master narrative, we can discern a distinct and alternate narrative through these other voices. Finally, I believe that the naming is important in that it strengthens the independence of these voices in a way that is not possible with indirect characterization. In effect, Lowell lives and dies by the sword of naming.

It is true that in *The Dolphin* the impulse to autobiographical confession begun with *Life Studies* breaks new ground with the naming and direct quotations, as Ward asserts (139). However, I would like to link the confessional impulse with another poetic strategy, which might help explain Lowell's use of naming and quotation. Lowell learned much about the juxtaposition of one voice with another in the years leading up to the publication of *The Dolphin* through his interest in drama. In the 1960s and early 1970s, Lowell turned to drama as a sister art, writing *The Old Glory* trilogy and producing translations (or imitations) of *Prometheus Bound*, *Phaedra*, and *The Oresteia*. For *Prometheus Bound*, he worked closely with director Jonathan Miller; *The Old Glory* won five Obie awards for the 1964–65 season, and Robert Brustein hailed Lowell as a "brilliant new dramatist" (*Old Glory* 218) as Lowell's plays were staged on both sides of the Atlantic. To an interviewer, Lowell said that, while writing plays, "I found it a great relief to have a plot and people who weren't me at all," and that he could "say things that were personal that I couldn't say in a confessional poem" (Alvarez 76). As he noted of confessional poetry to Ian Hamilton, "That vein of silver [eventually] gives out" (Lowell, "Conversation" 269). Drama also allowed Lowell to move in the direction of an increasingly public and polyphonic voice, something he felt necessary in the politicized 1960s.

But Lowell realized he lacked the invention—all his plays are translations or reworkings of short stories—and the objectivity required for original work on the stage. Never particularly comfortable with the medium, Lowell would write, "I now feel double-faced, looking on plays as some barbarian Gaul or Goth might have first looked on Rome, his shaggy head full of moral disgust, plunder, and adaptation" ("Poets" 177–8). Plunder and adapt he did, and the following comment to an interviewer gives us some idea of his direction:

> You know, I find fragments more interesting usually than whole plays. Plots are boring anyway. We all hate the sort of play where one thing leads to another and everything is drawn tight. [. . .]
> [R]ecently I read *Macbeth*, skipping all the places where he or his wife don't speak. What I found was that it would have made a great poem, one of the greatest, with all those plot elements removed. (Gilman 120)

This comment was made in 1968, one of the years named in Lowell's first collection of sonnets, *Notebook 1967–68* (pub. 1969). It is my contention that Lowell creates his own series of "fragments" in *Notebook 1967–68* and again in the expanded version, *Notebook* (1970). In both volumes Lowell quotes directly from a myriad of sources, some identifiable, some not. What he seeks is a collision of voices, his own interacting with others, and others interacting with each other. Ultimately Lowell uses these voices to create a dramatization of his life and circumstances; the dramatic voices are a means of debating the choices available to him as he goes through a midlife crisis, as he watches the 1968 Presidential elections unfold, and as he decides whether or not to continue in his marriage to Elizabeth Hardwick.[1] That process of dramatization is continued in *The Dolphin*, but it is intensified there because, while the *Notebook* poems included political, social, as well as personal debates about choices, *The Dolphin*'s voices concentrate on the choice he must make in his marriage. Thus the poems in *The Dolphin*, with their quotations, are like the "poem" *Macbeth*: the bridging plot is removed, and what is left are the voices. These voices are mostly Lowell's, Lizzie's, and Caroline's, although Harriet is also quoted, and there are occasional other voices as well. The voices not Lowell's own are signalled by quotation marks, or the quoted lines are in italics; sometimes both are used, as in the following, where Lowell quotes Caroline quoting from *Macbeth*: "'If it were done, twere well it were done quickly—/ to quote a bromide, your vacillation / is acne'" (*Dolphin* 53). The length of the quotation varies, ranging from half a line to whole sonnets. Context usually indicates who is speaking when Lowell does not tell the reader through the title or by other means.

Quotation theory allows us to take a dispassionate look at the inter-actions between these voices in *The Dolphin* and to draw different conclusions than have previous commentators and Lowell's immediate audience. Mikhail Bakhtin's distinction between monologic poetry and polyphonic prose is a useful place to begin, since I believe that the voices in *The Dolphin* are essentially polyphonic and that this is a departure from the monologic confessional volumes that precede *Notebook 1967–68*, despite Lowell's use of quotations in those early volumes. The novel-ist, Bakhtin argues, exploits the polyphony of alien meanings inherent in the prose word, turning such diversity to advantage, as he or she uses the various accents, characteristic speech patterns, and "social heteroglossia embedded in words" ("Discourse" 298) to animate the novel's different characters. Rather than expressing him- or herself, the novelist "exhibits" the discourses available to him or her through prose's polyphony: "The author does not speak in a given language (from which he distances himself to a greater or lesser degree), but he speaks, as it were, *through* lan-guage, a language that has somehow more or less materialized, become objectivized, that he merely ventriloquates" ("Discourse" 299).

In contrast, the poet, according to Bakhtin, works to rid language of "the intentions and accents of other people [by] destroying all traces of social heteroglossia and diversity of language" (298). Any diversity must be subordinate to the overpowering will to expression of the poet's intention: the "natural dialogization of the word" (285) is suspended, its alien utterances suppressed. Such is the nature of poetic language that "[e]ach word must express the poet's *meaning* directly and without medi-ation," Bakhtin argues, with the result that "*[e]verything that enters the work must immerse itself in Lethe, and forget its previous life in any other con-texts: language may remember only its life in poetic contexts*" (297, Bakhtin's emphasis). Even when the poet uses other voices, Bakhtin writes of those discourses that "no socially typical linguistic face (the possible personal-ity of the narrator) need peek out from behind them. Everywhere there is only one face—the linguistic face of the author, answering for every word as if it were his own. No matter how multiple and varied [. . .] one lan-guage, one conceptual horizon, is sufficient to them all" (297). However, Bakhtin's distinction between the monologic lyric and dialogic novel is largely qualified by his assertion that "[i]n an era when the novel reigns supreme, almost all the remaining genres are to a greater or lesser extent 'novelized'" ("Epic" 5). These newly novelized genres, including poetry,

> become more free and flexible, their language renews itself by incorpo-rating extraliterary heteroglossia and the "novelistic" layers of literary language, they become dialogized, permeated with laughter, irony,

humor, elements of self-parody and finally—this is the most important thing—the novel inserts into these other genres an indeterminacy, a certain semantic openendedness, a living contact with unfinished, still-evolving contemporary reality (the openended present). (7)

This last quality is especially evident in the *Notebook* volumes and *The Dolphin*.

Before he experimented with polyphony in *Notebook 1967–68*, Lowell's lyric voice was essentially monologic. Although Lowell sometimes incorporated other voices or wrote dramatic monologues, Bakhtin's objection is apposite: "Everywhere there is only one face—the linguistic face of the author, answering for every word as if it were his own" (297). As Axelrod notes, the dramatic voices in *Life Studies* "lack the power Lowell admired in Frost of getting within a character's skin and language" (103). But after Lowell's experiments with the theatre, the dramatic voices in *Notebook 1967–68* and the volumes through to *The Dolphin* are largely independent of Lowell's own. As suggested earlier, the voices present Lowell with choices he must make in his life, and the choice in *The Dolphin* is between Lizzie and Caroline.

Even so, Calvin Bedient argues that Lowell's experiment with novelized poetry is a failure:

That Lowell was both personally and poetically outrageous enough to compose whole poems from Elizabeth Hardwick's private letters to him may suggest a downright eagerness to violate what Bakhtin calls the "unitary and indisputable discourse" of poetry ("Discourse" 286); but Hardwick's words enter Lowell's volumes as depicted things, like the words of a character in an epistolary novel (Lowell's shamefaced "plot"), and I think Lowell begrudged every line lost to the language of others, even Hardwick's. (139)

I am not so sure. Lowell may have begrudged those lines, and he may have intended that they serve his need, but these other voices have a habit of resisting Lowell's intention. Take the following, in which Lowell quotes from one of Elizabeth Hardwick's letters:

"In London last month I encountered only
exhausted traffic and exhausting men—
the taxi driver might kill us, but at least he cared."
Cold summer London, your purer cold is Maine,
where each empty sweater and hollow bookcase hurts,

every pretext for their service gone.
We wanted to be buried together in Maine . . .
you didn't, "impractical, cold, out of touch."
The terrible postcards you bought and stamped for me
go off to Harriet, the Horseguards, the Lifeguards,
The Lord Mayor's Chariot, Queen Bess who could not bear—
true as anything else to fling a child. . . .
I shout into the air, my voice comes back—
nothing reaches your black silhouette.

("Letter," *Dolphin* 23)

Lowell's intention is that Lizzie's words should reflect unfavourably on her: she complains about traffic and "exhausting men"; the half line "but at least he cared" has the bathos of the abandoned lover. Lizzie is the one who refuses to be buried with Lowell; she buys "terrible postcards" (cliché-ridden) for Harriet; and the last two lines, culminating with "your black silhouette," complete the picture of a rejected wife deaf to the pleadings for release from the husband who has found happiness elsewhere.

Small wonder that Bishop and Rich found Lowell's use of Hardwick's letters cruel and mean-spirited. But we should take a second look at Lowell's attempted appropriation of Hardwick's voice. One word that is repeated in this sonnet is "cold," which Lowell attempts to associate with Lizzie: "Cold summer London, your purer cold is Maine." There are "empty sweater[s]" in Maine, and Lizzie refuses to be buried with Lowell in Maine: "impractical, cold, out of touch." Yet the rhythm and substance of the lines in which Lizzie speaks are far from cold; in fact, it is Lowell's lines that are decidedly cool, even detached. "But at least he cared" has passion in its pain, while "Cold summer London, your purer cold is Maine" immediately following it is analytical, aloof. Instead of agreeing with Lowell about the "terrible postcards" in judging Lizzie's character (you are what you buy), we should notice the next few words: "you bought and stamped for me." Who comes across as generous and thoughtful here? Not only does Lizzie buy Lowell postcards so he can play the dutiful father, she even stamps them for him. Lowell's word "fling" in the line "true as anything else to fling a child" gets tangled up entirely in those "alien value judgments and accents" Bakhtin says surround words ("Discourse" 276). "Fling" in other contexts means to cast aside or discard; it can also mean a brief period of indulging one's impulses, such as a sexual tryst. Inadvertently the sonnet says something other than what the dominant discourse

would like it to say, and Lizzie's quoted voice has much to do with
that change.

Other sonnets are equally powerful records of Lizzie's voice:

" . . . That new creature,
when I hear her name, I have to laugh.
You left two houses and two thousand books,
a workbarn by the ocean, and two slaves
to kneel and wait upon you hand and foot—
tell us why in the name of Jesus."

                    ("Voices" 23)

"I love you, Darling, there's a black black void,
as black as night without you. I long to see
your face and hear your voice, and take your hand—"

                    ("In the Mail" 41)

"You're not under inspection, just missed . . .
I wait for your letters, tremble when I get none,
more when I do. Nothing new to say."

                    ("Foxfur" 69)

            "I got the letter
this morning, the letter you wrote me Saturday.
I thought my heart would break a thousand times,
but I would rather have read it a thousand times
than the detached unreal ones you wrote before—"

                    ("Records" 31)

Ward says that his "first reaction was shock at the trivial and conventional tones of these complaints, as if the language of the abandoned
wife was too familiar to admit of poetry." He says his second reaction
was his "suspicion that by including this material Lowell was trivialising
the person he had offended, turning her into a stock character but pre-
tending to protect her integrity by seeming to quote her" (141). There
is something in this, certainly. However, Ward's later comment is problematic, as he discusses the last sonnet quoted above, "Records": "[T]he
nature of her words makes it easy for us to dismiss her. The casual quality of the woman's language, the repetitiveness and exaggeration, make
the poem's statements seem deliberately trite in tone and commonplace

in content. [. . . H]er heart seems to break a thousand times, but rather than not read his letter she'll have it break a thousand times" (143). But is this entirely so? Subversively, does casting Lizzie in the role of the conventional abandoned wife not also deny Lowell anything but the conventional role of the philandering husband in the "common novel plot"? I think Ward is right when he argues that Lowell fails to create a grand and rejuvenating passion out of his relationship with Caroline that justifies his invasion of Elizabeth Hardwick's privacy in *The Dolphin*, but it is partly the language Lizzie uses that anchors the volume in the "common novel plot" and not in the transformative metaphor of Caroline-as-dolphin-as-saviour, as Lowell may have wanted. Marie Maclean's observation is important here: "The problem in the use of quotation is that while it is a means of asserting textual power (one only quotes what one wants to), it involves the loss of textual control as the voice of the original speaker can still be heard even when its values are being questioned" (135).

In *Changing Voices: The Modern Quoting Poem*, Leonard Diepeveen explores at length the subversiveness of quotations within quoting poems. He argues that a quotation's "exact texture" introduces a "profound disruption" in the borrowing poem (4). As a result, "quotation injects competing strategies into a single text, and often these strategies do not resolve as much as they subvert the quoting text" (18). This is especially evident when the quotation is lengthy, as in *The Dolphin*, because:

> The more extensive the quotation becomes, the more readers look for the poetic voice in the quotation itself, and less in the relation of the quotation to the rest of the poem. The quoted voice stays long enough to acquire complexity and establish several characteristics within itself, and so its texture can neither be easily written over by a single strategy, nor subordinated to another voice. (105)

Lowell would appropriate Lizzie's voice for his purpose of reducing her to a stock character, but he doesn't succeed. The triteness Ward sees has a curious power as it accumulates in the volume. There is a kind of authenticity in that voice, too pained to grope for metaphor, too hurt and too unselfconscious to seek originality of expression. In times of stress and distress we fall back on the formulas that come to mind first, and these clichés, ironically, become more moving than the fancy-dress and calculating metaphors Lowell employs. Lowell may deliberately choose conventional language for Lizzie, but the result is a loss of control, as Maclean says, and this loss has unpredictable consequences. As it turns out, Lizzie's voice, because of the alien texture of the quotations, becomes a powerful contrast to Lowell's own. David Lodge notes that "[a] corollary of Bakhtin's insight is that language which in itself is flat, banal, clichéd and generally automatized can become vividly expressive when mimicked, heightened, stylized, parodied and played off against other kinds of language in the polyphonic discourse of the novel" (93). Conventionally, we expect heightened language in a sonnet sequence, but when contrasted in this context with the "generally automatized" language Lizzie uses, Lowell's tropes seem strained and worked-up, while Lizzie's flatter, less demonstrably figurative speech becomes "vividly expressive": "tell us why in the name of Jesus."

But this observation does not apply only to Lizzie's words, as in the examples above. Take the following poem, where Lowell anguishes over the difficult choices he faces:

> From the dismay of my old world to the blank
> new—water-torture of vacillation!
> The true snakepit isn't monodrama Medea,
> the gorgon arousing the serpents in her hair;
> it's a room to walk with no one else, to walk,
> take thought, unthink the thought and listen for nothing:
> "She loves me too much to have my welfare at heart . . .
> *they just aren't up to your coming home*
> *three weeks, then leaving for a year. They just aren't.*
> *They can't stand much more of anything,*
> *they are so tired and hurt and worn. They go on,*
> *knowing your real sickness is a fretful*
> *deafness to little children . . . and suspect*
> *it's impossible for anyone to help you."*
>
> ("Pointing the Horns of the Dilemma" 42)

This is an interesting and complex poem, in terms of the kinds of voices used, and it is a refinement of the polyphonic lyric and Lowell's attempt to control the quoted word. Lowell acknowledges that facing the invective of his wife ("monodrama Medea" is probably Lizzie, the "Monster loved for what you are" of *Near the Ocean*) is far easier than the "water-torture of vacillation" he is subject to when alone, where he can only "take thought, unthink the thought and listen for nothing." But he does in fact listen, at first to himself: "She loves me too much to have my welfare at heart . . . " Bluff, defensive, even self-deceiving, Lowell here tries to convince himself that whatever Lizzie wants him to do is for her sake and is not in his best interest. As if in response are the italicized words, almost certainly paraphrased from a mutual friend; because they are in italics and enclosed within the same quotation marks, they seem to emanate from Lowell's own memory and echo in his mind. The contrasts between the voices demonstrate the dynamics of the polyphonic lyric: we see the reflective, vacillating Lowell; then his self-quotation, the attempt to convince himself of Lizzie's selfish interest and thereby resolve his vacillation; and finally the echoing voice describing Lizzie's private agony and pain. Lowell's language is again figurative: the difficulty of choosing is "water-torture," the adversarial woman is "monodrama Medea, / the gorgon arousing the serpents in her hair." In direct contrast is the unadorned prose of the italicized portion: "*they are so tired and hurt and worn.*" Again, this italicized portion seems more honest, direct, and uncluttered by the strategies of self-deception that the figurative language encourages (the rejected wife as virago). The one false note in the italicized portion is the closest that section comes to what is conventionally deemed "poetic": Lowell's "real sickness" is described as "a fretful / deafness to little children." This seems to me to be another evasion on Lowell's part; by focusing on the children, and by using the weakly censorious "fretful" ("frightful" would have been more appropriate), Lowell evades censure for his actions toward Lizzie and Harriet. The line stands out for its poetic qualities that ring false in the context of the italicized passage. Notable is the assonance of short e's and i's ("*fretful deafness to little children*") and consonance of f's, l's, d's, and t's ("*fretful deafness to little children*"). Conspicuously melodic in a context that is otherwise unremarkable, these combinations of words sound hollow, suggesting an evasion on Lowell's part. We should note again that these words, because in italics, are depicted not as a direct quotation, *per se*, but as a quotation recalled as it echoes in Lowell's mind. This leaves the quotation vulnerable to changes, such as Lowell appears to make to limit the damage; nonetheless, the language itself holds him accountable.

Even some of the most damaging poems, from Lizzie's perspective, are less grievous when reexamined. Take, for example, "During a Transatlantic Call":

We can't swing New York on Harry Truman incomes—
the bright lights dragging like a ball and chain,
the Liberal ruined by the Liberal school.
This was the price of your manic flight to London—
the closed provincial metropolis, never

> an asylum for the mercurial American mind. . . .
> They say fear of death is a child's remembrance
> of the first desertion. My daughter knows no love
> that doesn't bind her with presents, letters, visits,
> things outward and visible. . . . I've closed my mind
> so long, I want to keep it closed, perhaps—
> I have no faith in my right to will transcendence,
> when a house goes, the species is extinct. . . .
> They tell me to stop, they mustn't lose my money.
>
> (*Dolphin* 47)

The two italicized lines are supposed to be Lizzie's voice on the telephone from New York, as she demands more income support. She is represented here, through these one-line excerpts from her conversation with Lowell, as the stereotypical ex-wife, ever asking for more of her husband's money, exacting financial revenge, the "price" of his desertion. However, from another perspective, what the italicized lines do, in Diepeveen's terms, is "ensure that readers are aware of two struggling forces: the quotation's previous existence and something of the quoting poet's hold over the quotation" (50). The quotation's distinct texture subverts Lowell's intended purpose and loosens his hold—and his control—over Hardwick's words. Furthermore, Bakhtin reminds us that reported speech is not the same as direct speech. Hence, Bakhtin writes, quoting Leo Spitzer, "When we reproduce in our own speech a portion of our partner's utterance, then by virtue of the very change in speakers a change in tone inevitably occurs: *the words of 'the other person' always sound on our lips like something alien to us, and often have an intonation of ridicule, exaggeration, or mockery*" (*Problems* 194). Isolated, out of context, and made prominent by the device of italics—often used for emphasis (as in Spitzer's quotation), but in the sonnet apparently to denote reported speech—Lizzie's lines do sound exaggerated, and as readers we can't help resenting the hidden polemic in Lowell's appropriation of Lizzie's voice here. "Any sly and ill-disposed polemicist," Bakhtin says, "knows very well which dialogizing backdrop he should bring to bear on the accurately quoted words of his opponent, in order to distort their sense. By manipulating the effects of context, it is very easy to emphasize the brute materiality of another's words" ("Discourse" 340). The sensitive reader will have already discounted the shrillness of the italics, knowing that context is all important. Without knowing the rest of the conversation on the phone, how can we judge these two statements? Moreover, the language used in the sonnet rebounds on Lowell in other ways. The "bright lights dragging like a ball and chain" initially seem to be connected with Lizzie's impoverishment: she is attracted to the "bright lights" despite her less-than-adequate income, and thus restricted, she demands more money from Lowell. ("Swing" is especially damaging here, with its overtones of both "manage" and "be up-to-date.") But "like a ball and chain" is a simile most often used to denote an unsatisfactory state of marriage. So, instead of reflecting on Lizzie, this simile betrays Lowell's discontent with his marriage. Lizzie and Harriet's financial drain on Lowell is his ball and chain. It is not surprising that the reported speech quoted in italics is particularly malicious and exaggerated.

A second point is that the whole sonnet betrays Lowell's anxiety over money and finances. Despite his attempt to make it seem that money is Lizzie's preoccupation, the sonnet intimates that it is Lowell's anxiety as well. Behind this sonnet is the question of what will happen to Harriet, and Lowell's answer takes the form which emphasizes his financial worries: "They say fear of death is a child's remembrance / of the first desertion." Who is "they" here? Are they child psychologists Lowell has been reading, generalized and casual "experts" (as in "They say it's going to be a cold winter"), or, more likely, complicated fears disguised as casual knowledge? In any event, the remark precipitates as if in answer a defensive rejoinder about Harriet knowing "no love / that doesn't bind her with presents, letters, visits, / things outward and visible," things which are concrete and tangible evidence that Lowell has not deserted her. However, the lines also suggest strongly their opposite: that desertion is in fact more about those things inward and invisible, which Lowell does not want to face: "I've closed my mind / so long, I want to keep it closed, perhaps—." When in the final line the outward and visible is again in the foreground ("They tell me to stop, they mustn't lose my money"), the petulance of the remark confirms our sense that the inward and invisible is sadly amiss in Lowell's relationship with his daughter.

I want to return to the debate over naming as my final point. Bakhtin argues that in monologic poetry, "*Everything that enters the work must immerse itself in Lethe, and forget its previous life in any other contexts*" (*Dialogic* 297). But in naming, and in quoting from known sources, Lowell forfeits the right or the ability to make language forget its previous contexts. Since Lizzie *is* in many senses Elizabeth Hardwick, and since her words are, in many cases, Hardwick's own, Lowell by necessity must embrace polyphony and risk the loss of control this entails. Had he created characters that stood for himself and the two women, and had he invented the letters, he would have been better able to structure the reader's response to the "common novel plot." However, these letters and conversations are not a poetic creation; they have resonances and contexts beyond his narrative. For one, we can check the original contexts of the letters and compare them with the poems, noting where Lowell changes the material for his own purposes, and noting also what he has left out. Furthermore, the naming of Hardwick and Blackwood leads us naturally to the Hamilton and Mariani biographies, where Hardwick is portrayed sympathetically as a long-suffering, patient, and understanding woman, a portrait that comes through only in part in *The Dolphin*, at least as Lowell attempts to portray her. This is the extra-literary baggage that Lowell's naming carries and that he then cannot control. He recognizes this, in a small way, in the poem "Draw," from the sequence "Doubt": "Should revelation be sealed like private letters, / till all the beneficiaries are dead, / and our proper names become improper Lives" (*Dolphin* 42)? Clearly Lowell thought not, although the last line indicates that he worried about how he would be depicted, and even if biography had a place in the interpretation of poetry. "Improper Lives" carries the connotation of both "inappropriate lives" (the poet lives in his work) and "unseemly lives" (Lowell's personal life was in turmoil). In other words, it suggests that readers in the future will be more concerned with the poet's life (which is improper) than with his work (the proper focus of the reader). Nonetheless, Lowell chose to use "proper" names—personal names, suitable names, and names as props. Whether or not Lowell was justified in the name of art in invading Hardwick's and Blackwood's privacy is a matter of debate; personally, I am inclined to agree with Elizabeth Bishop that Lowell violated a trust when he used the women's letters and conversations in his poetry. In Lowell's defence, it may be argued that by naming and by quoting Lowell wanted to create an authentic drama of voices, and in this he succeeded. Less successful, precisely because of his naming and quoting, is his attempt to control those voices. Lizzie in particular rises from the "common novel plot" to challenge the role Lowell assigns her, and it is her voice that we listen to by the end of the volume. By reading *The Dolphin* as a polyphonic poem we can recover Lizzie's voice from the "deliberately trite" tone Lowell gives her, and find a subversive authenticity that resists assimilation into Lowell's larger agenda.

Notes

1. In *"Notebook 1967–68*: Writing the Process Poem," Alex Calder demonstrates how Lowell's preoccupation with his fiftieth birthday led him to write a poem that eventually became the sequence "Half a Century Gone" in *Notebook*

1967–68. Calder goes on to argue that Lowell's intense concern with the passage of time permeates *Notebook 1967–68.* In *Robert Lowell's Language of the Self,* Katharine Wallingford notes that Lowell "defined himself personally and poetically through his relations with writers, living and dead" (96). This self-fashioning in the *Notebook* volumes is achieved primarily through debate, I would argue, and the many quoted voices in the poems provide Lowell with options to explore as he ponders his life at 50. I explore the influence of the drama on Lowell's sonnets more fully in "Drama and Dramatic Strategies in Robert Lowell's *Notebook 1967–68*" (*Twentieth Century Literature* 44 (1998): 53–81).

Works cited

Alvarez, A. "Robert Lowell in Conversation." *Observer* 21 July 1963. Rpt. in *Robert Lowell: Interviews and Memoirs.* Ed. Jeffrey Meyers. Ann Arbor: U of Michigan P, 1988. 74–8.

Axelrod, Steven Gould. *Robert Lowell: Life and Art.* Princeton: Princeton UP, 1978.

Bakhtin, Mikhail. "Discourse in the Novel." *The Dialogic Imagination: Four Essays by M. M. Bakhtin.* Ed. Michael Holquist. Trans. Caryl Emerson and Michael Holquist. Austin: U of Texas P, 1981. 259–422.

——. "Epic and Novel." *The Dialogic Imagination: Four Essays by M.M. Bakhtin.* Ed. Michael Holquist. Trans. Caryl Emerson and Michael Holquist. Austin: U of Texas P, 1981. 3–40.

——. *Problems of Dostoevsky's Poetics.* Ed. and trans. by Caryl Emerson. Minneapolis: U of Minnesota P, 1984.

Bedient, Calvin. "Illegible Lowell (The Late Volumes)." *Robert Lowell: Essays on the Poetry.* Ed. Steven Gould Axelrod and Helen Deese. Cambridge, UK: Cambridge UP, 1986. 139–55.

Bell, Vereen M. *Robert Lowell: Nihilist as Hero.* Cambridge, MA: Harvard UP, 1983.

Calder, Alex. "*Notebook 1967–68*: Writing the Process Poem." *Robert Lowell: Essays on the Poetry.* Ed. Steven Gould Axelrod and Helen Deese. Cambridge, UK: Cambridge UP, 1986. 117–38.

Diepeveen, Leonard. *Changing Voices: The Modern Quoting Poem.* Ann Arbor: U of Michigan P, 1993.

Gilman, Richard. "Life Offers No Neat Conclusions." *New York Times* 5 May 1968. Rpt. in *Robert Lowell: Interviews and Memoirs.* Ed. Jeffrey Meyers. Ann Arbor: U of Michigan P, 1988. 119–23.

Hamilton, Ian. *Robert Lowell: A Biography.* New York: Random, 1982.

Lodge, David. *After Bakhtin: Essays on Fiction and Criticism.* London: Routledge, 1990.

Lowell, Robert. "A Conversation with Ian Hamilton." *Collected Prose.* Ed. Robert Giroux. New York: Farrar, Straus & Giroux, 1987. 267–90.

——. *The Dolphin.* New York: Farrar, Straus & Giroux, 1973.

——. *For Lizzie and Harriet.* New York: Farrar, Straus & Giroux, 1973.

——. *For the Union Dead.* New York: Farrar, Straus & Giroux, 1964.

——. *History.* New York: Farrar, Straus & Giroux, 1973.

——. *Life Studies.* New York: Farrar, Straus & Cudahy, 1959.

——. *Near the Ocean.* New York: Farrar, Straus & Giroux, 1967.

——. *Notebook*. 3rd ed. New York: Farrar, Straus & Giroux, 1970.
——. *Notebook 1967–68*. New York: Farrar, Straus & Giroux, 1969.
——. *The Old Glory*. Rev. ed. New York: Farrar, Straus & Giroux, 1968.
——. *The Oresteia of Aeschylus*. New York: Farrar, Straus & Giroux, 1978.
——. *Phaedra and Figaro*. Jean Racine and Pierre Beaumarchais. Trans. Robert Lowell and Jacques Barzun. New York: Farrar, Straus & Cudahy, 1961.
——. "Poets and the Theatre." *Collected Prose*. Ed. Robert Giroux. New York: Farrar, Straus & Giroux, 1987. 175–8.
——. *Prometheus Bound*. New York: Farrar, Straus & Giroux, 1969.
Maclean, Marie. *Narrative as Performance: The Baudelairean Experiment*. London: Routledge, 1988.
Mariani, Paul. *Lost Puritan: A Life of Robert Lowell*. New York: Norton, 1994.
Wallingford, Katharine. *Robert Lowell's Language of the Self*. Chapel Hill: U of North Carolina P, 1988.
Ward, John A. "'Not Avoiding Injury': Robert Lowell." In *American Declarations of Love*. Ed. Ann Massa. New York: St. Martin's Press—now Palgrave Macmillan, 1990. 137–54.

6

Poetic Address and Intimate Reading: The Offered Hand

William Waters

> It is not difficult to imagine a . . . model of literary
> history and criticism in which writing is deliber-
> ately taken as a gift to others . . . or as an exercise
> in generosity, and where this feature is energetically
> foregrounded. In such a reading the theme of com-
> munication (reaching out to those known and those
> unknown alike) interlaces in paradoxical and sweet
> ways with the theme of love.
>
> > (Virgil Nemoianu)

> This hour I tell things in confidence,
> I might not tell everybody, but I will tell you.
> > (Walt Whitman, "Song of Myself," §19)

Reading an unfamiliar poem in the "you" form, most of us will be preoccupied with the question of who is being addressed. Is it we ourselves,
or someone else? For example, at the opening of Galway Kinnell's poem
"Wait," we read:

> Wait, for now.
> Distrust everything if you have to.
> But trust the hours. Haven't they
> carried you everywhere, up to now? (127)

The claims of the poem, its direction and force, vary greatly with the
addressee we settle on. Experienced readers quickly seek clues in the

---

A longer version of this essay originally appeared in *Literary Imagination* 2.2
(2000): 188–220. It is reprinted here by permission of Oxford University Press.

remainder of the text that might identify the addressee, as if the poem could be weighed and understood only after this question is resolved.

This need to pin down poetry's "you" has left an enduring mark on poetry criticism. Especially the possibility that an ambiguous poem is directly addressing its reader makes some critics uncomfortable: if another explanation for a poem's "you" can be found, it will often be preferred. "The poet . . . turns his back on his audience," wrote Northrop Frye, so adding what has become his own much-cited brick to the bulwark against reader address which J. S. Mill's similar assertion—"poetry is *over*heard"—unwittingly founded (Frye 250; Mill 348).

This essay, taking up several poems that say "you" to someone who might or might not be the reader, works at describing certain ways in which literature presses for a close relation with those into whose hands it may fall. The inquiry could be seen as a kind of literary history, but not a familiar kind: including our own act of reading in the consideration of a text's life, taking our own experience as our example of how texts come to and exert influence upon later readers, we could find that our account of these matters proves not strictly rational, shot through with affective interest. To feel this interest is to begin to acknowledge the claims made on us as individuals by our engagement with poems. Criticism which serves poorly that level of personal engagement misses something essential, something that, for me at least, speaks to why poetry matters to us and how we might come to feel answerable to it.

After a short excursus on the literary-critical background of the inquiry into poetry's "you," the discussion turns to examples of works whose reading, as I hope to describe it, may enact a reach through history, a gesture of touch everywhere attended, but nowhere held fast, by the play of time.

The topic of poetry's addressees—and the larger questions it raises, about what kind of "communication" a poem really is, and about how we should take what is said there—have attracted modest scholarly attention. Mill's notion that poetry is overheard opened and shut the case for many later critics, since by these lights all poetic "you's" must be apostrophic in the rhetorician Quintilian's sense: they turn aside (ἀπὸ–στρέφειν) to someone, or something, that is not the principal listener (4.1.69). After Jonathan Culler's seminal 1977 essay "Apostrophe," most modern criticism on the topic of poetic address has taken this type of addressee ("O wild West Wind") as its object.[1]

But a comparative study of the extraordinary range of interlocutors in lyric would be alive to distinctions between what linguistics has termed "receiver," "target," and "addressee," would register multiple addressees within a single poem (rather the rule than the exception?), and would concede uncertainty in the plentiful cases where a "you" eludes definition. This is difficult ground. Typologies familiar from the relatively well-researched field of second-person narrative are helpless before poetry's freedom to move between communicative frameworks with a suddenness, or disregard, unexampled in any other genre or use of language.[2] The awkward fact is that poetry, from the brash parlando of Archilochus to the pronominal lability of John Ashbery, enacts—for us, as readers, now—not so much a stable communicative situation as a chronic hesitation, a faltering, between monologue and dialogue, between "talking about" and "talking to," third and second person, indifference to interlocutors and the yearning to have one.

Part of the reason for this instability lies in the complex historical and cognitive shift between oral delivery and writing as modes of poetic transmission.[3] This shift (whose still active forces can be felt if one tries discussing poetry without metaphors of voice or speech) is lastingly implicated in what we readers experience as poetry's "désancrage," or "uprootedness," from any specified communicative situation. Who is speaking (or writing), to whom, in what context? It is difficult to answer these very basic pragmatic questions with respect to a poem. The resulting kinds of ambiguity have become integral to the modern written genre, so that to read a poem is to enter an underspecified communicative act.

I mean to present the viewpoint of a reader who cannot, or will not, free myself from the unsettling feeling that certain poems might intend me as their addressed recipient. In an important sense, after all, whether a poem can be said to address its reader depends as much on the individual reader as it does on the individual text. The readings that follow do not play up the inevitability that disillusionment and irony will obtrude upon absorption and belief. Some critics have asserted that when literature seems to say "you" to individual readers, this moment of readerly identification is a ruse, always recognized as such the instant afterward, and so ironized and mediated virtually as it happens.[4] This study takes a different tack: irony, quick in our habits of critical thought, is here stayed by the conviction that real reading is as much a matter of absorption as it is of distance. My readings here attempt to hold open, long enough at least that it can be recognized, the moment when a reader feels addressed by poetry's "you."

At the same time, theoretical discussions of "positionality," although preoccupied with the coercive "you" of ideological authority (Althusser's "hey you there!": by definition the shout of the police [48–9]) and too little aware of the "you" of intimacy, have usefully demonstrated how written texts tacitly propose to their readers—notwithstanding these readers' final freedom—certain choreographies.

1

One of the strongest testaments—in more than one sense of that word—to the unsettling power of ambiguous address remains Keats' late poem or fragment "This living hand":

> This living hand, now warm and capable
> Of earnest grasping, would, if it were cold
> And in the icy silence of the tomb,
> So haunt thy days and chill thy dreaming nights
> That thou would wish thine own heart dry of blood
> So in my veins red life might stream again,
> And thou be conscience-calm'd—see, here it is—
> I hold it towards you.

(384)

Overwhelmingly, this writing wishes to reach someone. But to ask who that someone is, is already, in my view, to dodge the extended hand and the strange thrall that must grip a reader who accedes to the hailing of the poem and so becomes the intended interlocutor of the dead. Earlier Keats criticism proposed to discover Keats' fiancée Fanny Brawne in this addressee; later conjecture took the lines to be material for a play; but to hold that the force of this poem's "you" is a spectacle only, or that it expended itself wholly on some third person in the past, seems to me a willful impoverishment ensuring that critics will remain immune to the haunting power of the works they study.[5]

Keats spins these lines over the oral / written dichotomy mentioned earlier as foundational to the modern lyric. The poem starts with an obliquely self-referential gesture: "this hand" is, while not the same as "this poem," its immediate metonym for the writer, and thus with these words the text points to its own status as a written thing. Conversely, the poem's last lines abruptly flout this fact by using language that belongs to a face-to-face, oral situation of utterance ("see, here it is—").[6] The poem exploits and sharpens its paradox also in another, still stronger way: it founds its power—its animate "reach," we might say—on the trust that poems, as written things, as inanimate artifacts, may outlive their authors.

"This living hand" is the hand Keats saw before him as he wrote the handwritten poem, as the deictics "this" and "now" confirm. It is the agent of his expression, "warm and capable" of earnestly grasping, among other things, his pen. Against the sense of himself as there, as real and capable of exerting an effect upon the world, Keats develops a counterfactual, imaginary antithesis. The verb "would" splits his first lines exactly in the middle, doubling the familiar and alive with its own self strange and dead. The lines foreshadow the features of the uncanny that Freud delineated in 1919: the strangeness of what was before familiar, the uncertainty as to whether a thing is alive or inanimate, and the disruption of identity through doubling. When at length the poem breaks off the increasingly intricate grammar of this long subjunctive scenario, and we emerge abruptly into "—see, here it is—/ I hold it towards you," then how can we describe what has happened? I want to argue that the first answer must be sought in the field of pronoun reference, what linguists call, in such cases, anaphora.[7] We must ask, that is: what do these instances of "it" refer back to?

It would seem natural to arrive at an answer by bracketing that long hypothetical middle altogether. The poem started with the words "This living hand," and surely it's the same hand that is presented at the end of the poem. Reasonably, in other words, we could identify the key elements of the poem's syntax as follows:

> This living hand, now warm [etc.]
> [. . .]
>   —see, here it is—
> I hold it towards you.

But of course what is striking about this skeletal version of the poem's syntax is that it so obviously fails to show the skeleton in the poem. The chilling effect clearly depends on having what is omitted above, namely the hypothetical subjunctives, present.

Must we reason, then, that when the poem breaks into "see, here it is—I hold it towards you," the anaphoric references point back to the earlier "it" of line 2 ("if it were cold . . . "), to the fictional dead hand? Unlikely, since then we'd be faced with the logical and syntactic incoherence of the poet claiming he holds towards us the merely hypothetical hand he has imagined would be (but is not) in the tomb.

We are, in other words, caught in an anaphoric muddle. The reader is left (possibly without noticing the fact) with a cloudy sense of whether it's the living hand or the dead one that the poem tries to hold towards us; and if the poem does succeed in haunting us, we can find the origin of that haunting exactly in our uncertainty (carefully prepared by the poem's grammar) as to whether the crucial shape in the poem is living or dead.

I mentioned above that this text is written under the aegis of the age-old promise that poems may still be read when their authors are gone. Keats' poem, we might say, goes further: it is written in a way that incorporates the death of its writer. The force of the poem depends on the way that time is figured into it. The long conditional scenario in the middle of the poem—"would, if it were cold / . . . / So haunt"—is motivated not only by fantasy, but also by the thought of mortality, which was never far from John Keats' mind, given his doubtful tubercular prognosis. The thought of death, in writing a poem, is the thought of, in Shakespeare's words, the "eyes not yet created" that will "o'erread" this text, later (as if reading an epitaph) when the writer is gone.[8] At this time of later reading, the grammar of Keats' poem will be at odds with fact: the living hand will be dead and the imagined one (the one in the tomb) true.

The agency of this inversion of the poem is the poet's own empirical death. The truth of the living hand gave way to the truth of the cold, dead one upon Keats' death in 1821. It is, in other words, history that makes the indicative into a falsehood and the subjunctive true. But this infolding of temporality, although it is at the very heart of the poem, is not something its writer could bring about, nor is it something for which the reader is responsible either. Rather Keats' relation to his own mortality in writing this poem is best characterized by saying that he relied on it. Writing with his living hand, he relied on his own death, his own absence; and so the poem at every point counts on being turned inside out by time.

Although it is a grammatically subjunctive hand which lies in the icy silence of the tomb, nevertheless the possibility of presenting this dead hand in actuality—the possibility, in other words, that the "it" of

—see, here it is—
I hold it towards you

could be holding out as much the dead hand as the living one—this possibility is realized by the reader who recognizes how time has turned Keats' imagined death into prosaic fact, and how the poem's intention reaches, impossibly, through exactly this dimension, out of poetry into reality, "through" death into actual being. Keats is dead and gone, but his poem knows that, and this is the source of its unquiet power.

The change from "thou" to "you" has baffled critics.[9] But it is another element of the poem's gradual revelation that the living reader is implicated: where "thou" is poetical, "you" was for Keats the address to a contemporary, "outside" of literature. (This observation would also argue against the proposal that the lines were composed for a play.)

Again, coming across any poem addressed to an unidentified "you," we are likely to ask whom the poem is written to—and it is plain that ready answers often lie close at hand (as we consult the author's letters, journals, or other "paratexts"). Yet we can also see that asking the question already put us in a third-person relationship with the poem; our own reaction has made us what Mill suggests readers of poetry are, "overhearers."[10]

But the astonishing force of this Keats poem is its intense "addressivity": it is about the possibility of haunting someone after the poet dies, haunting by means of a hand which is extended in the very medium of the poem. To haunt by means of a poem, one must have readers. What this poem requires, in any way of looking at it, is an other, a "you" to haunt. It demands the presence of a reader as a poem has seldom demanded it. And to my way of thinking, who that reader is is much less important than that a reader be there, becoming absorbed in reading, suspending his or her empirical life (as Jonathan Culler says in remarking on this poem) to perform exactly the transfusion—at least in imaginative terms—that the poem predicts, giving life to Keats in the act of reading, and being haunted.[11]

Jonathan Culler brought Keats' poem to the notice of a comparatist readership by including it at the end of his 1977 essay "Apostrophe," revised in *The Pursuit of Signs*. That context (though Culler clearly grants that Keats' poem "eschews apostrophe for direct address" [153]) has generated lingering confusion about how much this poem shares "the time of the apostrophic *now*" (153) or other features of apostrophe understood as address to non-hearing entities:[12]

> this poem, whose deictics—"This living hand, now warm . . . ," "see, here it is"—give it the special temporality of apostrophic lyrics, is a daring and successful example of the attempt to produce in fiction an event by replacing a temporal presence and absence with an apostrophic presence and absence. (153–4)

The strain of pressing reader address into service as the crowning example in a discussion of apostrophe is evident if we reflect how much more radical Keats' "temporality" is than what apostrophe displays. What gives his poem its chill is not its insistence on the "*now* . . . of writing," "beyond the movement of temporality" (152), but its incorporation of the immediate presence, by definition, of any written text to its reader. Temporality is not "neutralized" but rather enlisted; this poem, in contrast to what Culler claims for apostrophe, depends for its effect wholly on the real-world passage of time. "The poem is underway," as Paul Celan wrote, and "the writer stays with it."[13] It is the *now* of *reading*—and in equal measure the "here"—that Keats exploits, by yoking them to the time and scene of writing. And this, his poem's central accomplishment, is not shared with poetic apostrophes nor remotely approached by them. One critic misidentifies both "the first and last lines" of Keats' poem as showing "the deictic movements of the present writing," "a 'present' that is clearly fictional in the manner of Culler's 'apostrophic *now.*'"[14] But the hand *was* warm and capable while writing—line 1 is no fiction—and the final lines appeal more emphatically to the time of reading, which is not fictional either.

As a way of generalizing the kind of readerly stance I have been trying to describe in Keats' poem, I turn to an essay titled "On the Interlocutor," published in 1913 by the Russian poet Osip Mandelstam.[15] "At a critical moment," writes Mandelstam,

> a seafarer throws into the ocean waves a sealed bottle, containing his name and an account of his fate. Many years later, wandering along the dunes, I find it in the sand, read the message, learn the date of the event and the last will of one now lost. I had the right to do so. I did not open someone else's mail. The message sealed in the bottle was addressed to the one who would find it. I found it. That means I really am its secret addressee. (234–5)

This message in a bottle provides Mandelstam with his governing metaphor for the way poetry is "sent" and "received." Here the question of "answer" may seem foreclosed: the tides have made the bottle's path from its origin to our beach unknowable, and in any case the date of the message assures us the writer is dead and gone. There is neither means to answer nor anyone to answer to, much less anyone expecting answer; the message is in this sense gratuitous, extra; it leaves us free.

And yet the curious sense that by the act of finding, one has really become the "secret addressee" of this message—this sense does hold us somehow. Mandelstam goes on to describe the feeling of receiving a poem that is mindful, like the message in a bottle, of its eventual and unknown reader:

> Reading this poem . . . I experience the same feeling as I would if such a bottle had come into my hands. The ocean in all its great element has come to its aid, has helped it fulfill its destiny; and that feeling of providence grips the finder. (235)

The word "providence" captures the paradoxical feeling: on the one hand it is the unlooked-for event, something that is not made to happen but just comes; it exerts no claim and exacts no return. On the other hand, "providence" suggests the sudden thought of vast and unseen patterns—intentions—at work behind the seeming accidents of precisely your life. It is an overwhelming feeling of "intendedness" that, as Mandelstam says, "grips" one. It is the sense that the ocean has helped the poem to fulfill its "destiny." Mandelstam's word here is "prednaznachenie," which suggests something like "earmarking": the poem has incessantly sought its true addressee, the one for whom it is meant, and in finding and reading it, you are discovered as (made into) that one. "I would like to know," writes Mandelstam, "who among those chancing to read [such a] poem . . . will not start with that joyful and uncanny shiver one experiences when one is unexpectedly hailed by name" (235). The poem chooses you, the poem's "you" becomes your name and the poem singles you out by calling it. At this point the quite reasonable thought that really, anyone at all could have found the message, that it was after all addressed to no one—this thought is set aside, forgotten, or even no longer true. Once you have found the message, there will be no other addressee. In this way you become answerable for it.

Remarkably, then, the sense of unimaginable distance in the intervening oceans of time and space is at the same time, without losing any of that distance, a feeling of unexpected nearness. When such a message comes into your hands, the abysses separating you from its sender dramatically intensify the feeling of a "providential" closeness to him (in Mandelstam's unsentimental use of that word).

Mandelstam's metaphor can serve as a *point d'appui* for my argument, which aims to bring out this sense in which certain poems seek an interlocutor (the *sobesednik* of Mandelstam's title); and criticism, in this case, must work to imagine the act of reading that could acknowledge such claims and so give answer to the poem. This line of inquiry also begins, of its own accord, to touch upon the tricky question of what we now call readerly "answerability," through this "providential grip" of the message encountered by chance and engaged with as necessity.

2

. . . I extend my hand and feel in the same moment inseparably: You and I, I and You.

                      (Friedrich Heinrich Jacobi)

The figure of the offered hand appears again in a short unpublished fragment of Rilke's, written at Muzot (Switzerland) in 1925, a year before his death.

> Aber versuchtest du dies: Hand in der Hand mir zu sein
> wie im Weinglas der Wein Wein ist.
> Versuchtest du dies.

Edward Snow's translation (233) reflects something of the strangeness of the German:

> But if you'd try this: to be hand in my hand
> as in the wineglass the wine is wine.
> If you'd try this.[16]

This poem is about contact; it's about the relation between "I" and "you," which is to say about the attempt to get "I" and "you" right—right in their relation to each other, first; and so each right in itself. As a poem, it is about wanting someone to be present to the poem, and about someone wanting to be present to it: about the endeavor to find the second person who will, in answering, find the poem's first person.

All this does not make the text a metapoetic commentary—a poem about poetry—so much as something closer: it is an attempt at nearness and an offer. As we ourselves become interested in the poem, we may begin to feel—not altogether rationally, but compellingly—that we are also implicated in it.

This poem opens with the word "but," an adversative, which at once presupposes (simultaneously sets up and reveals) some antecedent scenario or, more exactly, some foregoing alternative to which the poem opposes itself. The shape of this implied context—what must "have preceded" this opening of the poem—may be pieced together as the converse of what the text itself presents.[17]

If we imagine the first-time reader pausing at the caesura (punctuated here with a colon), we can inquire once again what would be at stake in that reader's tentatively, even fleetingly, putting on the poem's "you."

> But if you'd try this:

At this point, the line can work at a very general level: since it is a question of *versuchen*, of attempting something, we could surmise that here being "you" is about having not reached some goal, having already attempted without success, or having sought without finding.

Being addressed by this poem's second person pronoun, then, means accepting the implication that one feels, personally, a history of endeavor and failure, or uncompleted search. Some of the pull of this line—"But if you'd try this"—is the sense that one could really get it, that the sought-for thing (whatever it might be) is within reach. But at the same time, the repetition of this phrase to end the fragment has a tinge of wistfulness. It is uncertain whether the addressee will ever make the attempt. So while it would be missing the mark to call this particular freestanding conditional ("if you'd try") a wish contrary to fact—it need not be really contrafactual, say in the manner of a past perfect hypothetical—the poem is accompanied by the thought that what it proposes will not necessarily be taken up. This thought, in turn, accords with the original implicature of "If you'd try this," the presupposition of a history of failures or misfires.

It is in this tone and against this background, then, that the poem proposes something. Once again the poem offers its addressee the poet's hand, but here it is a gesture at once more intimate and milder than Keats' pointed and disquieting reach.

> But if you'd try this: to be hand in my hand
> as in the wineglass the wine is wine.
> If you'd try this.

Strictly speaking, it may be misplacing the emphasis to say a hand is offered here, since the first line attributes the agency unmistakably to the addressee. In this respect the line reflects the peculiar pragmatics of written address generally, where—in contrast to oral communication— it lies with the reader or addressee, not with the "sender," to set the communicative transaction going. That is to say, the line is true to the reading situation. Yet the reader is also faced with the same pragmatic impasse on which the Keats poem was centered: he or she is invited to hold hands, but by a written text. But if the reader does not falter at the impasse; if, in the privacy of a reading moment, the desire for contact seems to matter more than the literal absurdity of it—then you may attempt to discover for yourself (even if it is finally for yourself alone) what motions of the mind or heart might count as taking up the offered hand of the dead.

The invitation is elaborated in the poem's second line; but it is a line apt to be misread, in a way that points up the unexpected turn of thought in Rilke's simile. It would be easy to alter the line unconsciously to "wie im Weinglas der Wein ist." It was, in fact, just here that the seemingly indefatigable Rilke translator J. B. Leishman nodded, so publishing this misreading forth into libraries everywhere: "as in the wineglass the wine" (Rilke, *Poems* 341). In this rendition Leishman, as it were correcting the original to "Wie in dem Weinglas der Wein," further ignores the striking way Rilke's addition of the (grammatically superfluous) verb "ist" deliberately derails just that easy meter and rhyme.

If this were how the poem went, it would do some of the same things that Rilke's poem does, but not all. This hypothetical, simpler version of the poem would invite repose and offer supporting encirclement, mapping the wine resting in the wineglass's embrace onto the image of your hand resting in the hand of the poem's speaker. The repetition of the same word *Hand* in line 1 would modulate directly into the echoing, but importantly differing, pair *Wein–Weinglas*. And so on.

But Rilke's lines read otherwise, in ways I hope the false variant just considered will help to make apparent:

> Hand in der Hand mir zu sein
> wie im Weinglas der Wein Wein ist.

> to be hand in my hand
> as in the wineglass the wine is wine.

Added here is the metrically obtrusive repetition of the word *Wein*. The addition fundamentally changes the grammar of the simile: instead of a predicate of location (der Wein ist im Weinglas), Rilke has a predicate of identity, or tautology (der Wein ist Wein). The location ("im Weinglas") only designates a site for this tautology. The phrase emphasizes first how *in* such a clasp of hands, each hand becomes more itself, experiences itself as what it is. I take the poem to be claiming that the same is true not just of lover and beloved, but also of reader and writer, even reader and poem.

In "Hand in der Hand," the two instances of *Hand* represent two separate entities meeting: the second *Hand* is not the same as the first. But they are two entities of one kind. *Wein*, on the other hand, is not a countable noun. In a sense, the different syntax of the two images reflects and presents this difference: two clasped hands inherently retain a "prepositional" relationship with one another, but wine—even two wines poured together—is wine.

The thought of the poem's second line—"as in the wineglass the wine is wine"—is remarkable (and Rilkean) in the "Aufeinanderbezogenheit," the interrelatedness, interdependence, mutual constitution of identity that it expresses. The wine is known as wine by being found in the wineglass, as at the same time the wineglass is a wineglass because of the wine it contains. Human beings are not human in and of themselves, but become what they are by saying "you," which is to say by way of the second-person claims they make and acknowledge. I am, in the end, completely myself only in and because of my relation to you.[18] This is Rilke's Communion.

But those who find themselves in relation may also lose themselves there. This we can see when we take the step of mapping this image of "wine as wine in the wineglass" back onto—here Snow's translation cannot accompany us so well—the phrase "Hand in der Hand." For the two distinctive roles, the individual players, are masked in the phrase "Hand in der Hand"; one cannot determine, so to speak, which hand belongs to the "I," which to the "you." It's as if the invitation were to an intimacy where the concepts "my" and "your" would drop away from the phrase "my hand in your hand," leaving just some hand in some hand: a kind of loving bewilderment of forgotten identity. This is the resolution sought, as well, in George Herbert's poem "Clasping of Hands," where after 18 lines of address to God which track the instability of the categories "mine" and "thine" in the experience of prayer, the poet finds the clasp of hands in "not mak[ing]" this knowledge of which is which:

> O be mine still! still make me thine!
> Or rather make no Thine and Mine!

> (Herbert 142)

In the case of Rilke's poem, the bewilderment is extraordinary because of the asymmetricality, or even radical disjunction, of the roles it forgets: reader and writer, living and dead. The poem's opening "but" clause, with its entailment of a certain specific history (a history of fruitless search) on the part of the "you," goes some distance toward selecting its addressee in a way that might lay groundwork for the kind of trust that such forgetting as this exacts. It is trust: in the touch of hand and hand, one hand does not know the other (it is not "knowledge"). Intimacy in touch is partly the quality of awareness that the other is exactly *what* one does not know, is the boundary to any hope of certainty.[19]

The attempt (*Versuch*) is therefore an uncertain one; but if you as reader of the writer's poem can forget which is which, who is who, and just rest "Hand in der Hand," one clasped with the other, knowing no more than that one is clasped with the other, then—the poem promises—you will find this is like wine being wine:

wie im Weinglas der Wein Wein ist.

But as we sit with the text before us, no hand actually appears; and more than that, Rilke is gone: the caring and fellowship offered here are no one's, only intermittent vestiges of a dead man's capacity for feeling. If the hand that any poem extends to us is both living and dead, is it wise to lay ourselves open to the poem's address, to invest ourselves in the call of this "no one"?

The experience of intimate engagement with a "you" poem always occurs in such double vision: one responds to the address, and finds no one calling; you answer to the fellow human emotion that really does seek answer, but in the end you remain alone, answering. This being left alone is what Rilke's poem enacts, as the companionship of the first line (hand in hand) falls away, leaving the singular identity of the second (wine is wine); where "mir" ("to me"; Snow's "my") promised meeting, it evaporates or withdraws, and what is held within the wineglass is finally one thing, in the right place, and just itself.

It could sound like failure. But discerning in the poem even the trace, the hollow form of the poet's living hand, we may find that this matters. We find ourselves accountable to the gesture that we have stumbled across in this way. The poem really does impart something; it becomes a space for the virtual transformation of the reader—the wineglass within which wine may, despite everything, find itself to be wine. In return for this gift, the poem's urgent claim is that we hold to it, that we press towards our own answerability as we read. Perhaps, though our obligation has been awakened by receiving something from the hand of a historically real other, the obligation comes not directly from accepting what is offered so much as from that other moment, the moment of knowing—as we must—that we are still alone, reading.

Detained by a poem, one finds with growing seriousness of attention that the poem meets and responds to just that quality of one's attention; one finds it still capable at the level of one's own most searching capabilities. The decisive moment occurs when at some point you unexpectedly get something from the poem that is not locatable within any of the poem's parts, but which emerges from the many parts working all at once and has, as well, crucially to do with your own reading presence, your investment of an attention that you experience as yours. You see something that cannot be said. This place where reader and text touch is like the unnameable point of contact between two of Rodin's sculpted bodies, as Rilke saw it: "A hand which makes contact with the shoulder or thigh of another no longer belongs wholly to the body from which it came. Out of it and the object that it touches or grasps there comes into being a new thing, one thing more, which has no name and belongs to no one; and then it is a matter of *this* thing, which has its own boundaries" (SW 5.165, my translation). Since you cannot "pass it on," at that point, the buck (so to speak) stops with you. You can't tell anyone else what you have seen, not whole, not the way you got it. It is, just as Whitman says, "in confidence" that something has been vouchsafed to you (*Song of Myself* §19; 1: 24).

The crucial fact is that for all you know, no one else has ever seen what you have seen. And no matter how inclined one is to check one's reading experiences against others', or to defer to some putatively more expert reader than oneself, these possibilities are closed. For all one can know, this gift that is the poem may be going unopened through the world like a sealed letter. The thought is accompanied by the loneliness, then, that you who receive this message cannot share it either: the true privacy of reading.

What is at stake, again, is our ability to acknowledge the claims made on us by the works of art with which we engage. These are the claims of the aesthetic. In the acknowledgement (the "admission") of one's simple awe or gratitude lies, as I see it, the very closest and so easiest to overlook of that rich gamut of ways in which texts matter across time.

A moving testimony to the force of these claims appears in a speech by the poet Paul Celan in which he writes as, one might say, Osip Mandelstam's unknown reader. Though Celan dedicated (in both senses) a volume of his own poetry to Mandelstam (*Die Niemandsrose* [1963]) and translated the Russian poet's work into German, it is in one of Celan's rare speeches that he expresses most clearly his closeness to Mandelstam, whose name however does not appear in the speech.[20] Here Celan cites Mandelstam's essay "On the Interlocutor" without citing him, sending out the message of—specifically—the message in a bottle just as if it were his own (which it then must have become). This act is also the concern of the message itself, namely the meeting of two people ("conversers," *sobesedniki*) over, through, and in the message, which becomes in this way time's corridor.

A poem, since it is an instance of language, hence in its essence dialogic, may be a letter in a bottle thrown out to sea in the—surely not always strongly hopeful—belief that it may sometime wash up somewhere, perhaps on a shoreline of the heart. In this way, too, poems are underway: they are headed toward something.

Das Gedicht kann, da es ja eine Erscheinungsform der Sprache und damit seinem Wesen nach dialogisch ist, eine Flaschenpost sein, aufgegeben in dem—gewiß nicht immer hoffnungsstarken—Glauben, sie könnte irgendwo und irgendwann an Land gespült werden, an Herzland vielleicht. Gedichte sind auch in dieser Weise unterwegs: sie halten auf etwas zu. (*GW* 3: 185–6)[21]

Celan did not know Mandelstam, who had died twenty years before in transit to Siberian exile. Reaching through time, the work reaches through the writer's own death and so always appears as a gift held in his absent hand, a thing offered by someone not there. By the graces of that contract we hold with the texts we call literary, then, when Celan reaches in faithfulness back to Mandelstam, he likewise reaches through Mandelstam, not only, then, in gratitude but also "out of" gratitude, out to unknown others.

The assertion that the bottle cast out to sea not merely is "underway," but is heading for something ("Gedichte . . . halten auf etwas zu") represents for the poet a kind of trust in (to use Mandelstam's word once again) providence; or, we could say, it represents the incorporation, backwards into the bottle's path, of the astonished perspective of its eventual receiver. It is with respect to its finding that the bottle can be said to have been "heading for" something, for—as Celan puts it—a shoreline of the heart, for a "reality," for you:

Poems . . . are headed toward something.
Toward what? Toward something open, inhabitable, an addressable "you" perhaps, an addressable reality.
Such realities are, I think, at stake in a poem.

Gedichte . . . halten auf etwas zu.
Worauf? Auf etwas Offenstehendes, Besetzbares, auf ein ansprechbares Du vielleicht, auf eine ansprechbare Wirklichkeit.
Um solche Wirklichkeiten geht es, so denke ich, dem Gedicht.

Thinking of poetry as a means of real contact in this way is, again, not a rhetorical effect. It is the experience of someone who "carries his existence into language," as Celan concludes his speech; and this means, in equal part but wholly dark to one another, separated by the written language with which they touch, both poet and reader.

Invoking this point of contact calls up Celan's own reflection on the proximity of the human hand to the poem it writes, or holds in order to read. In stressing the fundamental importance of "craft" to the poet's work, Celan here restores the hand latent in the German word for craft, *Handwerk*.

> Craft means handiwork, a matter of hands. And these hands in turn belong to just one person, that is, to a unique and mortal soul searching for a way with its voice and its dumbness.
>
> Only real hands write real poems. I cannot see any basic difference between a pressing of hands and poem.
>
> Handwerk—das ist Sache der Hände. Und diese Hände wiederum gehören nur *einem* Menschen, d.h. einem einmaligen und sterblichen Seelewesen, das mit seiner Stimme und seiner Stummheit einen Weg sucht.
>
> Nur wahre Hände schreiben wahre Gedichte. Ich sehe keinen prinzipiellen Unterschied zwischen Händedruck und Gedicht. (*GW* 3: 177–78)

Celan brings the abstraction of "Handwerk," craft, into focus as "Hand-Werk," the work of hands, which are always the two hands of one single human being, a being tentative, partly mute, and finally mortal. The writing of real poems, it is said, requires real hands; and these real hands, seeking a way, accompany the poem, indeed *are* the poem to such an extent that Celan finds the poem to be a "Händedruck." This word "Händedruck" is extraordinary, partly by virtue of its apparent ordinariness: it is, first, the common word for "handshake" (if less breezy than that American word). A handshake greets, but it also seals, and affirms; it verifies something, or testifies to it. In this sense the "Händedruck" may be the guarantor of the hands' "Wahrheit," their "truthfulness," their "reality."

But this reality must be found on both sides, as Mandelstam agreed, in words that press upon Celan's thought here: "Only a reality can call into life another reality" (240). If only real hands write real poems, surely only real hands can receive them, or can return the pressure of the poet's writing hand. The translation "handshake" in the passage above was rejected partly for reasons of tone, partly because if Celan dismantles "Handwerk" in this same passage, then we must be alert, also, to the components of "Händedruck," namely "hands" (*die Hände*) and "pressure" (*der Druck*). And we must see, also, how the sentence's willed superposition of *Händedruck* and poem pulls forth the other meaning of *Druck*, "printing," which reveals itself as—perhaps—the sentence's original starting point. The extent to which a handshake (*Händedruck*) is an impressing (*Eindruck*), or an expression (*Ausdruck*) by hand, may undergird the sense in which a poem is not just printing (*Druck*) of something handwritten but also an impression of the writing hand, and the hand's expressive pressure. With this word, then, that joins together the touch of hands and the unguided drift of the printed page through the contingencies of time and space, Celan brings together the two metaphors for the private reading of poetry that have occupied us in this passage. The "Flaschenpost," the letter in a bottle, is a matter of vast distance, great uncertainty, and perhaps reaches of time necessarily entailing the death—the absence from the world—of the writer who sought human contact in this way. If in any communication, even face-to-face, there is always the possibility that our intended message will not receive the proper uptake from our interlocutor, then the message in a bottle raises that uncertainty to its highest power.

A clasp of hands would seem altogether different. This is communication where two bodies touch, where misgivings about response may evaporate. As Celan says, it is (or can be) a matter of *presence*, of reality; two human beings sharing, with their pronouns "I" and "you," the same ontological space. But here we find ourselves again in the territory of the uncanny, where people incalculably distant, even dead, may appear immediately present; where the fixity of the printed word can stir, and reach, and call; where the strange and the familiar come together in one shape. "Poems are also gifts," as Celan puts it, "—gifts to the attentive" ("Gedichte, das sind auch Geschenke—Geschenke an die Aufmerksamen"); but they can give of themselves precisely because they are not timeless, but are the vessels of time's lapse, as that lapse is felt; they are the registers of those same losses that make them more worth keeping. "The poem," writes Celan, "admittedly makes a bid to have no end. It tries to reach through time—through it, not around it."[22] The consciousness of our own reading's historical singularity (it will not come again, nor come to others as it does to us, now) is the thought that may move us, sometimes, to take responsibility for being the poem's reader.

> But if you'd try this: to be hand in my hand
> as in the wineglass the wine is wine.
> If you'd try this.

Astonishingly, someone made this thing; and at the heart of such a speaking gift lies, palpably, the maker's wish that it be received by someone. It is you who are that "indefinite" but utterly particular recipient.

Any feeling of obligation here will be your feeling, not a burden imposed by another. If, trusting, you make the attempt, and reach to take the offered hand, it is of yourself you become aware, open, obliged, held as if coincident with yourself in the poem's hollow form

> wie im Weinglas der Wein Wein ist.

3

It is futile to try to enumerate the imaginative positionings a reader can take up with respect to a poem's elements—say, for our purposes here, with respect to its pronouns "I," "you," or the third person—because the array is infinite, illimitably nuanced, and only in part conscious, like the ways we relate to other people. Poems cast wholly in the first or third person may draw us to an imaginative participation as vivid as what a "you" poem can elicit. Address can recall me to my own presence—to myself, as it were, seen from the point of view of the poem—and so foreground acts and styles of reception. Or it can suspend the border between poetry and reality to give place, if not to their coincidence, then to a mutual self-reference of poetic fiction and readerly fact.

In a much-cited poem Emily Dickinson writes, "This is my letter to the World / That never wrote to Me—" (1: 527–8). Here, as it does in some other fascinating poems, Dickinson's "this" points to the body of her poetry, or to the very poem that says "this." It is another mode of access to the reader, since the demonstrative refers with equal precision to the poem beneath the poet's pen circa 1862 and to the instantiation of it that I, now, hold to read. Such is the line of the poem's own thought, as the poet writes that her

> Message is committed
> To Hands I cannot see—

Surely, as Virginia Jackson movingly writes, "Reading Emily Dickinson here and now, ours are the unseen hands most deeply 'committed'" (98). That commitment is like our willingness to bear the self-reflexive force of "this." The poem gestures to the page you hold open ("*this* is my letter"): yours are the hands that the poet knows of—or rather trusts in—but "cannot see." It is not evident, given her oeuvre, that Dickinson was other than serious about the "letter to the World." If it seems important that this degree of caring about something be, in some way, met, then we cannot justifiably assume that another has discharged the responsibility that Dickinson's work gives into the hands of its reader. Not finding a way to assure my superfluity in this respect, I must—and what could sound like egoism is grievously humbling, an experience of utmost inadequacy—come to the text as if my presence mattered to it.

Literary reception is generally a matter of what Mandelstam calls the ocean, the complex social forces that convey poems like Dickinson's to other writers and to a collective readership. But now and then a reader will stumble into a reception both personal and immediate, a sudden understanding of him- or herself as exactly the poem's "secret addressee." To take on a work in this way means to discover that something has "made" you, as Hans-Georg Gadamer writes, into "the person to whom the text was originally addressed" (333); such a reception—privately, fleetingly—lets factual knowledge go dark; and in the reluctant moment you find, disbelieving, the elision of history in the poet's unseeing nearness to your own reading hands.

Notes

The notes throughout this essay reflect the date of this essay's first appearance in a different form in 2000. My book *Poetry's Touch: On Lyric Address* (2003) includes, alongside fuller discussion of this same topic, a longer bibliography but one likewise limited by its date. The intervening years have seen much relevant work on poetic address and related themes.

1. There are exceptions to the emphasis on apostrophe: T. S. Eliot's "The Three Voices of Poetry"—in part an answer to Gottfried Benn's proclaiming the triumph of "monologic lyric"—had considered various aspects of poetic address, but focused on poetic drama. Jonathan Holden polemicized against excessive use of an ambiguous "you" in 1970's American poetry. Gudrun Grabher's study of "you" in Plath, Levertov, and Ammons carries a quantity of philosophy (Husserl, Heidegger, Buber, Sartre), behind which the poems recede. Criticism of Ashbery and Celan, special cases, is hard to apply more generally, though Bonnie Costello's "John Ashbery and the Idea of the Reader" is a notable exception. Good beginnings which one could wish got further are Caroline Masel's "The Tutelary *You*: A Reading of the Act of Address in Stevens, Yeats and Eliot" and Vance R. Holloway's "El tú en la poesía de Antonio Machado"; in a different way the same is true of Marianne and Michael Shapiro's venture to bring Bakhtinian dialogism to the study of the lyric. Tenney Nathanson's treatment of Whitman, that most insistent of all poets when it comes to hailing the reader, is the fullest study of reader address in poetry. As an astute precedent in Whitman criticism,

C. Carroll Hollis's *Language and Style in* Leaves of Grass deserves mention (see especially "Audience Involvement, 1855–1860," 88–123). John Hollander takes up "Poetic Imperatives," and Virginia Jackson and Olivia Rosenthal provide valuable insights into the figure of address in Dickinson and in sixteenth-century French lyric, respectively. Finally, Anne Ferry's *The Title to the Poem* sheds light on the history and rich interpretive implications of those dimensions of address relating to how poems are titled (see especially "Who 'Hears' the Poem," 105–36).

2. For the linguistic terms, see Levinson, *Pragmatics* 61–73. Concerning the "you" of narrative fiction, Monika Fludernik's "Second-Person Narrative: A Bibliography" and collection of essays (*Second-Person Narrative*) provide good orientation.

3. The accumulated scholarship on the relationship between literature's forms and orality-and-literacy is vast. To mention a handful of starting-places: the classic works are by Eric Havelock, Jacques Derrida, and Walter Ong. See also Jesper Svenbro and Rosalind Thomas on ancient Greek. On medieval Europe, see Paul Zumthor and A. N. Doane & Carol Braun Pasternack. Florian Coulmas takes up various aspects including ideographic vs. alphabetic cultures; Konrad Ehlich discusses deixis; and Dennis Tedlock provides an anthropological view. On contemporary poetry, see Charles Bernstein.

4. Stephen Owen evokes this moment of disillusionment well and retains a rare sense that disillusionment is not the only interesting part of the story (96–101, 198–201). Irene Kacandes, discussing the readerly "you" of postmodern fiction, notes that "the address doesn't precisely call us" and that (this is Owen's point) "even when the literary text really is 'talking' to me . . . I'm aware I'm not the only reader" (14). I grant the concern; but my emphasis is the intermission of that awareness.

5. For the history of speculations about the poem's composition, see Walter Jackson Bate, *John Keats* 626. These alternative views are fruitfully discussed by Lawrence Lipking 180–4 and by Brooke Hopkins 37–8. See also Timothy Bahti 219–20.

6. This description, like some that will follow, simplifies certain intricacies which could be more precisely detailed (but at some cost to readability) in the terminology of pragmatics.

7. Confusingly, classical rhetoric knows anaphora as repetition of an initial word. But in keeping with the term's literal meaning of "carrying back," i.e., pointing to an antecedent, linguistics has designated anaphora, together with its pair cataphora ("pointing" forward in the text), as technical terms for the referential operations of pronouns.

8. Sonnet 81. Most pertinent to Keats' poem is the very long tradition of epitaph poems, such as those collected in Book 7 of the Greek (or "Palatine") Anthology, which call or "reach" out to the passer-by, e.g. #342, κάτθανον, ἀλλά μένω σε [I am dead, but await thee]; cf. also #280–1. Paul Friedländer nominates two sixth-century Attic inscriptions (his #82, 83) not included in the Greek Anthology as the "earliest specimens" (1) of this address to the wayfarer; in both, the command is στῆθι καί οἴκτιρον [stand and weep] (186–7). Horace's ode I.28 includes the "conscience calm'd" topos. For the tradition, see the entry and bibliography under "Epitaph" in *The New Princeton Encyclopedia of Poetry and Poetics*.

There are fascinating ways in which lyric poetry is epitaphic in a general sense. Some aspects of the topic occupy the following works: Karen Mills-Courts' promisingly titled but to me unhelpful tome *Poetry as Epitaph: Representation and Poetic Language*; Paul de Man's essay "Autobiography as De-Facement"; Lawrence Lipking's *The Life of the Poet* 138–91; Geoffrey Hartman's *Wordsworth's Poetry, 1787–1814* 3–30; Wulf Segebrecht's "Steh, Leser, still!"; and not least T. S. Eliot's "Little Gidding" in *Four Quartets*.

9. An exception is Richard Macksey (854, 881).

10. In current terminology, we adopt the "footing" of "bystanders" to the communication. See Erving Goffman 124–59. Stephen Levinson, *Pragmatics* 61–73, suggests what seems at present the most usable array of terms for discussing the complexities of "participant roles," though his later work introduces confusions about the essential term "target" ("Putting"). Herbert Clark sketches a diagram (*Using* 14–15) to complement his psycholinguistic work on the topic (*Arenas of Language Use* and, with Thomas B. Carlson, "Hearers and Speech Acts"); and William F. Hanks situates deixis in culture.

11. Andrew Bennett argues that the poem's logic strictly entails that "the reader must have died" (12), which presupposition he finds central to (English) Romanticism generally. His description of how readers handle this presupposition in the Keats poem is unconvincing at certain junctures (e.g., to refuse the logic is to become a "non-audience," which in turn means that "for this poem at least, the audience has died" [12]).

Startlingly exact for "This living hand," by contrast, is Georges Poulet's description of literary reading generally: "une oeuvre littéraire, tant qu'opère en elle cette insufflation de vie provoquée par la lecture, devient elle-même, aux dépens du lecteur dont elle annule la vie propre, une manière d'être humain, c'est-à-dire une pensée consciente d'elle-même et se constituant comme le sujet de ses objets" (285).

12. Cf. the critiques in Balz Engler and in L. M. Findlay.

13. "Das Gedicht ist . . . unterwegs. Wer es schreibt, bleibt ihm mitgegeben" (3: 198). Further references to Celan are to the *Gesammelte Werke*, cited as *GW*.

14. Macksey 854. Macksey goes on to claim that "This living hand" represents "direct address that 'becomes' apostrophic . . . through the prolepsis of the 'if' clause." Since Macksey does clearly take the reader to be the poem's addressee, this sentence is hard to make sense of unless he has confused apostrophe with prosopopoeia (the figure of making the dead speak), a trope which Culler, citing de Man, also introduced into his discussion of Keats. This part of Macksey's confusion could originate with de Man, since de Man too twice identifies apostrophe with prosopopoeia ("prosopopoeia, the fiction of apostrophe" [75, 78]). For classical definitions and examples, see Heinrich Lausberg's *Handbuch der literarischen Rhetorik* 377–9 and 411–13. See also J. Douglas Kneale, who claims that Culler misidentifies apostrophe to begin with.

15. Throughout, translations from Mandelstam's essay are mine.

16. To my knowledge there exists no critical commentary on these lines. Quotations from Rilke are to the *Sämtliche Werke*, abbreviated *SW*.

The obvious rendition "hand in hand to be mine" is avoided because "Hand in der Hand mir" is not a German idiom, but Rilke's coinage, and also because the original pointedly evades rhyme. Snow's "hand in my hand" is not literal, though, and I depart from it where necessary below.

17. In linguistic terms, there is an uncertain boundary here between conventional implicature (the fixed function of contrast in the word "aber") and conversational implicature (the specific "contour" and character of that adversativity in a given utterance). On implicature, a concept developed by H. P. Grice, see Levinson's *Pragmatics* ch. 3, esp. 127–8.

18. Martin Buber's book *I and Thou*, together with his essay "Dialogue," are foundational reflections on this topic. Similarly, Hans-Georg Gadamer's *Truth and Method* touches on it repeatedly. Steven Kepnes, writing on Buber, expresses dismay that Gadamer nowhere cites Buber as the source of his ideas (27), but the complaint is fallacious, since the I/You relation is not a concept and need not come from study.

19. This opposition between knowledge and more intimate kinds of experience ("nearness") is explored in Christopher Benfey's thoughtful *Emily Dickinson and the Problem of Others*.

20. Martine Broda's *Dans la main de personne* is an eloquent meditation on *Die Niemandsrose* and on Celan's relationship to Mandelstam.

21. "Ansprache anläßlich der Entgegennahme des Literaturpreises der Freien Hansestadt Bremen" (*GW* 3: 185–186). Some phrases in the translation here are borrowed from Rosmarie Waldrop's *Paul Celan: Collected Prose*. Subsequent quotations from Celan are (except as noted) Waldrop's, with small modifications.

22. "Gewiß, [das Gedicht] erhebt einen Unendlichkeitsanspruch, es sucht, durch die Zeit hindurchzugreifen—durch sie hindurch, nicht über sie hinweg." "Ansprache," my translation.

Works cited

Althusser, Louis. "Ideology and Ideological State Apparatuses (Notes towards an Investigation)." *Essays on Ideology*. Trans. Ben Brewster et al. London: Verso, 1984. 1–60.

Bahti, Timothy. "Ambiguity and Indeterminacy: The Juncture." *Comparative Literature* 38 (1986): 209–23.

Bate, Walter Jackson. *John Keats*. Cambridge, MA: Harvard UP, 1963.

Benfey, Christopher. *Emily Dickinson and the Problem of Others*. Amherst: U of Massachusetts P, 1984.

Bennett, Andrew. *Keats, Narrative and Audience: The Posthumous Life of Writing*. Cambridge, UK: Cambridge UP, 1994.

Bernstein, Charles, ed. *Close Listening: Poetry and the Performed Word*. New York: Oxford UP, 1998.

Broda, Martine. *Dans la main de personne*. Paris: Cerf, 1986.

Buber, Martin. *Ich und Du*. 1923. Heidelberg: Lambert Schneider, 1983.

——. *Zwiesprache* [Dialogue]. Berlin: Schocken, 1932.

Celan, Paul. *Gesammelte Werke in 5 Bänden*. Ed. Beda Allemann and Stefan Reichert. Frankfurt am Main: Suhrkamp, 1983.

Clark, Herbert. *Arenas of Language Use*. Chicago: U of Chicago P, 1973.

——. *Using Language*. Cambridge, UK: Cambridge UP, 1996.

——. and Thomas B. Carlson. "Hearers and Speech Acts." *Language* 58 (1982): 332–73.

Costello, Bonnie. "John Ashbery and the Idea of the Reader." *Contemporary Literature* 23 (1982): 493–514.

Coulmas, Florian. *Über Schrift.* Frankfurt am Main: Suhrkamp, 1982.

Culler, Jonathan. "Apostrophe." *The Pursuit of Signs.* Ithaca: Cornell UP, 1981. 135–54.

De Man, Paul. "Autobiography as De-Facement." *The Rhetoric of Romanticism.* New York: Columbia UP, 1984. 67–81.

Derrida, Jacques. *Of Grammatology.* 1967. Trans. Gayatri Chakravorty Spivak. Baltimore: Johns Hopkins UP, 1976.

Dickinson, Emily. *The Poems of Emily Dickinson.* 3 vols. Ed. R. W. Franklin. Cambridge, MA: Harvard UP, 1998.

Doane, A. N., and Carol Braun Pasternack, eds. *Vox intexta: Orality and Textuality in the Middle Ages.* Madison: U of Wisconsin P, 1991.

Ehlich, Konrad. "Text und sprachliches Handeln. Die Entstehung von Texten aus dem Bedürfnis nach Überlieferung." *Schrift und Gedächtnis.* Ed. A. Assmann et al. Munich: Fink, 1983. 24–43.

Eliot, T. S. *Four Quartets.* New York: Harcourt, Brace and Company, 1943.

——. "The Three Voices of Poetry." *On Poetry and Poets.* London: Faber & Faber, 1957. 89–102.

Engler, Balz. "Deictics and the Status of Poetic Texts." *The Structure of Texts.* Ed. Udo Fries. Tübingen: Narr, 1987. 65–73.

Ferry, Anne. *The Title to the Poem.* Stanford: Stanford UP, 1996.

Findlay, L. M. "Culler and Byron on Apostrophe and Lyric Time." *Studies in Romanticism* 24 (1985): 335–53.

Fludernik, Monika. *Second-Person Narrative.* Special issue of *Style* 28.3 (1994).

——. "Second-Person Narrative: A Bibliography." *Style* 28.4 (1994): 525–48.

Freud, Sigmund. "The Uncanny." *The Standard Edition of the Complete Psychological Works of Sigmund Freud.* Ed. James Strachey. London: Hogarth P, 1953–74. 17: 219–52.

Friedländer, Paul. *Epigrammata: Greek Inscriptions in Verse.* Berkeley: U of California P, 1948.

Frye, Northrop. *Anatomy of Criticism.* Princeton: Princeton UP, 1957.

Gadamer, Hans-Georg. *Truth and Method.* 1960. Trans. Joel Weinsheimer and Donald Marshall. 2nd ed. New York: Crossroad, 1992.

Goffman, Erving. "Footings." *Forms of Talk.* Philadelphia: U of Pennylvania P, 1981. 124–59.

Grabher, Gudrun. *Das lyrische Du: Du-Vergessenheit und Möglichkeiten der Du-Bestimmung in der amerikanischen Dichtung.* Heidelberg: C. Winter, 1989.

Greek Anthology. Trans. W. R. Paton. Vol. 2. Loeb Classical Library. Cambridge, MA: Harvard UP, 1958.

Grice, H. P. "Logic and Conversation." *Syntax and Semantics, Vol. 3: Speech Acts.* Ed. P. Cole and J. Morgan. New York: Academic P, 1975. 41–58.

Hanks, William F. *Referential Practice: Language and Lived Space among the Maya.* Chicago: U of Chicago P, 1990.

Hartman, Geoffrey. *Wordsworth's Poetry, 1787–1814.* Cambridge, MA: Harvard UP, 1971.

Havelock, Eric. *The Muse Learns to Write: Reflections on Orality and Literacy from Antiquity to the Present.* New Haven: Yale UP, 1986.

——. *Preface to Plato.* Cambridge, MA: Harvard UP, 1963.

Herbert, George. "Clasping of Hands." *George Herbert and Henry Vaughan.* Ed. Louis Martz. New York: Oxford UP, 1986.

Holden, Jonathan. "The Abuse of the Second Person Pronoun." *The Rhetoric of the Contemporary Lyric.* Bloomington: Indiana UP, 1980. 38–56.

Hollander, John. "Poetic Imperatives." *Melodious Guile: Fictive Pattern in Poetic Language.* New Haven: Yale UP, 1988. 64–84.

Hollis, C. Carroll. *Language and Style in* Leaves of Grass. Baton Rouge: Louisiana State UP, 1983.

Holloway, Vance R. "El tú en la poesía de Antonio Machado." *Explicación de textos literarios—Hispanic Press* 16 (1987–88): 70–84.

Hopkins, Brooke. "Keats and the Uncanny: 'This living hand.'" *The Kenyon Review* 11.4 (1989): 28–40.

Jackson, Virginia. "Dickinson's Figure of Address." *Dickinson and Audience.* Ed. Martin Orzeck and Robert Weisbuch. Ann Arbor : U of Michigan P, 1996. 77–103.

Jacobi, Friedrich Heinrich. *Auserlesener Briefwechsel.* Leipzig: G. Fleischer, 1825–27. 1: 330.

Kacandes, Irene. "Are You in the Text? The 'Literary Performative' in Postmodernist Fiction." *Text and Performance Quarterly* 13 (1993): 139–53.

Keats, John. *Complete Poems.* Ed. Jack Stillinger. Cambridge, MA: Harvard UP, 1982.

Kepnes, Steven. *The Text as Thou: Martin Buber's Dialogical Hermeneutics and Narrative Theology.* Bloomington: Indiana UP, 1992.

Kinnell, Galway. *Selected Poems.* Boston: Houghton Mifflin, 1982.

Kneale, J. Douglas. "Romantic Aversions: Apostrophe Reconsidered." *ELH* 58 (1991): 141–65.

Lausberg, Heinrich. *Handbuch der literarischen Rhetorik.* Munich: Max Hueber, 1960.

Leishman, J.B., trans. *Poems 1906 to 1926.* By Rainer Maria Rilke. New York: New Directions, 1957.

Levinson, Stephen. *Pragmatics.* Cambridge, UK: Cambridge UP, 1983.

——. "Putting Linguistics on a Proper Footing: Explorations in Goffman's Concepts of Participation." *Erving Goffman: Exploring the Interaction Order.* Ed. Paul Drew and Anthony Wootton. Boston: Polity P, 1988. 161–227.

Lipking, Lawrence. *The Life of the Poet: Beginning and Ending Poetic Careers.* Chicago: U of Chicago P, 1981.

Macksey, Richard. "Keats and the Poetics of Extremity." *Modern Language Notes* 99 (1984): 845–84.

Mandelstam, Osip. "O sobesednike." *Sobranie Sochinenii v trekh tomakh.* Ed. G. P. Struve and B. A. Filipoff. 2nd ed. New York: Inter-Language Literary Associates, 1971. 2: 233–40.

Masel, Caroline. "The Tutelary *You*: A Reading of the Act of Address in Stevens, Yeats and Eliot." *New Comparison* 9 (1990): 158–69.

Mill, John Stuart. "Thoughts on Poetry and Its Varieties." 1833, 1859. *Collected Works of John Stuart Mill.* 33 vols. Ed. John M. Robson and Jack Stillinger. Toronto: U Toronto P, 1981. 1: 343–77.

Mills-Courts, Karen. *Poetry as Epitaph: Representation and Poetic Language.* Baton Rouge: Louisiana State UP, 1990.

Nathanson, Tenney. *Whitman's Presence: Body, Voice and Writing in* Leaves of Grass. New York: New York UP, 1992.

The New Princeton Encyclopedia of Poetry and Poetics. Ed. Alex Preminger et al. Princeton: Princeton UP, 1993.

Ong, Walter. "*Maranatha*: Death and Life in the Text of the Book." *Interfaces of the Word: Studies in the Evolution of Consciousness and Culture*. Ithaca: Cornell UP, 1977. 230–71.

——. *Orality and Literacy: The Technologizing of the Word*. London: Methuen, 1982.

Owen, Stephen. *Mi-Lou: Poetry and the Labyrinth of Desire*. Cambridge, MA: Harvard UP, 1989.

Poulet, Georges. *La conscience critique*. Paris: Corti, 1971.

Quintilian. *Institutio Oratoria*. Books 1–3. Trans. H. E. Butler. Loeb Classical Library. Cambridge, MA: Harvard UP, 1980.

Rilke, Rainer Maria. *Sämtliche Werke in sechs Bänden*. Ed. Ernst Zinn. Frankfurt am Main: Insel, 1955–1966.

Rosenthal, Olivia. "Présences du lecteur dans la poésie lyrique du XVIᵉ siècle." *Poétique* 105 (1996): 71–85.

Segebrecht, Wulf. "Steh, Leser, still! Prolegomena zu einer situationsbezogenen Poetik der Lyrik, entwickelt am Beispiel von poetischen Grabschriften und Grabschriftenvorschlägen in Leichencarmina des 17. und 18. Jahrhunderts." *Deutsche Vierteljahrsschrift für Literaturwissenschaft und Geistesgeschichte* 52 (1978): 430–68.

Shapiro, Marianne, and Michael Shapiro. "Dialogism and the Addressee in Lyric Poetry." *University of Toronto Quarterly* 61 (1992): 392–413.

Snow, Edward, trans. *Uncollected Poems*. By Rainer Maria Rilke. New York: North Point P, 1996.

Svenbro, Jesper. *Phrasikleia: An Anthropology of Reading in Ancient Greece*. Trans. Janet Lloyd. Ithaca: Cornell UP, 1993.

Tedlock, Dennis. *The Spoken Word and the Work of Interpretation*. Philadelphia: U of Pennsylvania P, 1983.

Thomas, Rosalind. *Literacy and Orality in Ancient Greece*. Cambridge, UK: Cambridge UP, 1992.

Waldrop, Rosmarie, trans. *Paul Celan: Collected Prose*. By Paul Celan. Riverdale-on-Hudson: Sheep Meadow P, 1986.

Waters, William. *Poetry's Touch: On Lyric Address*. Ithaca: Cornell UP, 2003.

Whitman, Walt. *Leaves of Grass: A Textual Variorum of the Printed Poems*. 3 vols. Ed. Sculley Bradley et al. New York: New York UP, 1980.

Zumthor, Paul. *La lettre et la voix: De la "littérature" médiévale*. Paris: Seuil, 1987.

——. *La poésie et la voix dans la civilisation médiévale*. Paris: Seuil, 1987.

7

Hasidim in Poetry: Dialogic Poetics of Encounter in Denise Levertov's *The Jacob's Ladder*

Temple Cone

For her collection *Poems 1960–1967*, Denise Levertov added a Hasidic tale to the reprinted text of her 1961 volume, *The Jacob's Ladder*. The tale, printed under the title "The Ladder," was drawn from Martin Buber's collection of Hasidic sayings and stories, *Tales of the Hasidim: Later Masters*, and it recalls Jacob's vision, in Genesis 28:12, of a ladder between heaven and earth on which angels were rising and descending:

> Rabbi Moshe (of Kobryn) taught: It is written: "And he dreamed, and behold a ladder set up on the earth." That he is every man. Every man must know: I am clay, I am one of countless shards of clay, but "the top of it reached to heaven"—my soul reaches to heaven; "and behold the angels of God ascending and descending on it"—even the ascent and descent of the angels depend on my deeds. (2)

That Levertov chose a tale from Buber's collection should come as no surprise. Besides drawing deeply from the concrete, celebratory spirit of Hasidism, Levertov had familial connections to Hasidism and Martin Buber himself. The poet's paternal ancestor, Schneour Zalman, founded the Habad branch of Hasidism, while her own father, Paul Levertoff, a translator of the Zohar, directly influenced Buber's writing of the *Tales* with his essay *Die Religiose Deukweise den Hasidim* and his distinct approach to the Hasidic stories (Hallisey, "Revisited" 166). While Levertov herself was raised a Christian (her father having converted and become an Anglican priest), she claimed that "I was always . . . very conscious of being Jewish" (Andre 61). The tale of Jacob's vision reveals Levertov's concern with the consecration of the mundane and the momentary, drawing on the Hasidic belief that worldly things and beings are

123

"shards" in which sparks of the original divine substance lie trapped, awaiting release. As Joan F. Hallisey has written in her examination of the Hasidic influence on Levertov:

> Given the Hasidic belief concerning "sparks" and her understanding of the consciousness that the poet must bring to his/her work, it appears that Levertov is telling us here that it is the duty and privilege of the poet to discover or uncover and to "translate" the sacred that is found in the secular. ("Illustrious" 265)

While much has been made of the worldly celebration of the divine in Levertov's work, the ways in which her poetics embody and actualize this celebration deserve further attention. Similarly, the emphasis on Buber's *Tales of the Hasidim* as an influence for Levertov has overshadowed the ways in which his religious philosophy, drawn from Hasidic lore but individually refined, permeates her work. This essay, therefore, will consider two main issues. First, it will examine the thematic significance of Buber's idea of the dialogic encounter (treated most fully in his major philosophical work, *I and Thou*) for Levertov's poetry. Second, it will demonstrate how Levertov's poetics, in particular her kinetic lineation and depersonalizing (though not destabilizing) of the subject, enact the dynamic of the I–Thou relation. By reading Levertov through the lens of Buber's philosophical system, we gain a critical vocabulary that may be applied to the whole of her work.

Before turning to the poems, we might examine further the tale Levertov borrowed from Buber for *The Jacob's Ladder*. The qualities Buber ascribes to the author of the tale, Rabbi Moshe of Kobryn, may be applied equally to Levertov, who would have had access to this description, which appears in the introduction to *Tales of the Hasidim: Later Masters*. They thus provide an entry into the discussion of the Hasidic element of her work; about Rabbi Moshe Buber writes:

> I do not hesitate to count this little-known man among the few late-born great men which the hasidic movement produced in the very midst of its decline. While he did not enrich the teaching, his life and words and the unity between his life and his words lent it a very. personal, refreshingly vital expression.
>
> Three sayings suffice to give the gist of his philosophy: "You shall become an altar before God"; "There is nothing in the world which does not contain a commandment"; and "Just as God is limitless, so his service is limitless."

These teachings are integrated with a life which by imaging and exemplifying them, sometimes recalls the early masters of hasidism. (23)

It is pleasant to think Levertov might have read this passage, either before or after adding "The Ladder" to her collection, and recognized the affinities between Rabbi Moshe and herself. Levertov's work recalls that of an "early master," William Carlos Williams, whose ideas on the line as a score for the breath and whose "*evocative* sense of *how things are*" ("Affinities" 3) provided her an early poetic foundation. Levertov's lifelong commitment to activism, both in poetry and personal protest, testifies to the union of her life and words. But most importantly for this discussion, the three sayings Buber identifies with Rabbi Moshe convey major thematic concerns in Levertov's poetry: attention to the world as a vessel of divinity; an absolute personal investment in relation to God; and recognition of the many forms of worship besides ecstatic mysticism.

The reverent openness to the world of which Rabbi Moshe and many other Hasidic rabbis spoke had powerful implications for Buber's philosophy. Human relations with the world, he claims in *I and Thou*, may be characterized by the attitudes of turning-toward and leaning-away-from beings in the world. These relations, which he terms I–Thou and I–It, respectively, determine the self and the non-self (or "other") in radically different ways. The I–Thou relation may be described as one of immediate, reciprocal presence, or intersubjectivity. One enters into the I–Thou in the fullness of one's own being, and encounters another in the fullness of their being, affecting and affected without coercion. Buber writes, "Relation is reciprocity. My [Thou] acts on me as I act on it. Our students teach us, our works form us. The 'wicked' become a revelation when they are touched by the sacred basic word. How are we educated by children, by animals! Inscrutably involved, we live in the currents of universal reciprocity" (67). This relation vivifies the present moment, since it is undistracted by any need to categorize or locate the encounter within a surveyable "history." By contrast, the I–It relation objectifies, treating world and subject as things to be known, experienced, organized, and used, never encountered in the present (in the sense of both the present moment and physical presence), but existing always already in the past.

Within human life, the two relations alternate naturally. While Buber does not condemn the I–It relation (he acknowledges that humans must enter into it in order to make their world habitable), its propensity to dominate human attitudes towards the world makes it a potential threat. To throw one's whole being into an encounter and thereby enter the I–Thou is difficult, but only in that encounter can the mutual respect of a non-utilitarian morality come about. "Love is responsibility of an I for a [Thou]" (66), Buber writes, suggesting both responsiveness (attention to the *presentness* of the other) and duty (in this case, a Kantian moral imperative). For Buber, failure of responsibility would have disastrous consequences: a totalized I–It relation would amount to the complete isolation of the subject from the subjectivity of all beings, including, ultimately, its own.

For Buber, God is the Thou who never becomes an It (and, conversely, never enters into an I–It relation, which would objectify humankind). A person enters completely into their being in relation to God, and when the relation ends (i.e., becomes an I–It), it is because one no longer speaks to God, but about him. Since all I–Thou encounters are direct relations (that is, unmediated and focused on the present moment), then the character of the lowliest relation contains within it an aspect of the highest. Any direct relation, whether to other humans, works of art, animals, or nature (for one may enter into the I–Thou with all of these, according to Buber), allows for a glimpse of the eternal Thou of God. If we recall the second saying attributed to Rabbi Moshe—"There is nothing in the world which does not contain a commandment"—we find a simple example of the bond between Buber's theological system and the Hasidic lore he devoted himself to. The dialogic encounter of the I–Thou valorizes the relationality emphasized in Hasidic lore; the world, if addressed correctly, can reveal itself with the impact of a commandment.

After immersing herself in the *Tales* during the fifties, Levertov produced *The Jacob's Ladder* (1961), her most direct engagement with Buber's ideas (Andre 60).[1] One of the book's principle themes is the achievement of an "authentic" relation (Levertov's term) with the outside world. Avis Hewitt connects this desire to Henry David Thoreau's notion of "a poetic or divine life" when he writes that "[a] 'divine' life makes quotidian reality holy, makes it sacred by the infusion of that which quickens the spirit; early on, Levertov named that source 'the authentic'" (67). In our terms, this relation may easily be described as the I–Thou, its primary concern being openness to a presence. Levertov writes in "Matins":

> The authentic, I said
> breaking the handle of my hairbrush as I
> brushed my hair in
> rhythmic strokes: That's it,
> that's joy, it's always

a recognition, the known
appearing fully itself, and
more itself than one knew.

(16–23)

While the speaker is not engaged here with another being, the attention she gives to her actions is indicative of the state of mind needed to enter into a dialogic relation. Alertness to physical sensation situates her in the moment, which, undistracted by temporal matters, is thereby intensified. Characteristic of this intensification in Levertov's poetry is her use of kinesthesia, the most physically "active" of the senses: "breaking the handle of my hairbrush as I / brushed my hair in / rhythmic strokes." The act of brushing hair does not seem like one of many acts in a day; were it so, the broken brush would be a problem for the speaker, not a vivid encounter. As Hewitt remarks, "Breaking is, paradoxically, the way to wholeness" (103).

In her thematic treatment of the I–Thou, Levertov alternately represents the relation with images of durability and ephemerality, suggesting that the dialogic encounter, real as stone while one is in it, can shift almost unnoticed into the I–It, where it still remains as a possibility. Levertov's shifting representations of the I–Thou ultimately reflect its persistence, the way in which it may easily be resumed if one assumes the right attitude. As Buber himself wrote:

> There are moments of the secret ground in which world order is beheld as present. Then the tone is heard all of a sudden whose uninterpretable score the ordered world is. *These moments are immortal; none are more evanescent.* They leave no content that could be preserved, but their force enters into the creation and into man's knowledge, and the radiation of its force penetrates the ordered world and thaws it again and again. (82, emphasis added)

In "The Thread," the speaker's sensation of being pulled by a connecting thread figures the ebb and flow between relations which Buber recognized as natural to human experience. The speaker's wonder at the persistence of the connection she thought was lost suggests the alienation resulting from immersion in the I–It, and implicitly criticizes the rational, categorizing mind that presumed to understand relationality:

Was it
not long ago this thread

> began to draw me? Or
> way back? Was I
> born with its knot about my
> neck, a bridle? Not fear,
> but a stirring
> of wonder makes me
> catch my breath when I feel
> the tug of it when I thought
> it had loosened itself and gone.
>
>   (8–18)

Having described the thread pulling her as "finer than cobweb and as / elastic" (5–6), the speaker contrasts its gentleness with other, harsher means of connection: "No barbed hook / pierced and tore me" (7–8). This harshness one might associate with the manipulative quality of the I–It relation that deindividualizes and objectifies the other. The fine, silk-like thread serves as a bridle for the speaker, suggesting that a rider (perhaps God) holds her by reins. In the implied figuration of the speaker as horse, Levertov unites energy and tranquility, that combination of activity and passivity with which Buber characterizes the I–Thou: "The [Thou] encounters me. But I enter into a direct relationship to it. Thus the relationship is election and electing, passive and active at once: An action of the whole being must approach passivity, for it does away with all partial actions and thus with any sense of action, which always depends on limited exertions" (62). If the master holding the reins is indeed God, then the poem hints that the Thou— eternal, ever-present and yet hidden—can always reveal itself, if only in glimpses. The lines alternately break across grammatical units ("as / elastic," "Or / way," "my / neck") and with them, the poem's rhythms convey the almost unnoticed shifts of relation, from I–Thou to I–It and back, that occur in human life.

While the bond of the I–Thou seems numinous in "The Thread," "The Jacob's Ladder" emphasizes its material reality for those who experience it. What was gentle and tenuous as a strand of spider web in the former poem is granted a metaphorical hardness in the latter, against which "a man climbing / must scrape his knees, and bring / the grip of his hands into play" (16–18). Levertov writes:

> The stairway is not
> a thing of gleaming strands
> a radiant evanescence

for angels' feet that only glance in their tread, and need not
touch the stone.

It is of stone.

(1–6)

As in Rabbi Moshe's "The Ladder," angels move up and down this stair,
hardly touching its steps. But here, a man (in the sense of "human")
may also ascend, though suffering difficulty and physical pain along the
way. While the figure of the climber seems to stand in for the poet in the
experience of composing a poem (the final line: "The poem ascends"),
this difficult advance along a stair between heaven and earth also implies
the challenge of entering and maintaining the dialogic relation. The
cost, however, is redemptive: "The cut stone / consoles his groping feet"
(18–19). The angels, for whom the direct relation would always be open,
cannot share in the wonder the human feels when the I–Thou resumes.
Ironically, the angels are always presented as descending—"One sees
that the angels must spring / down from one step to the next" (13–14)—
while only the man climbs. Doing so, he feels "wings brush past him,"
as if he were being paid homage, or were receiving the angels' blessings.

In keeping with the way a being, in entering the I–Thou, is wholly
engaged in that relation, Levertov's lineation enacts what she treats
thematically and imagistically. In her essay "On the Function of the
Line," Levertov writes, "The most obvious function of the linebreak is
rhythmic: it can record the slight (but meaningful) hesitations between
word and word that are characteristic of the mind's *dance* among per-
ceptions but which are not noted by grammatical punctuation" (79,
emphasis added). That she describes the play of perception embodied
in line-breaks as a dance is not meant to feminize or beautify Levertov's
poetics (indeed, she herself often refers to this dance-like quality in her
work), but to point out their kinetic quality, the sense of living activity
which arises out of the dialogic encounter. While the speaker in "The
Thread" ruefully criticizes herself for missing this pattern, the lineation underscores the powerful effect of resuming the I–Thou; one reads
that "a stirring / of *wonder makes me*" (14–15), as if the self remained
unformed until it entered into a direct relation with the world.

Rhythmically, Levertov's frequent enjambment across grammatical
units resists the weightiness conveyed by the end-stopped line. Such
weightiness can provide a tone of pronouncement, and at the time *The
Jacob's Ladder* was written, one of the developing strains of American
poetry, the Deep Image, was beginning to make full use of this effect. In

order to resonate across gender, racial, and cultural divides (as Robert Bly suggested this form of poetry could do), the Deep Image poem needed a tone of wisdom; frequent end-stopping gave even individual lines the impact of a significant utterance. By contrast, the Black Mountain School (with which Levertov is generally associated, though she shares affinities—particularly an attention to the natural world—with the Deep Image) concerned itself less with the resonance of individual utterances and more with the interaction between the mind and the poem's subject. As Charles Olson, whose ideas on the line influenced Levertov's own, writes in "Projective Verse," " . . . all the thots [sic] men are capable of can be entered on the back of a postage stamp. So, is it not the PLAY of a mind we are after, is not that that shows whether a mind is there at all?" (19).

For Levertov, lineation scores the play of the mind, marking shifts of perception and consciousness. As a result, the poem resembles the working of an individual mind in response to its world; each line-break records a moment of hesitation, doubt, excitement, etc. In this way, the speaker becomes more present to the reader, and the I–Thou relation which the poem treats thematically is further authenticated. Moreover, by limiting her use of expressly autobiographical detail, Levertov depersonalizes the subject without destabilizing it, allowing the reader to substitute herself for the speaker. In "On the Function of the Line," Levertov claims:

> When the written score precisely notates perceptions, a whole—an inscape or gestalt—begins to emerge; and the gifted writer is not so submerged in the parts that the sum goes unseen. The sum is objective—relatively, at least; it has presence, character, and—as it develops—needs. The parts of the poem are instinctively adjusted in some degree to serve the needs of the whole. And as this adjustment takes place, excess subjectivity is avoided. Details of a private, as distinct from personal, nature may be deleted, for example, in the interests of a fuller, clearer, more communicative whole. (85–6)

Because Levertov seems to invite the reader to identify with the speaker, the poems often read like prayers. The experience described is transformed, metaphorically, into our experience, through the reading. Take, for instance, the opening of "The Fountain":

> Don't say, don't say there is no water
> to solace the dryness at our hearts.
> I have seen

> the fountain springing out of the rock wall
> and you drinking there.
>
> (1–5)

Addressing the despair felt for "the dryness at our hearts," the speaker offers herself as a witness, claiming that there is "water / to solace the dryness," and that she has already seen those who are troubled "drinking there." It is a mystical vision, and therefore private in some respects, but by using her vision to comfort others, the speaker is implicitly healed, too, for this water will "solace the dryness at *our* hearts."

We might contrast this instance of Levertov's externalized concern with a more ego-centered poem, Robert Bly's "Driving Toward the Lac Qui Parle River," the first section of which reads:

> I am driving; it is dusk; Minnesota.
> The stubble field catches the last growth of sun.
> The soybeans are breathing on all sides.
> Old men are sitting before their houses on carseats
> In the small towns. I am happy,
> The moon rising above the turkey sheds.
>
> (1–6)

Here the focus rests entirely on the subject's experience. While attention is turned to the outward world, the speaker watches from his own car seat, and while his vision results in happiness, it is a happiness shared with no one but himself. The lines themselves emphasize this staidness; heavily end-stopped, each one seems sufficient unto itself, like utterances in a void or claims of great solemnity. By contrast, more than half of Levertov's lines are enjambed, resulting in a whirling play between the linear unit as an individual vessel of meaning and the reader's expectation of completing the sentence: "the fountain springing out of the wall / *and you drinking there. And I too* / before your eyes // found footholds and climbed" (3–6, emphasis added). Her speaker speaks in a comforting tone to an unseen companion, allaying doubts about the existence of such solace for dryness (which may figure ennui, or pain, or despair). The dryness is commonly suffered; unlike Bly, Levertov's self-concern is situated within a communal context. Because of the speaker's isolation in "Driving," the ephemerality of the epiphany is heightened; while he becomes "[t]he moon rising above the turkey sheds," he has also entered a cycle (both daily and seasonal—i.e., the sheds are used for the autumn turkey hunt) that will end, inevitably, with a descent from happiness. But the fountain, on which an implied community depends ("our hearts," recalling Buber's notion of love as "responsibility"), remains ever-present, constantly renewing itself; Levertov writes:

> it is still there and always there
> with its quiet song and strange power
> to spring in us,
> up and out through the rock.

> (17–20)

Bly's egoistic position denies him connection with the world. While he may look out on the Minnesota farmland and experience a moment of happiness, the world does not gain reciprocally from this relation. In "The Fountain," engagement with this source transforms those who go to it; they become new ground from which the water can spring. Here, as in many poems, we begin to understand Levertov's idea of subjectivity. She cannot deny her personal presence absolutely, for to do so would conclude in an absolute embrace of the I–It relation, in which even one's own self is objectified. But an over-emphasis on the ego negates the reciprocal openness the authentic I–Thou relation demands. Though the point-of-view remains in the first person, the speaker's concern is not with her own experience, but with others'; Levertov abnegates an expression of experience-focused ego for an enactment of the dialogic encounter.

The loosening of the ego, which results in a perspective with which the reader can easily identify, was earlier characterized as prayerful. This quality, characteristic of many of the poems in *The Jacob's Ladder*, sometimes results in an actual prayer, as is the case in "Come Into Animal Presence." The poem illustrates how attention to the mundane world can occasion a correspondence with the divine. Beginning with an imperative that is also an invitation—"Come into animal presence"— Levertov describes several animals (the serpent, the rabbit, the llama, the armadillo) whose response to human contact is at most indifferent. These animals are less "noble" members of their kingdom: ugly, close to the ground, they ordinarily would arouse few feelings of devotion or praise. Yet Levertov suggests that the right relation to even a lowly animal would transform its apparent indifference into the full expression of its nature ("the snake has no blemish"). And though she does not state it explicitly, her reverential tone suggests such an encounter would transform the human participant as well. She writes:

> Those who were sacred have remained so,
> holiness does not dissolve, it is a presence
> of bronze, only the sight that saw it
> faltered and turned from it.
> An old joy returns in holy presence.
>
> (21-5)

Having entered the I-Thou, the speaker claims, one recovers a joy "in holy presence," and this presence, unlike Bly's soon-to-set moon, is durable, lasting, "a presence / of bronze." Such a direct relation, Buber claims, reveals not only the being of the other, but also offers a glimpse of the eternal Thou. One rejoices that this relation, wherein one's self is most authentically itself, can be continued forever in the presence of God. Levertov writes in the poem "Joy" (from the 1967 collection *The Sorrow Dance*):

> we cloud-wander
>
> away from it, stumble
> again towards it not seeing it,
>
> enter cast down, discovering ourselves
> 'in joy' as 'in love.'
>
> (12-15)

Throughout *The Jacob's Ladder*, attention to the presence of another is identified with the dialogic encounter. The very word "presence" appears frequently throughout Levertov's poetry; in "Primary Wonder" (from *Sands of the Well*), she writes that "once more the quiet mystery / is present to me . . . / the mystery / that there is anything, anything at all" (8-11). The persistence of the word suggests its importance for Levertov's moral and aesthetic vision, which may be one and the same, given Buber's belief that one's stance towards a thing will determine how one acts towards it. Buber's conception of love as responsibility for keeping a Thou from becoming an It seems parallel to the notion advanced by Rainer Maria Rilke, whom Levertov also read closely, of love as a mutual guarding of solitude (*Letters* 150). Such a form of love can be a political as well as a spiritual determinant in the construction of the self; refusal to enter the I–Thou risks an obfuscation of individuality, from which any number of abuses may spring. At the close of *The Jacob's Ladder*, Levertov portrays such a decline in "During the Eichmann Trial," and follows it by reasserting the I–Thou in "A Solitude."

Writing about Robert Duncan's epigraph to "During the Eichmann Trial" ("When we look up / each from his being"), Harry Marten remarks that "[t]he poet seems to suggest that it is something not often done" (82). As we have seen earlier in the discussion of Buber, the authentic I–Thou relation, which requires a person to enter fully into his or her being with respect to another, depends on outwardness, a reciprocal engagement with others. It is not that one enters into the I–Thou in order to gain this sense of self (though it follows); one enters the relation to gain a true sense of what is outside oneself. As Paul Lacey remarks, "[T]here is another kind of meditation, found in the poetry of Robert Bly, James Wright, and Gary Snyder as well as in Denise Levertov, where the discovery or creation of the self is unimportant, and only *seeing* matters" (117). For Levertov, the egoistic, ultimately solipsistic mind breeds an indifference to life, the consequences of which can be catastrophic, as emblematized by Eichmann's "banality of evil."

In his remarks on the "lack of a serious treatment of evil" (117) in *The Jacob's Ladder*, Lacey writes that although Levertov does base "During the Eichmann Trial" on a contemporary instance of human evil, she focuses "on the appropriate inner response to the issue rather than arguing a course of action" (118). In fairness to Levertov, the trial preceded the Vietnam conflict, which proved the impetus for her political activism, though Levertov's response to the trial certainly falls in line with an Augustinian view of evil as an abeyance of good (rather than the Manichean view of evil as co-existent with good). Later in her career, Levertov did use her poetry to pursue political causes, even reprinting an information sheet for demonstrators in her 1971 collection *To Stay Alive* (*Poems 1968–1972*, 154), though she did eventually unite the political and spiritual trains of her verse. "As is noticeable in her writing of the last several decades she [. . .] acknowledges that the poet with a vision believes *and* acts," writes Hallisey ("Unheard" 88). "During the Eichmann Trial" represents an attempt, within her religious sensibility at the time, to address the issue of evil.

Because all humans are capable of entering into the I–Thou and I–It, and because all are capable of rejecting the I–Thou as being too difficult to enter into and maintain, all are complicit in Eichmann's crimes against the Jews. Though the product of Eichmann's crime far outstrips

any crime of omission, the objectifying attitude out of which his crime
arose is enacted by many:

> He had not looked,
> pitiful man whom none
>
> pity, whom all
> must pity if they look
>
> into their own face.
>
> (1–5)

The first section, "When We Look Up," serves as a tonic to the series,
implying that acts of evil originate with an individual failure to relate
directly with an other. The sections that follow treat of Eichmann's
murder of a Jewish boy for stealing a peach and of *Kristallnacht*, the
pogroms that began the Holocaust. While Levertov does not aim at a
facile equation of one individual's death (the boy's) with the deaths
of several million, the implication that the spiritual attitude (i.e., I–It)
required to commit a single murder is little different from that required
to commit a million cannot be missed. In each case, it is suggested, the
crime arises from Eichmann's indifference to the faces

> into which the gaze wanders
> and is lost
>
> and returns to tell
> **Here is a mystery,**
>
> **a person, an**
> **other, an I?**
>
> (13–18)

As Marten points out, at the moment Eichmann expresses his apathy,
the poet sees "a spring of blood / [gush] from the earth" (52–3), which
washes over all humanity, drowning and condemning all with the sin
of his murders: "he, you, I, which shall I say?" (65). The poem represents Levertov's attempt to reassert the eminence of the I–Thou in the
wake of the Holocaust. To do so, she must not only restate the potential for destruction implicit in any I–It relation, but try to understand
Eichmann's own rejection of the I–Thou: "Pity this man who saw it /
whose obedience continued" (63–4).

The second section, "The Peachtree," allegorizes Eichmann's con-
fessed murder of a Jewish boy for stealing a peach from his orchard,
the lapsarian undertones of the poem equating the obfuscation of the
I–Thou with original sin. Initially, the poem is narrated in the third
person while describing the boy, but it switches to Eichmann's perspective ("mister death") at the moment of the theft. The utter refusal of the
poem to return to the boy's position suggests how Eichmann objectifies
him, all for the sake of an object (the peach): "mister death who signs
papers / then eats / telegraphs simply: **Shoot them**" (27–9). Ultimately,
of course, such objectification numbs the self and blights the world it
turned to for sustenance; Eichmann, who "would have enjoyed / the
sweetest of all the peaches on his tree / with sour-cream / with brandy"
(34–7), now finds that "there is more blood than / sweet juice / always
more blood" (43–5). At the moment he was apprehended, the boy stood
before Eichmann in utter vulnerability—as a thief, a young boy, and a
Jew, he could have no power—his being completely revealed: for Buber,
the sort of "meeting" through which the I–Thou could be entered. But
Eichmann, out of greed, perhaps, or perversion, cruelty or simple indifference, saw the boy instead as one more entity in a world of unrelated,
useful "things," and denied him. The third and final section, "Crystal
Night," follows almost as a result of this rejection of the intersubjective
relation. From a single denial of "love," as Buber and Levertov understand it, can arise a "Night of Broken Glass," the historic beginning of
the Nazi pogrom against the Jews.

If "During the Eichmann Trial" represents the consequences of the
denial of the I–Thou, then "A Solitude," the final poem in *The Jacob's
Ladder*, attempts to re-present the power of that relation in the world.
Although the title now bears a terrible historic implication for Levertov
(Eichmann's evil having been an act of utter disconnection or solitude),
it also recalls Rilke's claim that "a good marriage is that in which each
appoints the other guardian of his solitude" (150). Chronicling the
poet's encounter with a blind man on the subway, whom she briefly
guides on his way, the poem's narrative frame distinguishes it from
much of the volume. It is as if, after addressing Eichmann's failure to
engage with other humans and the destruction that resulted, Levertov
sought the structure of narrative to restore a pattern to the world.

The poem begins with an act of voyeurism: the speaker staring at
a blind man on the subway. Because of the man's blindness, he cannot respond to her gaze, and the speaker delights in gazing without
cease, a liberty ordinarily deemed improper. The man's status as object,
however, leaves the speaker unsated: "O, strange joy, / to gaze my

fill at a stranger's face. / No, my thirst is greater than before" (4–6). Disappointed by the experience of the I–It relation, the speaker suffers a thirst for contact, reinforced by "the quiet of people not speaking" (16) and by the isolation of the man's blindness. His blindness prohibits the sort of ordinary encounter sighted people could expect—"he doesn't know / what **look** is" (25–6)—but it guarantees that a genuine exchange could take place, because one would have to act outside of ordinary means (i.e., within the day-to-day, experiential world of the I–It) to make contact.

Finally, the speaker is not content to relate passively toward the man:

> When he gets out I get out.
> "Can I help you towards the exit?"
> "Oh, alright." An indifference.
>
> But instantly, even as he speaks,
> even as I hear indifference, his hand
> goes out, waiting for me to take it,
>
> and now we hold hands like children.
>
> (31–7)

The indifference heard in his voice recalls that of the lowly creatures in "Come Into Animal Presence," whose dissociation from human contact is transformed when met in the right relation: "What joy when the insouciant / armadillo glances at us and doesn't / quicken his trotting" (10–12). Having offered help, guidance, and company to the man, the speaker finds that though there is no change in his voice, the man readily accepts her offer, and a touch signals their new relation. Its intimacy recalls the concreteness of Levertov's motif for the I–Thou relation, the Jacob's Ladder ("The cut stone / consoles his groping feet": Levertov's choice of simile), while "and now we hold hands like children" indicates that the objectification associated with the I–It has been purified. When they part, the blind man "continues / his thoughts alone. But his hand and mine / know one another" (49–51), revealing that even when the direct relation falls away, its impress remains. At last, the man is restored to the world beyond the train station, a world "filled / with presences" (56–7), and he says, "I am," recalling the Hebrew name of the Lord, Yahweh, and exemplifying Levertov's Hasidic belief that locked in the shards of reality is the divine, which waits for the right relation to set it free.

In commenting on "The Jacob's Ladder," James Breslin describes a poetic process that is not about "finding the 'true form' of a physical object, like a straw swan, but of making substantial a symbolic and spiritual conception" (162). What Breslin seems to be describing is *sacrament*, the physical embodiment of spiritual grace. Though the term derives from a Christian context, it depends on a faith that the physical world can reveal the spiritual, a faith not unlike Hasidism's belief that worldly beings and things are shards containing sparks of the original divine essence. Revelation or release of that essence depends on the way one tries to engage with the world: either objectifying or authentically meeting it. "The Depths," an early poem in *The Jacob's Ladder*, conveys Levertov's faith in the mundane:

> Plunging
> out of the burning cold of ocean
> we enter an ocean of intense
> noon. Sacred salt
> sparkles on our bodies.
>
> After mist has wrapped us again
> in fine wool, may the taste of salt
> recall to us the great depths about us.
>
> (8–15)

Glimpsed rightly, even salt, the most common mineral, can be transformed into a sacred covering. Its taste, suggesting ceremonial consumption, reminds us of the profundity of the world that humanity inhabits, the all-too-forgotten depths. For Denise Levertov, the poem, like the sayings of the Hasidic rabbis, offers a way to mindfulness.

Notes

1. The book, therefore, provides a sort of control against which later developments in this aspect of Levertov's art—including her activism during the Vietnam conflict and her formal conversion to Catholicism—may be measured.

Works cited

Andre, Michael. "Denise Levertov: An Interview." *Conversations with Denise Levertov*. Ed. Jewel Spears Brooker. Jackson: UP of Mississippi, 1998: 52–67.

Breslin, James E. B. *From Modern to Contemporary: American Poetry, 1945–1965.* Chicago: U of Chicago P, 1984.

Buber, Martin. *I and Thou.* Trans. Walter Kaufmann. New York: Charles Scribner's Sons, 1970.

——. ed. *Tales of the Hasidim: The Later Masters.* Trans. Olga Marx. New York: Schoken Books, 1948.

Gelpi, Albert, ed. *Denise Levertov: Selected Criticism.* Ann Arbor: U of Michigan P, 1993.

Hallisey, Joan F. "Denise Levertov Sings 'The Unheard Music of That Vanished Lyre.'" *Renascence* 50.1–2 (1997): 83–93.

——. "Denise Levertov's 'Illustrious Ancestors'." *Denise Levertov: Selected Criticism.* Ed. Albert Gelpi. Ann Arbor: U of Michigan P, 1993: 260–7.

——. "Denise Levertov's 'Illustrious Ancestors' Revisited." *Studies in American Jewish Literature* 9.2 (1990): 163–75.

Hewitt, Avis. "Hasidic Hallowing and Christian Consecration: Awakening to Authenticity in Denise Levertov's 'Matins.'" *Renascence* 50.1–2 (1997): 97–107.

Lacey, Paul. *The Inner War: Forms and Themes in Recent American Poetry.* Philadelphia: Fortress Press, 1972.

Levertov, Denise. "On the Function of the Line." *New & Selected Essays.* New York, New Directions Books, 1992: 78–87.

——. *Poems 1960–1967.* New York: New Directions Books, 1966.

——. *Poems 1968–1972.* New York: New Directions Books, 1987.

——. *Sands of the Well.* New York: New Directions Books, 1996.

——. "Some Affinities of Content." *New & Selected Essays.* New York, New Directions Books, 1992: 1–21.

Marten, Harry. *Understanding Denise Levertov.* Columbia: U of South Carolina P, 1988.

Olson, Charles. *Selected Writings.* Ed. Robert Creeley. New York: New Directions Books, 1966.

Rilke, Rainer Maria. *Letters of Rainer Maria Rilke 1910–1926.* Trans. Jane Bannard Greene and M. D. Herter Norton. New York: W. W. Norton & Company, Inc., 1969.

8
Reading the Process: Stuart Hall, TV News, Heteroglossia, and Poetry

James D. Sullivan

Although Mikhail Bakhtin insists that poetic style is a closed system, he acknowledges that real live poets have to live in a polyglot world:

> Of course this relationship to his own language (in greater or lesser degree) could never be foreign to a historically existent poet, as a human being surrounded by living hetero- and polyglossia; but this relationship could not find a place in the *poetic style* of his work without destroying that style, without transposing it into a prosaic key and in the process turning the poet into a writer of prose. (Bakhtin 285, original italics)

But poems, like poets, live in that real world in which they are necessarily "surrounded by living hetero- and polyglossia." Any reader's or hearer's encounter with a poem occurs within that polyglot context of real life. Bakhtin assumes, however—as do most literary scholars—that any literary text is an abstractable linguistic construct whose material realization does not matter.

But in order to encounter a poem, we must read it or hear it in a richly coded material setting. Somebody is reciting it, or it appears on a published artifact. The performer and the venue offer contexts within which the poem is uttered, or the printed artifact quotes the poem within a visual and tangible material context (such as a book or magazine in a reader's hands, a broadside on a wall). Before the poem-bearing artifact lands in a reader's hands, the text, commodity-like, has been manipulated through a series of steps and exchanged by a number of hands. Each of those steps and hands has a different relation to the text, and each leaves a further set of quotation marks around it: poet first of all, but then editor, designer, printer, publisher, distributor, and reader, too. By reading poetry as a cultural practice, as something people do—rather than as a series of abstractable texts, linguistic constructs removable from any material context—we can see that, as poetry gets passed around, it is necessarily a heteroglot practice.

Is all this social interaction around the text simply external to the text and thus extrinsic to Bakhtin's concern with literary style? I insist that there is no text at all without some sort of artifact or performance, something available to the senses. Even if there is some unitary lyric language at the heart of the poem, we must encounter it through the codes of the artifact that bears it and the social context, the semiotically rich situation in which we encounter it. Our encounters with poetry are always heteroglot; they always lie within a series of quotation marks.

British cultural theorist Stuart Hall's model of communication, developed in his essay "Encoding, Decoding," offers a method for seeing the multi-voicedness through which any published poem speaks. Although Hall was writing about television news broadcasts, he has seen his model as more broadly applicable. He told an interviewer, "I'm only doing it with media studies because I'm talking to media people, but we could talk about any literary text or any bureaucratic piece of writing or any set of rules—anything that is a kind of recodification of something which already exists" ("Reflections" 260). Any publicly available communication, whether a sonnet or the nightly news, passes through a series of hands on its way from origination to its ultimate audience. Each of those hands takes the text passed along to it, decodes it according to its own professional or otherwise socially situated language, and then for its own purposes re-encodes it for the next moment in the sequence. Bakhtin defines heteroglossia as *"another's speech in another's language*, serving to express authorial intentions but in a refracted way. . . . It serves two speakers at the same time and expresses simultaneously two different intentions: the direct intention of the character who is speaking, and the refracted intention of the author" (Bakhtin 324, original italics). Each use of a text in the communication process is a use of another's language repurposed toward a new end. A poet's impulse for writing the poem, an editor's motive for including it in an anthology, a teacher's goal in placing it on a syllabus, and a student's understanding of it may or may not line up. Each is using an utterance of the previous moment differently. Rather than transmit the poem in bright clarity, each refracts the text through its own codes and for its own purposes.

The first part of this essay reviews Hall's "Encoding, Decoding," laying out his understanding, as of the early 1970s, of how television news processes discourse through a series of transformations. The people at each "relatively autonomous" moment take the input from the preceding moment, transform it, then pass it along newly encoded for the people at the next moment to transform in their turn. Each moment decodes, via its own language, the text passed along to it, using the text for its own purposes even while the text that the various codes work upon may remain much the same. Each moment influences the others, but no one of them has complete control over the meaning of the news report. The images that flash across the TV screen are not the total sum of the news story, but simply the interface between two moments in the total news process.

The second part adapts this model for literary studies, noting that poetry is also a series of cultural practices in which writer, publisher, distributor, and reader each decode and re-encode a poem. Each moment, fulfilling a unique function within the overall cultural practice, processes poems in its own way and thus inevitably produces different meanings—different kinds of meanings—from the other moments. As a cultural practice, poetry is therefore inescapably heteroglot.

1   Television

Hall developed his model of how television news broadcasts work in order to break out of the "transmission" models of communication and the behaviorist models of audience response then current in communication research. He wrote the essay for a 1973 colloquium at the Centre for Mass Communications Research at the University of Leicester, in part as a polemic against the use there of such models ("Reflections" 253). In such research, based on what Hall called "one or another variant of low-flying behaviorism" ("Encoding" 94), audience response was measured as a fairly direct function of sensory input. The living room is a Skinner box, TV provides the stimulus, and the broadcast researcher's goal is to analyze the conditioned responses of the audience to the broadcast images. This behaviorist model relies on a theory of communication in which the message remains, throughout the whole process, a discrete package unchanged from production to reception and which both sender and receiver understand in the same way—a perfectly manipulable independent variable that, tweaked at the production end, produces an equivalent response at the reception end. One clear voice speaks. It's the sort of unitary language Bakhtin attributes to poetic style.

British cultural studies, however, was, at that time, shifting its orientation from empirical communications research over into literary theory. Hall particularly credits the work of Roland Barthes as an influence on his own understanding of coding processes and how they complicate communication ("Reflections" 254, 271). Audiences do not just passively receive stimulation, but decode it within various frames of reference, not all of which match the frames of reference within which the shows were produced. The encoding/decoding model shows the inadequacy of models in which producers create and consumers receive the same message. Rather, a broadcast involves a series of relatively autonomous moments (which Hall labels production, circulation, distribution/consumption, and reproduction) in which people encode the event, then pass it along for others to decode and re-encode in the next moment. Furthermore, the codes used may shift as reporters, producers, and viewers of television news each process the information passed along from earlier moments via codes appropriate to their own material situations and frames of reference. Sometimes in this game of media telephone, those codes match up from moment to moment, and sometimes they do not.

Production

A reporter, along with a camera crew, encounters raw data, an event. Something happens: a train wrecks (or a poet happens upon a field of daffodils). But as Hall writes, "A 'raw' historical event cannot, *in that form*, be transmitted by, say, a television newscast. Events can only be signified within the aural–visual forms of televisual discourse. . . . To put it paradoxically, the event must become a 'story' before it can become a *communicative event*" ("Encoding" 92, original italics). The reporter's verbal description and comment, the position of the camera, the framing of the image, the sounds, and the selection of which details of the event even count as reportable: all those, composed according to the prevailing codes of journalism (or, to be Bakhtinian about it, the *language* of journalism), place the inarticulate event into discourse and thereby endow it with meanings. The crew on the spot does the initial encoding.

When a story originates from industry, government, or some other hegemonic institution, however, the reporter finds it already encoded via dominant hegemonic codes, the codes by which powerful institutions make their authoritative pronouncements. A news story beginning, "According to the Pentagon . . . ," or, "Caterpillar, Inc., has announced . . . ," will convey information already encoded such that it represents the interest of the originating institution. In this case, the reporter reprocesses it through what Hall calls the professional code, a code that, for the most part, works comfortably within the dominant hegemonic code ("Encoding" 101). The announcement is treated as a newsworthy event itself, and the reporter's job is not to find ways of encoding an inarticulate event, but to package an already encoded message precisely *as* an event, reporting the fact of the statement rather than its content. The moment of production, therefore, treats the utterance of a hegemonic institution as though it were, in Bakhtin's sense, a poem: "In genres that are poetic in the narrow sense, the natural dialogization of the word is not put to artistic use, the word is sufficient unto itself and does not presume alien utterances beyond its own boundaries. Poetic style is by convention suspended from any mutual interaction with alien discourse, any allusion to alien discourse" (Bakhtin 285). The alien discourse of journalism passes along the press release or sound bite in all its lyric clarity without reprocessing it.

Circulation

Visible quotation marks now appear. The story the crew has encoded is then submitted to people with the technical capacity to put the story into circulation: the producers and technicians. While the functionaries at this second moment are likely to share with the crew who initially encoded the story some assumptions about the role and function of professional journalism in general, their specific interests and functions do not quite match up with those of the reporters. While the reporter's job is to give an initial articulation to raw events, the television producer's job is primarily to perpetuate the discourse of the show, to read the reporter's work for those images that will make a successful broadcast, to place those images into the pre-existing format of the show in such a way as to keep people watching and keep the ratings high so that the format may repeat itself for broadcast after broadcast, on into the foreseeable future. So television producers will not only cut a story to fit an available segment but also make other changes not necessarily consistent with the reporter's understanding of the event. They place it in a context of other events reported in that day's newscast, creating thereby juxtapositions by which stories may inflect one another. The anchor's lead in and lead out offer further interpretive context. Having decoded for their own purposes the story offered them, those with authority over circulation re-encode it for broadcast.

When the broadcast image is then distributed for public consumption, it is not exactly cast out with utter ignorance as to its fate, but with some idea of the codes people will use to decode the images on their television screens. As Hall notes, those involved in the earlier moments in the process have an interest in the audience's decoding the story in a way that corresponds to earlier encodings. That is, these two earlier moments are explicitly rhetorical and dialogic, anticipating and seeking to influence the responses of the later moments. Despite the theoretical inadequacy of the transmission model, it remains an ideal toward which reporters (and many poets) aspire. Those involved in the earlier moments (production and circulation) have an interest in the audience's decoding the stories with a minimum of distortion. Reporters learn to package their stories in such a way that editors and studio technicians will feel the least need to tinker. Studies of audience attitudes and viewing habits help those in charge of circulation craft their stories in such a way that they can minimize misunderstandings—that is, decodings via contrary codes. Expectations of later decodings are, therefore, embedded in earlier moments in the process. So even while transforming the languages of earlier moments, they include also the languages of later decodings. This is precisely what Bakhtin calls "the internal dialogism of the word": writers and speakers form their utterances in response to and out of already available languages and in anticipation of probable rejoinders and responses (280). The various moments, however, are relatively autonomous in that no moment can guarantee that the next will employ compatible codes, but determinate in that the output of each moment provides the input for the next.

Distribution/consumption

Earlier moments in the process—especially production and circulation— have an interest in anticipating and determining how later moments will decode what they have been handed. They therefore encode in such a way as to approach the transmission model. Decoding at the moment of consumption, however, is not answerable to the transmission ideal. The consuming audience need not decode the story in a way faithful to its encoding. But they usually do. Though misunderstandings and decodings via contrary codes do occur, most of the audience will decode the images offered them via the dominant hegemonic codes—the codes most familiar and most fully naturalized. Yet especially in coverage of policy debates, segments of the audience are likely to consume the broadcast via contrary codes. Hall concedes that literal misunderstandings occur, but he argues that they are not the primary means of contrary decodings:

> No doubt misunderstandings of a literal kind do exist. The viewer does not know the terms employed, cannot follow the complex logic

of argument or exposition, is unfamiliar with the language, finds the concepts too alien or difficult or is foxed by the expository narrative. But more often broadcasters are concerned that the audience has failed to take the meaning as they—the broadcasters—intended. What they really mean to say is that viewers are not operating within the "dominant" or "preferred" code. Their ideal is "perfectly transparent communication." Instead, what they have to confront is "systematically distorted communication." ("Encoding" 99–100)

Any broadcaster has an interest in diminishing "misunderstandings of a literal kind," but can never eliminate them altogether. Even among viewers perfectly attuned to the intellectual and ideological demands of the program, there remains a constant possibility for lapses of attention and distractions in the room that lead them to miss or mishear a key point in the argument, thus distorting their decoding. But according to Hall, those random distortions—"noise" in the transmission—trouble broadcasters less than do more systematic distortions.

Generally, people receive input clearly, and generally they decode it via the codes used to encode it, but Hall suggests that most distortions occur around two general clusters, a "negotiated code" and an "oppositional code." A negotiated code presumes the hegemonic code. It accepts the authority of the dominant view as globally and abstractly legitimate, but overlays that understanding with a more locally situated code that reads the local implications of that logic. What's good for the country as a whole is not necessarily good for me and people like me. Hall offers an example: "At the level of the 'national interest' economic debate the decoder may adopt the hegemonic definition, agreeing that 'we must all pay ourselves less in order to combat inflation.' This, however, may have little or no relation to his/her willingness to go on strike for better pay and conditions" ("Encoding" 102). Despite the general acceptance of the anti-inflation principle, that specific refusal of its local implications looks, from the perspective of earlier moments in the process, like a misunderstanding of the economic message.

Some viewers reject the dominant frame of reference altogether, producing a contrary re-encoding via an oppositional code. Hall describes "the viewer who . . . 'reads' every mention of the 'national interest' as 'class interest'" ("Encoding" 103). While use of negotiated codes indicates a continuing global identification with the hegemonic position, use of oppositional codes suggests an overall negation of the hegemonic position—not just a straying from it under the contingent pressure of local conditions, but an overall refusal to recognize its legitimacy.

Watching TV news is, therefore, not a purely passive, receptive activity, but as Hall sees it, a dialogic activity in which viewers deploy a repertoire of languages in response to the broadcast languages.

Reproduction

The discourse passes through a series of transformations, no moment sure that the next utterance will necessarily foreground or even preserve its meanings. At each point, however, "[i]f meaning is not articulated in practice, it has no effect" (Hall, "Encoding" 91). There is no meaning—that is, meaning is not produced or transformed by a further series of codings—if no reporter covers the event, if broadcast executives tacitly cut the story, or if people don't watch the show. At any point, the discourse can halt if the next moment simply fails to pick it up. Nor does it necessarily just end, however, when the broadcast image strikes the viewer's eyes and fires the neurons that decode it. If the process of signification ends when the viewer frames an understanding, then, too, the process comes to a halt.

One of the goals of the earlier moment—most particularly of circulation—is to keep the process running. They want to produce and circulate stories that keep enough people tuned in day after day so that they may keep their jobs. Without that reproduction of the process, the whole cycle winds down. From the broadcasters' perspective, the reproduction of the viewing habit is the most pressing concern. A less urgent, implicit concern is the maintenance of social structures on a broader level—the mode of production and the attendant distributions of power—that make the broadcast operation itself possible. This particular concern, however, lies so deep in the political unconscious that, in the current US context, it seldom rises to the consciousness of people busy with the everyday work of broadcasting. In societies facing radical social and political change, however, this issue rises to the forefront of media policy. The outcome of a revolution may determine not only the fates of the broadcasting institutions, but also the personal fates of the production and circulation personnel.

Analysis of reproduction, therefore, focuses on the broadcast's ultimate effects on audience behavior. What do people do in response to watching a TV show? Here the analytic lure of "low-flying behaviorism" becomes especially strong and must be countered with a rejection of any one-to-one correspondence between specific broadcast images and specific subsequent behaviors. In some sense, the ultimate meaning of the whole process lies here, in the social effects of the broadcast on the large, media-consuming public, how they re-encode the discourse into subsequent behavior. That meaning is never, of course, unified, because people will have a diversity of responses to any particular program, tending toward, but seldom limited to, simple reproduction of the viewing habit. The entire discourse, however, from production through reproduction, displays a tremendous diversity of signifying practices. One cannot reasonably focus on the final moment without considering the range of practices that provide the input for that moment. The significance of the discourse lies in that whole net of practices, codes, and quotations. The point of Hall's model of communication is to understand the broadcast not as a lisible text, but as a set of practices that transform a discourse many times throughout a process. Each moment quotes, and thus inflects, the ones before it, providing break-points where the application of different codes can disturb any direct transmission of ideology.

2 Poetry

Hall offers a model of TV news as a cultural practice, a chain of trans-formative codings by people in various relations to the news broadcast. This model may be adapted to a variety of communication practices, but it is particularly apt for an analysis of the cultural practice of poetry, an art form that, especially in the lyric mode, continues to create an impression of an unmediated voice, a direct communication between writer and reader. While Bakhtin treats this unmediated, unitary voice as the defining characteristic of poetry, he admits in a footnote that he exaggerates: "It goes without saying that we continually embrace as typical the extreme to which poetic genres aspire; in concrete examples of poetic works it is possible to find features fundamental to prose, and numerous hybrids of various generic types exist" (Bakhtin 287). While a genre as an abstract generality may aspire to such a unity of voice, "concrete examples of poetic works," real published poems, cannot, and Hall's model shows how heteroglossia enters the material cultural practice of poetry.

The model I am developing from Hall implies a disjunction between moments. Hall focuses on the *activity* of coding, which, in his model, looks like commodity exchange. Later moments take the work of earlier moments and manipulate it for their own purposes. Having taken up the product of a previous moment, a reader has no necessary respon-sibility to decode it according to the previous moment's expectations. Each moment transforms the material available to it around its own "preferred reading," which the next may or may not assume. They don't have to accept the earlier moments' readings as they quote the text passed along to them. Nonetheless, those earlier readings may remain legible within the quotation marks.

Poems are manipulated by people who stand in different material relations to them, each person decoding and re-encoding according to a different frame of reference. The poem is not fixed at a particular moment (the poet's final draft, the published page, the impressions of a first reading), but is a malleable object of cultural practice, something people approach and use in a variety of ways throughout a dynamic process. Poets (production) and publishers (circulation) encode the work. Institutions—most prominently booksellers, libraries, and schools—make the work available in specific settings and circumstances (distribution). And consumers of poetry decode it not only as readers (consumption), but also as citizens responding to its implications in their later behavior after they have set the book down (reproduction). This model focuses on the material life of the poem as an ever-shifting object of cultural practice rather than as a static text by which a poet speaks in an undistorted single voice to a reader.

Production

A poet writing a poem is like a reporter putting together a story, producing the initial encoding that will later undergo all the subsequent transformations. Just as a reporter encodes raw data into a story via the professional codes of journalism, a poet encodes observations via the conventions of genre. But while the journalists' professional code constrains them to relay institutional statements—from speeches, interviews, press releases, and press conferences—with a minimum of manipulation, poetic convention *presumes* subjective manipulation of the discourse. While modern journalism values objectivity and a suppression of the reporter's personality, since at least the Romantic era, we have valued precisely those signs of subjective manipulation in poetry. Analysis of the production phase, therefore, focuses on a poet's selection of objects for poems, selections of noteworthy details, and the process of encoding those selections into poetic discourse.

A reading of "Two Dedications" by Gwendolyn Brooks, for example, might focus on her choice to juxtapose her public verses upon the dedication of two very different works of public art in Chicago in August 1967: Pablo Picasso's sculpture for the Civic Center Plaza and a collaborative mural in and by the African American community of the South Side. In one case, she focuses her attention on the perplexity and alienation many citizens felt before the new, modernist object in the middle

of the Loop: "Does man love Art? Man visits Art, but squirms" (442).
The tone is ironic and detached from the artwork and the occasion:

> Observe the tall cold of a Flower
> which is as innocent and as guilty,
> as meaningful and as meaningless as any
> other flower in the western field.

(443)

In the other, she focuses not on the mural, but on the vitality of the
crowd come to celebrate its dedication:

> In front of me
> hundreds of faces, red-brown, brown, black, ivory,
> yield me hot trust, their yea and their Announcement
> that they are ready to rile the high-flung ground.
> Behind me, Paint.

(445)

And the tone is full of sensual pleasure in both the things described and
the language used to describe them:

> South of success and east of gloss and glass are
> sandals;
> flowercloth;
> grave hoops of wood or gold, pendant
> from black ears, brown ears, reddish-brown
> and ivory ears[.]

(444)

Much of the poem's meaning, therefore, is a function of the poet's selections: what, from all the raw data available to her in the occasions for
the poem, she chooses to relay—as well as the distinct tone, diction,
and form of each part.

Furthermore, Brooks takes previous discourse—the artworks and the
public response to them—as the focus of the poem. She uses and comments upon others' discourse in a heteroglot way. Brooks's language is,
thus, not self-contained, but responds to other artistic discourses: the
high modernist and the Black Arts-populist. Although in this poem
Brooks is clearly responding to two specific and contrasting cultural
traditions, any poet has to situate a poem in relation to a generic or

cultural tradition, using, manipulating, and responding to the characteristic languages of that tradition. Shakespeare, for another example, thus uses and comments upon the language of the Petrarchan tradition in his own sonnets. From Sonnet 130, "My mistress' eyes are nothing like the sun": the speaker's word "nothing" comments upon the artificiality of the Petrarchan language in the rest of the line. Or when his sonneteer asks, in Sonnet 18, "Shall I compare thee to a summer's day?" he again invokes Petrarchan language, but for a double purpose: first, the purpose internal to that language, praise for the beauty of the beloved, and second ("So long as men can breathe, or eyes can see / So long lives this" [lines 13–14]), as an objective demonstration of his mastery of that language, a language that he did not originate, but which he has taken and transformed for his own purposes.

Circulation

Publishers manipulate and contextualize poems; they keep the gates. Editors base their acceptance decisions on the specific goals and discourses of the magazine or publishing house. "Quality" is everybody's watchword, of course, but different publishers define that word differently. Poems of the highest quality are those that best fit or that extend the discourse of the publisher. Whatever decodings an editor may generate while reading a poem, the usual institutional output of that decoding is binary—to print or not. A thumbs up indicates an editorial decoding that has fit the poem into the publisher's discourse, a judgment that it furthers the publisher's marketing image and its goals. A magazine or a press known to have a particular political slant, for instance, can be expected to publish work consistent with that slant. Although some contemporary poets may get their work printed in or at least reviewed favorably in, for example, both *The Nation* and *The New Criterion*, some poets are more likely to show up in one than in the other. Or a book publisher has a particular aesthetic for which it is known, a particular kind of poetry readers expect to find in the books under that imprint. Glancing up at my bookshelf for an example, I see, standing side by side in alphabetical happenstance, the *Selected Poems* of both A. R. Ammons and David Antin. Establishment press W. W. Norton has published one, avant-garde and defunct Sun & Moon the other, respectively. Familiar with both books, both writers, and both presses, I cannot easily imagine the reverse. Accepting a poem for publication accepts it into a particular discourse. Poets exert some degree of influence over this decoding by submitting their work to or acceding to a request from a particular publisher—an encoding from the moment of production that reads the work into a particular publisher's discourse. The first major disjunction of codes, however, can occur at this point, when poets are unaware of or perhaps misread the preferred discourses of the publisher. Every editor who reads unsolicited manuscripts knows this disjunction—that pile of manuscripts that demonstrate little awareness of the publisher's focus or audience.

Contexualization in an anthology (via an introduction, annotation, or juxtaposition with other works), emphasis in a magazine (cover blurb? buried in the back? juxtaposed with what other poems or articles?), placement in a collection, illustrations and other graphics, as well as any advertisements or other promotions—all encode. When Robert Bly published Walt Whitman's "To the States" as the first poem of his anthology *Forty Poems Touching on Recent American History*, Whitman's disgust at "a filthy Presidentiad" and his warnings of the "gathering murk" (21) referred no longer to the political cowardice of Whitman's 1850s, but to the moment when Bly selected it, 1970. The poet's verse became the editor's utterance.

The quality of the printing, the paper, and the font all suggest the cultural status of the discourse, to what extent the publisher is encoding it as high art, low art, or anti-art—its status in the cultural hierarchy. Compare two periodicals from the 1960s: the gracefully crafted pages for the formalist verse of *Kenyon Review* and the typewritten, mimeographed pages for the open-form poetry in LeRoi Jones and Diane DiPrima's *The Floating Bear*. Whatever literary statement the poems make appears within the graphic statement the publication makes about its place and its content's place in the culture.

Distribution

As far as television is concerned, distribution and consumption are generally simultaneous: the broadcasters transmit the shows (circulation), which reach their public via TV screens (distribution), and the public watches them right there and then (consumption). The context of distribution (where the set sits, when it is switched on) is identical with the context of consumption; no other institutions usually mediate between the broadcasters and the audience. Other institutions besides publishers, however, also filter and re-encode poetic discourse. School curricula and course syllabi, for instance, have an enormous influence on students' exposure to poetry, contextualizing for them what poetry is and how it is read. Since the classroom is, for most Americans, the site of their most extended exposure to poetry, the poems selected for them in that context decisively shape their understanding of it. In their capacity as shapers of curricula and syllabi, educators use the goals of their programs and courses as the codes for a binary decoding of poems (to use or not). They then re-encode the work within a pedagogic context of other readings, class assignments, lectures, and so on. When we give our students a critical vocabulary for discussing poetry, we are encouraging them to read poems within that critical language.

Libraries, booksellers, and distributors also read in terms of their institutional missions and the potential market. A bookseller or library, considering whether to stock something, decides, in effect, whether to present it to the public as an utterance of the institution. What does it suggest about us that we carry such a work? Is it consistent with the sort of work people come here to find? Does it further our mission? They read the discourses of the work through their own institutional discourses and also through the prospective discourses of their clients. Most bookstores and libraries, of course, aspire to a correspondence between the utterances upon their shelves and the demands of their audiences. They aspire, that is, to a transparent transmission of the artifact from earlier moments toward the moment of consumption. However, although these institutions usually lack the more direct influence of editors and publishers over linguistic content and material form, publishers' expectations about what those institutions will buy affects what they publish and in what form. At one time these institutions had a near veto power, within a particular community, that publishers themselves lacked, though with the dominance of on-line megastores, that particular kind of influence may now be over.

Readers seldom access published poems except through some social mediation. A poem assigned at school, for example, will appear as part of the discourse of that institution, or at least of a particular class. The reputation of a bookstore provides a framework of expectations regarding the books one will find there. Even outside an institutional context, a book recommended or lent by a friend or family member will bear the mark of that person as one opens it. All books have a provenance. And the book, magazine, pamphlet, or broadside speaks from the discourse of that provenance, the artifact's material history, within which the reader comes upon the literary artifact.

Consumption

The readers of this fourth moment are the potentially heterogeneous group who decode not only the poem's words, but also the published artifact that bears those words.

The specific social and material setting of reading likewise inflects the decoding. In my study of American poetry broadsides of the 1960s,

I cite numerous examples of how that material setting—at an antiwar rally, in a radical bookstore, on a living room or bedroom wall, in a museum, in a special collections library, on a street corner, or on the quad at a moment of high tension on campus—encodes a poem, uses the poet's language in a context and for a purpose that the poet may not have imagined. Most books, magazines, and pamphlets, however, are so portable that this particular point of analysis is usually out of our reach as critics. Only in the case of very rare artifacts can we be certain of the conditions under which they are read, because access may be available only in a particular collection, perhaps during specific hours and only to people with certain credentials. In all reading situations, however conventional, the specific material and social conditions always produce meaning.

More readily available to critical scrutiny are the material qualities of the artifact. From production to circulation and from circulation through distribution to consumption, the discourse passes via some material embodiment, some artifact or performance that makes it available to the senses. Publishers receive from writers not just poems, but documents that embody poems—the manuscripts. Galleys, page proofs, and other correspondence may pass between them as documents that embody further elaborations or refinements of the text. Publishers, likewise, are in the business of making and distributing artifacts that further bear the discourse along to its audiences: books, periodicals, pamphlets, broadsides, postcards, websites, and posters for the overhead ad spaces on city buses. Audiences receive the discourse through some physical, sensual medium that inflects the decoding, that socially encodes the discourse in the binding and design of a book, the layout of a magazine, page design, editorial apparatus, the quality and colors of the paper and the ink, evidence of the technology used to print it, the font and size of the print. All these bibliographic codes, essential elements of the literary artifact, unavoidable elements of the sensual activity of reading, enter the hands and eyes of a reader not, in most cases, at the center of sensual or intellectual attention, but as a necessary part of it, a set of codes within which lie the literary codes, which are themselves inaccessible (non-existent, even) except through and with the bibliographic codes.

All these codes (provenance, site of reading, artifactual materiality, language) are liable, in much the same ways as news telecasts, to misunderstandings (that is, decodings inconsistent with the preferred readings of earlier moments). Despite all attempts at editorial annotation and classroom contextualization, "misunderstandings of the literal kind" are, if anything, far more common in the consumption of poetry than in the consumption of television news. Though such readings come to our attention most glaringly among the untrained readers of our introductory-level classes, "misreadings of the literal kind" occur among readers at all levels of sophistication. But beyond the intense critical attention we may bring to bear on a poem when preparing a critical essay or a class lecture, most people's literary experiences, even most reading experiences of critical professionals, lack the laser-keen focus and discipline of close reading. Heterogeneous codes, therefore, can sometimes enter the discourse at the point of consumption even among readers in closest ideological and intellectual harmony with poet and publisher.

While Hall presupposes that television news is encoded, in the moments of production and circulation, in clearly hegemonic terms, and while much, perhaps most, poetry may also fit quite comfortably within hegemony, a much greater share of poetry than of TV news falls outside it. Adrienne Rich and Lawrence Ferlinghetti, to pick two prominent examples, certainly employ oppositional codes (feminist in one case, anarchist in the other) at the moment of production. As publisher of the City Lights Pocket Poetry series, Ferlinghetti likewise has employed an oppositional code in the unconventional design of those square little books. They diverge from standard book shape and size, suggesting a divergence inside from mainstream poetics, and their design has become, since the 1950s, an icon for poetry associated with the Beat Generation.

Certainly, readers have decoded hegemonically encoded poetic texts in the three ways Hall suggests viewers decode TV news. Take, for example, that classic hegemonic poetic utterance: Robert Frost's reading "The Gift Outright" at John Kennedy's inauguration. Invocation for one of our highest civic rituals, uttered with the blessing of and as a blessing upon the pinnacle of political authority, by a writer popularly recognized as wielder of the authentic national voice—few American poems have commanded such a powerful position of cultural authority. You can't get more hegemonic than that. Decoded within the spirit of the inauguration (as most who heard it that day would have), it is a nationalist poem celebrating the national destiny toward which all present were to dedicate themselves:

> The land was ours before we were the land's.
> She was our land more than a hundred years
> Before we were her people. She was ours
> In Massachusetts, in Virginia,
> But we were England's, still colonials[.]
>
> (lines 1–4)

Hearers committed at the time to the integrationist spirit of the early civil rights movement, however, may have employed a negotiated code, accepting the poem's nationalist ideals, but recognizing the racial exclusions implicit in its anglocentrism; they may have recognized in it also the national sin of denying many citizens the benefits of those ideals. And in the decades since its most famous utterance, the poem has become a pedagogic chestnut, a handy example one can use to teach introductory level students about reading against the grain, focusing on the exclusion of all non-English immigrants who came to or were taken to the New World, but most flagrantly of the native population already here: "To the land vaguely realizing westward, / But still unstoried, artless, unenhanced, / Such as she was, such as she would become" (lines 14–16). As a sign of racist nationalism, it has become an exemplary tutor text for oppositional decoding. The languages within which the readers receive the utterance, therefore, change the statement.

Attention to counter-hegemonic verse is a sign of the misreading of culture. This is what the culture wars and the canon debates were about: "misunderstandings" of culture in precisely the way Hall shows TV viewers misunderstanding the news by employing negotiated or oppositional codes, only in this case, the apparently willful misunderstanding occurs at the very beginning of the decoding process, when a reader passes up the acknowledged masterworks and selects the wrong book. From this perspective, according serious scholarly and critical attention to the popular likes of Edgar Guest, Burma Shave signs, or Hallmark greeting card verse, for example (as Mike Chasar has done recently), looks like a clear error in judgment. Politicized readings of canonical works and writers are likewise "misunderstandings" of their intent and their cultural significance.

Reproduction

How does reading poems affect people's behavior? Magazine editors may hope it moves readers to pick up the next issue when it comes out. Teachers may hope the classroom experience of poetry encourages students to read more of it. Students may hope it earns them a grade, a credit, or a degree. A poet of any ambition tries to produce works that will make editors and readers want more. A good publication record and an MFA may even land one a teaching job—someone's reading of the poems would thus produce the meaning, "Hire this poet." From the perspective of some earlier moments in the process, the optimal effect includes the reproduction of a similar experience, developed into a reading habit, just as broadcasters try to reinforce the viewing habit. Another part of that process is to reproduce, at the broadest level of generalization—so broad as to seldom rise to consciousness—the social conditions that permit the production, circulation, distribution, consumption, and redistribution of more poetry.

Beyond the economic (buy more magazines or books) and the pedagogic functions (produce essays and class discussions, earn a credit), specific effects of poetry reading are usually as elusive as the effects of a TV show. Again, one must resist the "low-flying behaviorism" that connects specific texts with specific subsequent behaviors. Poets, editors, or teachers with specific agendas may hope reading will transform the social behavior of readers, but they certainly cannot predict the myriad sympathies and resistances among which the text will fall. Any sizable pressrun disseminates an edition to an untraceably diverse audience. Small editions with narrow and tightly focused distribution may reach an audience specific enough that one might hazard a guess as to its effects, but even then, the guess would have to extend through a whole range of effects as even a solidarity of readers apply all their peculiar, personal reading practices to it amid the disparities and distractions of their separate lives. And even in the spectacularly unlikely occasion that everyone at a political rally, receiving the same poem-laden handout, should—caught up as they might be in the soul-stirring rhetoric of the occasion—decode it in exactly the same way, its effects on their later behavior once they head home will be as various and untraceable as anything else at the rally. Even among readers who interpret political poetry with the greatest sympathy, the actual impact may extend no further than the delight they feel at reading such radical stuff.

Yet that delight reproduces the conditions for producing the poetry in the first place. Adrienne Rich, for example, could publish more feminist poetry, which could be fairly widely circulated by Norton, precisely because enough readers decoded her other work with satisfaction. That satisfaction reproduces the demand not (or not only) for poetry in general, but for the particular kind of poetry that produced that satisfaction. The reproduction of the desire to read similar works suggests the reproduction of sympathy with the ideological orientation of the work. The cultural work of the text may lie in reproducing, in the readers, the ideological conditions that led to the writer's producing the text. Or in the case of oppositional criticism (as in the example of reading Frost against the grain), the cultural work of the lesson may lie in reproducing the ideological conditions that might lead a reader to regularly employ oppositional codes. The desire to read more Rich with sympathy or the desire to read more Frost with skepticism is the result of a political poetic practice that reproduces an ideological orientation.

Hall wanted to show that a news broadcast is not a unified message. Each moment in the communication process does not just transparently pass along the message handed to it. Instead, each moment receives the text from the previous moment, then decodes it in its own language and for its own purposes, not necessarily according to the codes and preferred readings of any of the previous moments. It then re-encodes a text to pass along to the next moment, and neither the codes nor even the text are necessarily identical to the codes and texts from earlier in the process. Nor can a given moment be sure that later moments will employ the same codes or pass along an identical text. At each point in the process, new meanings can emerge, old ones get distorted or suppressed.

In poetry, on the other hand, the convention is to maintain a respect for the writer's words—even if later moments recontextualize and repurpose them—rather than manhandle them as the news broadcast process can do to a reporter's work. The different moments in the cultural practice of poetry use the text to produce different meanings. But the meanings possible at each moment are not wide open. Each moment relies on the text and context provided by the earlier moments, and for its own decoding and re-encoding it relies on the codes available to it, so while no moment is entirely answerable to an earlier moment, the materially realized texts provided by the earlier moments do partly determine what those moments can do.

If we therefore apply Hall's model of the communication process to poetry, it meshes nicely with Bakhtin's poetics. Because of this convention of respect for the original words, each moment ends up quoting the text provided by the moments before it. Uttered anew by a publisher, bookseller, teacher, or reader, the poem takes on new meanings in its new contexts while, through the quoted words, retaining traces of the earlier moments.

Discussing poetry, thus, as a cultural practice rather than as a fixed set of texts—discussing it as a practice in which people in a variety of relations to poetic texts pick them up, manipulate them, and pass them along in a new context—shows that any published poem is necessarily heteroglot. Without this cacophonous heteroglossia, without this blooming of quotation marks upon quotation marks on either side of every poem, I'd never be able to read these rows of poems on my shelves.

Works cited

Ammons, A. R. *The Selected Poems: 1951–1977*. New York: Norton, 1977.
Antin, David. *Selected Poems: 1963–1973*. Los Angeles: Sun & Moon, 1991.

Bakhtin, M. M. "Discourse in the Novel." *The Dialogic Imagination.* Ed. Michael Holquist. Trans. Caryl Emerson and Michael Holquist. Austin: U of Texas P, 1981. 259–422.

Bly, Robert, ed. *Forty Poems Touching on Recent American History.* Boston: Beacon, 1970.

Brooks, Gwendolyn. "Two Dedications." *Blacks.* Chicago: The David Company, 1987. 442–5.

Chasar, Mike. *Everyday Reading: Poetry and Popular Culture in Modern America.* New York: Columbia UP, 2012.

Frost, Robert. "The Gift Outright." *The Poetry of Robert Frost.* New York: Holt, 1979. 348.

Hall, Stuart. "Encoding, Decoding." *The Cultural Studies Reader.* Ed. Simon During. London and New York: Routledge, 1993. 90–103.

——. "Reflections upon the Encoding/Decoding Model: An Interview." *Viewing, Reading, Listening: Audiences and Cultural Reception.* Ed. Jon Cruz and Justin Lewis. Boulder: Westview, 1994. 253–74.

Shakespeare, William. *The Riverside Shakespeare.* 2nd ed. Ed. G. Blakemore Evans and J. M. Tobin. Boston: Houghton Mifflin, 1996.

Sullivan, James D. *On the Walls and in the Streets: American Poetry Broadsides from the 1960s.* Urbana: U of Illinois P, 1997.

9
Dialogic Poetry as Emancipatory Technology: Ventriloquy and Voiceovers in the Rhythmic Junctures of Harryette Mullen's *Muse & Drudge*

Andrea Witzke Slot

"A people is many individuals."

(Harryette Mullen)

With its multi-voiced arena, extreme word play, and remixing of images and voices, Harryette Mullen's 81-page poem *Muse & Drudge* is anything but easy. Sometimes the complexities of the text spin with such speed that readers wonder if they have inadvertently skipped lines or missed something crucial to interpreting the text. But the quick movement and constantly changing points of view are, in fact, the point—the crux of the poem's dialogic drive that emulates the social worlds in which we live. With its meeting ground of numerous subjective (and therefore ideological) positions, Mullen's poem produces new patterns that recognize and alter the subjugating narratives and ideologies that continue to pervade American culture, media, and history. More specifically, Mullen creates a double play of ventriloquy in *Muse & Drudge* to project the subjective positions of both the oppressor and the oppressed (and everything in between); in doing so, the text throws out the polarities of culture's rigged and racial typecasts and replaces them with a multidimensional matrix of possible selves. As these various perspectives become more defined and yet simultaneously altered through their engagement with one another, they begin to reshape the invisible power of habitual thought and media consumption that so often leads to unrecognized or unacknowledged (and therefore more insidious) forms of subjugation. In other words, a poem like Mullen's, if engaged fully, can change thought patterns and actions as readers gain an illuminated understanding of culture's ideological traps, which negatively impact society as a whole, no matter what one's race, color, class, or gender.

This essay will first examine how a poem's dialogic capabilities are made possible through its use of subjectivity and linguistic innovation. It will then demonstrate how these poetic properties work within Mullen's dialogic text, *Muse & Drudge*, and how they help the poem become a dynamic means of emancipatory technology of the kind Chela Sandoval explores in her work. Sometimes the dialogic engagement of ideologies happens within the sweeping overarching dialogic engagement in Mullen's poem, but so too does it happen in brief and powerfully packed dialogized passages—Bakhtinian words-with-a-sideways-glance. Ultimately, the poem's rhythm and movement become a way of allowing readers to enter its complex social realm even when they are unsure of meaning. In order to illustrate this point more clearly, the poem's structural and linguistic movement will be linked to Houston A. Baker's image of the railway juncture, a powerful metaphor for the complexities of voice in African American culture, history, and ideology. Using the musical elements of *train-wheels-over-track-junctures* images and sounds, the poem moves closer and closer to both the absent and the imagined bodies of a people (some of which never existed except in the fiction of media stereotypes), merging the representational with the literal as the text exposes and rewrites a difficult U.S. past and present. Although still relatively hard to find, and too often overlooked in multi-ethnic, post-colonial, cultural, gender, and even literary studies, dialogic poetry has the potential to incite change in the thought patterns that unwittingly uphold systems of subjugation and power by allowing us to see the past and the present in new ways. Mullen's *Muse & Drudge* is an example of just such a poem.

In order to understand how dialogism meets emancipatory change in Mullen's work, it is important to define dialogic poetry and examine just how it can be a force for ideological regeneration. First of all, dialogic poetry must be distinguished from polyvocal poetry. Polyvocal poetry, while multi-voiced, does not present the same kind of engagement between and among distinct subjective (and therefore ideological) positions. Like dialogic novels, dialogic poems use the clashing content of various ideological positions to loosen the power structures that are embedded in the language we use and the social spheres we occupy. This fundamental element of Mikhail Bakhtin's theories on dialogism is too often underplayed in the studies currently available concerning poetic dialogism. It is no secret that Bakhtin dismissed the possibilities of poetic dialogism, and while a number of critics have successfully addressed the dialogic and heteroglossic elements of poetry, many of these studies focus on excavating the various positions of a single self inside what many would see as monologic poetry, which is certainly not without value.[1] No current work, though, fully addresses what I see as the driving impetus of Bakhtinian dialogism in its application to dialogic poetry—namely, the incorporation of distinctly different ideological positions that simultaneously delineate and alter one another through their subjective engagement, which in turn creates constantly shifting modes of meaning. Moreover, few, if any, such studies focus on the range of emancipatory possibilities in specific dialogic poems.

Dialogism in poetry, in fact, has the potential to be even more powerful than in fiction due to two principal features that have always defined the poetic form. The first is poetry's subjectivity, or interiority of thought, the key reason for Bakhtin's dismissal of poetry's dialogic functionality, while the second involves the high-level linguistic play possible in the poetic form. To address the first, subjectivity, it is worth revisiting Bakhtin's theories concerning the utterance, the reply, and the creation of meaning in dialogism as applied to the novel. In his book *Dialogism: Bakhtin and his World*, Michael Holquist reminds us that for Bakhtin the relationship between utterance and reply (be it in "real time" or literary dialogue) gives the utterance *as well as* the reply meaning; in other words, the utterance and the reply must be set in motion for meaning to be enacted. This utterance and reply give each "I" or "self" context, especially when a plethora of "I"'s (characters, narrators, authorial interruptions) come into conversation as different voices. The *connective* and *defining* features of simultaneity cannot be emphasized enough; we are all isolated in the act of speech, Holquist reminds us, but this isolation is something we all share. And within this shared isolation lies hope of some kind for community and humanity, for, as Holquist writes, "in so far as my 'I' is dialogic, it ensures that my existence is not a lonely event but part of a larger whole" (38). Dialogism is about "multiplicity in human perspective" (22), and that multiplicity is the root of "shared loneliness," so to speak. Poetic dialogism (especially the kind that can initiate social change) is therefore not just a matter of identity but also of community as our individual voices are only created in a context of what lies beyond us—i.e., the *other*. "In Bakhtin, the very capacity to have consciousness is based on *otherness*," Holquist writes, as well as a "differential relation between a center and all that is not that center" (18). In relation to the "I," this means that the "center" is "a *relative* rather than an absolute term, and, as such, one with no claim to absolute privilege" (18). Thus, the concept of "self" is always constructed through context—through the relation of self to other, or, more precisely, the relation to a community of "selves," none of which has priority over the others. These subjective "I"s are democratized in a dialogic text, which allows the various voices (and ideologies) to *engage* with one another and not just talk *at* one another.

These various expressive selves link to the fundamental nature of subjectivity. Poetry, of course, has been defined by its subjective, singular point of view for centuries, with the concept of a single-voiced, monologic perspective being the long-time calling card of lyric poetry in particular. This perception of poetry continues to be held by many today even with the anti-lyric "I" stance that won approval among Language and experimental poets.[2] Definitions of lyric poetry continue to turn to such statements as Matthew Arnold's "poetry is a dialogue of the mind with itself" and John Stuart Mill's longer quote: "Eloquence is *heard*, poetry is *over*heard. Eloquence supposes an audience; the peculiarity of poetry appears to us to lie in the poet's utter unconsciousness of a listener. Poetry is feeling, confessing itself to itself in moments of solitude" (348). Bakhtin also believed that poetry presented this single-voiced, monologic world—and, in fact, saw this singular point of view as the fundamental limitation of the dialogic possibilities of poetry as he believed it represented a solitary and closed ideological vision. As he puts it in "Discourse and the Novel," "[l]anguage in a poetic work realizes itself as something about which there can be no doubt, something that cannot be disputed, something all-encompassing" (286). And yet if one looks closely at Mill's quote, there is the implication that even when the poet is speaking to himself, he is eliciting a response. The *response*, whatever it may be, is essential for the creation of each and every subjective voice in a poem. As Bakhtin sees it, though, there is a distinct (and even defining) lack of multiple voices in poetry; not only is there "just" the voice of the poet but that monologic voice is typically aligned with dominant ideology. In other words, there are not competing ideologies, but rather a single "self" that expresses a specific and individualized belief system that is (more often than not) representative of dominant ideology. Moreover, Bakhtin theorized that the language in a poem works within its own framework, within a single voice, *even if* working with contradictions or ambiguities, as he explains in "Discourse in the Novel": "The world of poetry, no matter how many contradictions and insoluble conflicts the poet develops within it, is always illumined by one unitary and indisputable discourse" (286). Granted, Bakhtin refers primarily to the epic poem when he refers to poetry, which is only part of the problem with his dismissal of poetry, but the crucial point is that

Bakhtin was completely right about poetry's ability to incorporate an intensive subjective position. What he wasn't right about, however, was that the subjective nature of poetry meant that poetry had to be always and necessarily monologic with a concurrent single ideological position.

In fact, the interior subjective qualities of a poem are exactly what give dialogic poetry its dialogic edge. How so? When a poem begins to assume more than one voice, not only does it *not* lose its subjective, singular realm, but rather, the intensely subjective, individualized positions in a multi-voiced poem become *more* defined when *many* interior "selves" are engaged in a social canvass of dialogue in which utterance is met with response. In other words, in the realm of others, each "I" becomes more deeply subjective and, yes, more individualized. Moreover, and with some irony, we are more likely to find dialogic poetry in places where critics now least expect it: the more experimental/avant-garde poems that were created in an attempt to erase the "I" of a text. Despite the attempt to eliminate the personal and subjective in some avant-garde poems, language rises from individual places in which readers engage with perspectives that always and necessarily represent an ideological perspective connected to an "I."

Mullen's poem is a case in point. *Muse & Drudge* is a fast-moving, experimental, book-length poem that not only does *not* erase the "I" but instead celebrates it. In the first fourteen pages alone, the reader encounters a chorus of women's voices. We meet not only Sapphire, who is introduced both through how others view her as well as through her own subjective and individualized alternative selves (and whose significance will be detailed below), but also a traveling Jane who reaches out in second person in the lines "your heart beats me / as I lie naked on the grass" (100); the shade of a battered woman who tells the reader that the "sun goes on shining / while the debbil beats his wife / blues played left-handed / topsy-turvy inside out" (104); and an abused woman who lives a different life "offstage," "battered like her face / embrazened with ravage / the oxidizing of these / agonizingly worked surfaces," even as a male figure (for whom the reader is given an omniscient or private point of view) looks on her from "that other scene offstage / where by and for her he descends / a path through tangled sounds / he wants to make a song . . . " (104). And these are just a few of the countless voices that flicker in and out of the pages of the text, each with various and changing addressers as well as addressees. Readers catch fleeting snippets of conversations and thoughts mid-stream as they enter the dialogic rhythms of the poem—voices talking to one another, to oneself, about others, and about oneself, in first, second and third person—and, yes, voices speaking in the unity of countless "interior" moments that become engaged with one another in the larger cultural and historical geography of the poem. Notably, though, readers encounter *multiple* and ever-shifting subjectivities of past and present, but these subjective positions are often voiced through the "mouthpiece" of unexpected (and deliberately deceptive) ideological perspectives, producing a sharp and complex ventriloquized effect. Interestingly, and relevant to Mullen's work and the idea of ventriloquism, Bakhtin did in fact admit the possibility of the dialogic in dramatic poetry, as he believed the dramatic poem comes closer to the recreation of the dialogic than narrative or lyric poetry because of the direct incorporation and interplay of "masks" in which more voices and characters, and, thus, ideological perspectives, could exist. Yet, I argue, the idea of the "mask," i.e., the persona, is a staple of all poems, lyric included, and is innately linked to poetry's intimate use of subjectivity. Mullen's poem, like many lyric poems, incorporates some of what Bakhtin admitted was possible in the dramatic poem, but the many masks and dramatic personae in the poem work within its definitive lyric framework. The dramatic meets the lyric head on in her work, so to speak, as numerous ventriloquized voices hide behind masks that represent various ideological positions.

But just how are these voices and various "selves" made dialogic in the realm of poetry? How does Mullen achieve the flickering dialogic creation of meaning among subjective and ventriloquized points of view? There are several answers to this, all of which involve innovative use of language, the second of the two defining features of poetry that provide the impetus for its dialogic possibilities. This defining feature is something that virtually every great poem has in common: play with language in innovative, surprising, vision-altering ways. These innovative linguistic techniques take many forms, including new syntactical structures, never-before-used contexts, fresh and surprising rhymes and rhyme patterns, parataxis, breakages, grammatical inventiveness, use of white space, line breaks, puns, double-entendres, plays on clichés—all techniques, by the way, that mimic the disorder of real-time dialogue and the nonlinear nature of multi-voiced discussion. Most of all, poetry has access to a very different use of the white space, something simply not available in the same way in the genre-defined *form* of the novel. When we do find experimental linguistic innovation in the novel, one could argue (as I do elsewhere) that it is the novel that is becoming more like poetry—a lyricization of the novel, so to speak, to play on Bakhtin's belief in the rare possibility of the novelization of poetry.[3] Most importantly, though, these linguistic switches in the text allow for more fluidity and slippage among voices and perspectives and between points of view. Perhaps the linguistic shifting in surprising and unexpected ways could be best defined by the incorporation of volta-type shifts in the text, which, although typically associated with sonnets, could be argued to appear in all strong poems. The volta, of course, is the "turn" in a poem and is utterly dependent on what comes before (regardless of the "type" of poem). Mullen's work is full of high-level, surprising, and serious play both in form and context, which makes the dialogic interchange and countless code-switching volte (in the plural sense) particularly rich and fast moving. Mullen's innovative linguistic techniques and code-switching set the poem's ventriloquized effects into play within particular lines and passages, but also keep the poem moving quickly forward.

It must be acknowledged here, too, that poets who create such code-switching, dialogic poems are not just any poets. They are practitioners of the methodology of the oppressed through their use of these dialogic techniques—becoming the emancipatory "trickster who practices subjectivity as masquerade" of which Sandoval writes (61.2). In her work *The Methodology of the Oppressed*, Sandoval explains that the realm of differential consciousness is indeed available to anyone, but also says that a true practitioner of emancipatory technologies has an exceptional and finely-tuned sensitivity to the codes and signs of conflicting cultural and social spheres due to their personal experience of "low-riding," as Sandoval puts it, between sign systems (113.4). Dialogic poetry, I argue, *is* the differential consciousness—the "process through which the practices and procedures of the methodology of the oppressed are enacted" (81.2), and the poet who writes such poems becomes the practitioner— the "re-creator"—of such differential consciousness. Thus, such poems can only be produced by someone who has the ability to "low ride" between sign systems *as well as* an exceptional and heightened ability to use language that recreates those various sign systems in a way that reveals and engages various ideological positions. In short, these poets create linguistically complex, dialogic poems that encounter as well as reveal the traps of ideology in startling new ways. In the course of *Muse & Drudge*, Mullen demonstrates that she is in fact the rare and qualified "differential practitioner of a theory and method of oppositional consciousness" (Sandoval 61.2) as she recreates a variety of ventriloquized sign systems and assumes the masks and mouthpieces of both the oppressor and the oppressed and everything in between.

On the first page of *Muse & Drudge*, readers meet one of the poem's most significantly loaded figures, a figure whose name is literally the first word of the poem and whose presentation is instantly fractured and yet also multiplied in meaning and voice. The first page of the poem also immediately showcases the linguistic play with interiority, which is achieved through the quick starts and stops of syntax, lack of punctuation, and unexpected switching of addresser and addressee:

> Sapphire's lyre styles
> plucked eyebrows
> bow lips and legs
> whose lives are lonely too
>
> my last nerve's lucid music
> sure chewed up the juicy fruit
> you must don't like my peaches
> there's some left on the tree
>
> you've had my thrills
> a reefer a tub of gin
> don't mess with me I'm evil
> I'm in your sin
>
> clipped bird eclipsed moon
> soon no memory of you
> no drive or desire survives
> you flutter invisible still

(99)

This first page alone conjures up a range of references and voices that assume various ideological positions, cultural sources, and attitudes in dialogic play beyond Sapphire's, including Bessie Smith's "If you don't like my peaches, don't shake my tree," Rudy Greene's song "Juicy Fruit," as well as Sappho's lines, "She was like that sweetest apple / That ripened highest on the tree, / That the harvesters couldn't reach" (Frost 471). Structurally, the poem first delivers, in third person, a *physical* description of "Sapphire" and her "lyre styles / plucked eyebrows / bow lips and legs" (99). This vision, however, shifts from the "I" of the implied outside "observer" to one that has omniscient insight—a subjective point of view of the *limbs* themselves, "whose lives," we are told, "have been lonely too." Notably, too, these lines imply that the limbs are not alone in their loneliness; the owner of these lips and legs it would seem is likewise lonely, perhaps, as the text implies, because of being objectified and perceived as body parts rather than as a whole woman.

In the second stanza, the reader then immediately encounters an inside view of Sapphire—an "I" whose "last nerve's lucid music" begins to talk directly to another addressee—and who is privy to the inner beliefs of that addressee: "you must don't like my peaches." And yet the coded, tongue-in-cheek message holds some irony as these "peaches" seem to have been taken, even if "there's some left on my tree." The third stanza then addresses the pleasure that the addressee—the "you"—has gotten out of her: "you've had my gin / a reefer a tub of gin." The other has been intoxicated by her, yes, and notably received pleasure from her, which this speaker directly acknowledges—but alongside this acknowledgement is a concurrent and clear warning (through the fast pace of three colliding, run-on sentences): "don't mess with me I'm evil / I'm in your sin." In this high-level play of subjectivities, the subsequent "I" responds to the voices and perspectives in the first stanza, calling out the "evil" that *others* believe she embodies—and yet the text spins it itself back on the perspective of the "other" the moment the "I" implicates the beliefs of the other "in [their] sin." Thus, the original image of Sapphire may have been constructed by *others*, but that image is now altered by her own engagement between subjective self and varied addressees. The direct hit at ideology is especially evident in the last stanza, in which the words and images are piled quickly on top of one another: "clipped bird eclipsed moon / soon no memory of you." The clipped bird in the fourth stanza implies, too, that the damage that the *other* has imposed will now be clipped and eclipsed, in terms of both content and context. Yet, even if "no drive or desire survives," this voice is fully aware that the other—this objectifier and its subsequent power—"flutter[s] invisible still," implying that the ideological damage continues to exist, even if insidiously.

What is fascinating here is not just how many perspectives function within these first 16 lines but also how they are ventriloquized first through a voice that first *describes* Sapphire and then through a series of voices that come from Sapphire herself—voices that are likewise ventriloquized through the mouthpiece of the poet. When we begin to excavate the troubled history of this figure of Sapphire, her possibilities for ventriloquy become even more rich and complex. Although her name has been reappropriated by black feminists to denote strength and defiance, notably by the poet and novelist who has taken the name "Sapphire," the name was first introduced to the American public through a fictional character who appeared in one of the first comedy series broadcasted by NBC in 1929, a 15-minute radio sitcom titled *Amos 'n' Andy*. Created and produced by two white vaudevillian actors known for their work in the minstrel tradition, the show had an astoundingly large audience—53% of the listening audience (some 40 million people living in America)—which meant that a huge number of white people (many of whom had little or no contact with African Americans) began to formulate an "understanding" of black people based on the stereotypes shaped by the show. Of course, many black people also tuned in to listen to the comedy, and while listening may not have necessarily meant acquiescence, as the historian Mark Newman notes, it was several years before the NAACP filed a petition against the production, specifically taking issue with the word "nigger" (a petition that in turn was ignored by the show's management). The potential for spreading the stereotyped, white creations of black figures through the program was particularly insidious because of the medium of radio, Judy Isaksen writes in her essay "Resistive Radio: African Americans' Evolving Portrayal and Participation form Broadcasting to Narrowcasting." After all, the black voices and characters were not only created by white actors but were *played* by them too—a particularly injurious form of blackface because of the lack of visual cues. Sapphire herself was known as "the shrewish, fat 'mammy' figure who was frequently shrill voiced and quick tempered" (Isaksen 756) and became a stereotyped figure with which black women have had to contend for decades, a figure often related to the "emasculating" black woman who robs men of power, one who is seen as always wanting a fight, and one who has been on the receiving end of blame, shame, and animosity rather than being seen as a figure of power. Mullen's entire poem pulls this image apart, admitting to the text elements of anger, but only as they appear alongside a range of emotions that constitute any complicated, real woman versus a stereotyped image that is rigged by invisible ideological power. Mullen replays the ventriloquized stereotypes hidden (and created by) the media of the past and present, but virtually every stereotype presented in the text is accompanied syntactically by sharply dialogic and insightful voice-overs that allow "real women" to engage with, occupy, and deteriorate the damaging ideological power of such images. The Sapphire stereotype could even be said to be in conversation with all the other voices and perspectives presented, confronted, and altered in the text, including but by no means limited to such typecasts and media figures as the Mammy, the diva, the lunatic muse, the prostitute, the drug addict, and the voodoo queen.

The inversion of the Sapphire stereotype also riffs on older texts that lie outside of American history, as seen in the epigraph of the book, in which we hear Callimachus's words and subjectivity evoked:

"Fatten your animal for sacrifice, poet / but keep your muse slender"
(97). The title of the collection *Muse & Drudge* is the first direct reply
to Callimachus's words as Mullen transports them into a new cultural
arena. The muse and the drudge, like Sapphire, Sappho, and the numerous voices of the text, throw polarities out and replace them with a
multidimensional matrix of possible selves, proving that even (and
maybe especially) these labeled, typecast figures are not necessarily
"set" but are nonetheless representative of enduring stereotypes whose
effects are still being felt in our society today.[4] In other words, both
the muse and the drudge have traditionally been denied subjectivity
as they have been "looked upon" as opposed to doing the "looking."
In reference to the text, Mullen has said that the muse and the drudge
are indeed cast as polarities, the "extreme oppositions that we see in
representations of black women in the media. Either the fabulous diva
or the mother using crack, the prostitute. The super-skinny black model
versus Aunt Jemima" (Bedient 660). Mullen, in other words, is specifically "interested in more of a continuum, filling in or troubling those
kinds of oppositional constructions of black women" (660). The entire
text seems to be a commentary on this double play of women's voices,
and it is no accident, given Mullen's commentary, that the text moves
from this epigraph straight to the Sapphire character, who begins to
splinter such polarities from the very first lines.

Interestingly, in addition to the ventriloquized voices, authorial
interruptions also enter the text and directly address the problematic
relationship of these polarities. In the lines below, for example, the nar-
rator/persona makes a complicated observation and offers direct advice,
on which so many of the poem's voices and images might turn:

> muse of the world picks
> out stark melodies
> her raspy fabric
> tickling the ebonies
>
> you can sing their songs
> with words your way
> put it over to the people
> know what you doing

(115)

The "muse" is first revealed here in the third-person voice of an omniscient narrator that seems to be speaking to a general audience and/or

the reader directly. But by the second stanza, the narrator/lyric persona quickly moves to the addressee of the muse herself, telling her directly that she "can sing *their* songs with words your way" (my italics). The addressee is likewise cautioned to "know what you doing," though, which implies that a careful strategy is needed, one that is necessarily riddled with challenges. As Mullen herself explains, "[p]artly what the poem is doing is reclaiming the black woman's body, so that the body is hers, something that she can enjoy, because so many people have tried to define and limit and imprison her body and her sexuality. The idea is that she can be in charge: she can play her own instrument, and she can play the tune that she wants" (Bedient 659). I would take this a step further and say that the singer is not only her own instrument, but she will also play the instruments of others—the racial stereotypes—in new ways, occupying and changing them through artfully subverted and empowered means. By engaging them in dialogue there is a sharper means of resistance—a talking "with" which infiltrates and reclaims power versus talking "to."

Part of the ability to slide between points of view, as seen in the two stanzas above, lies in the lack of punctuation in the poem, again something not readily possible in the movement of a genre-driven novel (unless, again, the novel incorporates the lyric). But the poem's dialogic movement is also directly dependent on poetry's innate musical and rhythmic features, which are likewise made possible by innovative linguistic possibilities. Importantly, these musical and rhythmic features create a greater potential for readers to engage with the challenging movement of dialogic poems even when meaning is not obvious or clear. After all, an emancipatory dialogic poem cannot be emancipatory if readers do not enter the poem with a commitment to engaging with the text in its entirety. The poem's skilled and constant rhythmic movement provides the catalyst for the mixing of voices and ideologies through the tight musical structure of the line lengths, internal rhymes, and the graphic design of the poem itself, in which dozens of allusions, many of which will not be caught by readers, are found. Mullen is fully aware that there is much in the poem that many readers won't be privy to, but she celebrates her use of these allusions and obscurities, knowing that "you can also heighten paradox and contradiction when you compress together things that come from very different registers or different lexicons [as] they jostle each other." This not only creates more tension in the text but, paradoxically, also creates more "elasticity in the utterance" (Bedient 656–7). It means, too, that no one reader or voice gains dominant control, or, as Elizabeth Frost puts it, Mullen's "continual allusions rule out the possibility of any single reader's mastery over her text" (468), democratizing the voices and perspectives of readers as well as the voices in the text.

The poem's musical drive is embedded in its overarching design as well as in countless individual passages and phrases of the poem. In an interesting link to theories explored in Houston A. Baker's work, we find these passages in the poem alluding to the sounds of movement found in the trope of the train juncture in particular. In his book *Blues, Ideology, and Afro-American Literature: A Vernacular Theory*, Baker writes about the railway juncture and how it serves as a powerful interpretive lens for African American history, culture, and thought. Baker creates a revealing vision of a multitude of "black blues singer[s] at the railway junction lustily transforming experiences of a durative (unceasingly oppressive) landscape into the energies of rhythmic song" (7), which is certainly evoked in Mullen's poem in terms of voice as well as musical movement. Mullen's poem is, like Baker's train juncture, "[p]olymorphous and multidirectional, scene of arrivals and departure, place betwixt and between (ever *entre les deux*)" (7). Even more illuminating is how this image of the train juncture connects directly with the redressed images of oppression and subjugation that appear in the larger landscape of *sounds* in the poem. Baker reminds us of the range of sounds "heard" in the railway juncture and what these mean in relation to the blues tradition:

> If onomatopoeia is taken as cultural mimesis, however, it is possible to apply the semiotician's observations to blues by pointing out the dominant blues syntagm in America is an instrumental imitation of *train-wheels-over-track-junctures*. The sound is the "sign," as it were, of the blues, and it combines an intriguing mélange of phonics: rattling gondolas, clattering flatbeds, quilling whistles, clanging bells, rumbling boxcars, and other railroad sounds. (8)

Language necessarily recreates sound as a means of song as well as voice in the poem, recalling Umberto Eco's ideas on music as explored in Baker's theories on the blues and African American ideology.[5] As Eco writes and Baker expounds, there is a lack of "content plane" in music, "sometimes called the 'abstractness' of instrumental music" (7) that, in turn, allows the folding in of voices more easily in a dialogic text. From the very beginning of *Muse & Drudge*, in phrases such as the "last nerve's lucid music" and in words such as "thrills" and "invisible still," we hear the beginning of the *train-wheels-over-track-juncture* sounds of the poem, which also, Baker argues, play with the idea of *training*; as Baker puts it, "only a trained voice can sing the blues" (8). Perhaps it is just such training as both a poet and a reader of varied cultural systems and thought that has given Mullen the ability to become the practitioner of emancipatory technology through her poetic works.

Readers encounter this *train-wheels-over-track-juncture* movement through the overarching architecture of the poem and, intriguingly, even the graphic shape of the poem. The poem could be said to mimic the train cars themselves as each page consists of four quatrains with the lines in each stanza being roughly equal in length. In addition, each line has three, four, or (occasionally) five heavy rhythmic beats, providing a kind of backbeat that feeds into the *train-wheels-over-track-juncture* movement forward. This means, too, that the poem looks and sounds traditional in many ways in terms of stanza usage, meter, and rhyme, and yet likewise houses an intensely experimental dialogic content— countless voices that emerge in these train cars as they move through various junctures. This clash of old style versus new in terms of poetic form and tradition is yet another play on perspectives in dialogue and ideologies in the text. Note the rhythms in the lines below that show this experimentation within traditional rhythmic and rhyming form:

> ain't had chick to chirp nor child to talk
> not pots to piss in, no dram to drink
> get my hands on money marbles and chalk
> I'll squeeze 'til eagle grin, 'til pyramid wink
>
> tussy-mussy mufti
> hefty duty rufty-tufty
> flub dub terra incog
> mulched hearts agog
>
> (146)

The end rhyme in these two stanzas shifts subtly from ABAB to CCDD, but the lines likewise shift significantly in terms of speed of movement—as if a train is pulling to a stop but changes its mind and speeds up instead. These lines are also almost celebratory in the sheer play with alliterative language in terms of consonance and assonance and tongue-twisting syntactical moves that play off numerous clichés. More importantly, though, they embed subtle dialogic engagement, as the subjective experience of the first "I" (in the first stanza) is met with the answer of a second speaker (in the second stanza)—albeit they work with such speed that the reader might not be initially aware of the multitude of voices. The sounds as well as the imagery of the first stanza imply the lack of ownership of anything—hinting at this in relationship to songs, food, alcohol, and even one's children. And yet, the voice says, "I'll squeeze 'til eagle grin, 'til pyramid wink"; in other words, this persona will do what is necessary to find the dollar bills (as inferred by the eagle and pyramid which are, interestingly, also imbued with a subjective, personified perspective) to live, subtly implicating the stereotype of the welfare mother here, too, who is often at the receiving end of blame in politics and beyond. The second stanza embeds sounds that not only reflect the terra incognito, the unexplored land, but also call forth more violent imagery in the lines "mulching of hearts," all through musical sound and word play. Lacking an implied new "I," we hear the resistance through celebratory rhyme and the "flub dub" of a heart that will continue to beat, find new places to go, even as the voice recognizes the "mulched hearts agog." The poem gains momentum as it moves forward in this way, page after page, with shifts in rhyme patterns and sounds, addressers and addressees.

Interestingly, the music of the poem is also contained in brief passages throughout the text in which readers likewise "hear" meaningful reverberations. Ventriloquized, subjective voices are embedded in fleeting, much shorter passages, too, recalling Bakhtin's concept of the "word-with-a-sideways glance," in which even a single word can be shared by very different perspectives of an addresser and addressee and, even more importantly, by a third participant whose presence is required for the two-sidedness to be set into play.[6] Many of these brief but loaded passages also directly relate to music, for instance as readers "hear" the "plucking" of eyebrows and lyre strings (99), a piano with the "blues [being] played left-handed" (103), someone "tickling the ebonies" (115), the sounds of machines and drums mixed in "outlaw beat machines / yet the drums roll on" (152), and a "start strangled banjo" (116). To take just one of these phrases, "tickling the ebonies," we see a multitude of possible interpretations, attitudes, and voices moving within. Readers encounter both a playfulness and a more sinister element embedded in the three words. One could see the inverted (racist) justification of the so-called "playfulness" of the passage, for example, in the allusion to blackface as well as the "toying" with (and concurrent rigging of) black bodies by white ideology (recalling how black artists were "played" by white DJ ventriloquists who introduced their work through taking on "black-sounding" personae on the radio). But readers also encounter reclamation of black bodies in these same lines through the syntactical inversion of *the expected* in the lines as they encounter in the very same moment the resistant and revised inversion of the phrase "tinkling the ivories." This means one voice and/or addresser recreates the old while another *simultaneously* makes it new by code switching the "expected"; meanwhile readers, the third and necessary perspective of the word-with-a-sideways-glance, must bring their own knowledge of the original phrase "tinkling the ivories" for any of this to be set into play. And yet, it is the jarring of the mind out of the expected, even while recalling the expected, that gives these phrases such power.

This complicated three-way dialogism is also embedded in the music of scatting and verbal play in such lines as "mutter patter simper blubber / murmur prattle smatter blather / mumble chatter whisper bubble / mumbo-jumbo palaver gibber blunder" (155), as it is in the lines mentioned above, "tussy-mussy mufti / hefty duty rufty-tufty / flub dub terra incog" (146). In rhythmic switching of a kind, we also encounter slower sounds that hint at slave songs, which expose and then rewrite the legacy behind such songs: "I didn't went to go / swing slow zydeco / so those green chariots / light your eyes up" (155). In these particular lines we have, again, the view of the once-dominant ideology in an image of slavery that the song "Swing Low, Sweet Chariot" inevitably conjures, but we also have the original, expected lines reworked in a voice that uses black dialect and refuses to be contained by the expected: "I didn't went to go," the speaker says, directly addressing a you, "so those green chariots / light your eyes up." Again, the readers' knowledge of "Swing Low, Sweet Chariot" and the concurrent images of religion—especially as a way of bearing the pain of being enslaved—are necessarily conjured up in the reading of the poem for the ideological views to be released and then code-switched. These sounds go on to mix with misogynist elements of rap, with a certain amount of criticism and even warning, as in the lines "rap attacks your tick / cold fusion licks / could make you sick / nobody's dying in this music" (161), which likewise typify the loaded Bakhtinian words-with-a-sideways-glance in a high-level form of punning and linguistic play.[7]

Throughout the work, the musical substance of the poem incorporates the voices of white ventriloquists as well as the voiceovers that respond and invert power. These *train-wheels-over-track-juncture* sounds, though, ultimately lead the reader from the idea of representational voice to the concept of ownership. By this, I mean ownership of one's voice as well as one's creativity, memories, cultural history, and, most importantly, body. Indeed, most critical studies of Mullen's *Muse & Drudge* ultimately explicate how the text enters the ground of ownership of the black body and the legacy of slavery.[8] This physical ownership of one's body and the accompanying rights of every individual entail a *rewriting* of many kinds the text implies, even as it *performs* this very rewriting. Mullen deals explicitly with women's double bind of ownership here—in the context of both white society and the African American community itself. We see this played out in such lines as these that recall Zora Neale Hurston's "mule of the world" analogy for the hardship black women have had to bear:

> mule for hire or worse
> beast of burden down when I lay
> clean and repair the universe
> lawdy lawdy hallelujah when I lay
>
> tragic yellow mattress
> belatedly beladied blues
> shines staggerly avid diva
> ruses of the lunatic muse

(119)

In these lines, we encounter bodily ownership educed by images of slavery and servitude, as well as the Mammy and Sapphire characters embedded in such lines as "lawdy lawdy," which also mix with hints of rape (tragic yellow mattress), in which a (woman's) body's rights are openly violated. And yet, even if "belatedly," the "blues shines staggerly," which conjures both a drunken and/or damaged image as well as the controlled resistance and ownership of the blues. The "avid diva" image is also a loaded term, in which we have a glance of the criticism of the Sapphire-type woman as well as the glance toward not just a diva but an "avid diva," which suggests one who is awake and aware and avidly ready to assume and reappropriate any position *imposed* on her. With this, too, is an implied and innate ability to escape such "mammy" voices that have been ventriloquized in movies and books and have inhabited imagined and typecast black women's bodies for centuries. Notably, Mullen also brings back the image of the muse here as she inverts Hurston's "mule of the world" metaphor for black women to "muse of the world." In doing so, Mullen moves through juncture after juncture of the muse and the drudge images, drawing them closer to the topics of abuse and slavery in the poem without ever naming them as such.

The poem consequently moves into places in which arrival of the past is unavoidable, but there is defiance here, too—even if resistance itself is something that doesn't always gain as much change as it should, as we hear in the voices that say, "yes I've tried in vain / never no more to call you name / and in spite of all reminders / misremembered who I am" (165), directly addressing an invisible "you" that seems to embody a ghost-like figure that continues to haunt so many cultural images, white and black. Those voices have occupied stereotyped, white-created, fictional characters throughout black cultural history, past and present, even as the subject of who is "misremembered" goes missing in the grammatical context of this phrase. The text, in other words, enters into the suffering of bodies that were hijacked literally as well as figuratively by a dominant ideology that assumed power through legalizing ownership of slaves, as well as later through a hijacking of imagined black bodies through ventriloquized typecasts. If we reshuffle these visions back to the first stanzas, we are reminded of the "clipped bird eclipsed moon" and the implication that the *memory* of those who have instigated the oppression of others will also be eclipsed, re-envisioning history as well as reclaiming ownership of the body. Even so, the whispering of the clipped bird of the past will continue to be felt distantly, as the reader encounters in the first poem: "no drive or desire survives / you flutter invisible still" (99). The history of the past will be haunted by this fluttering even as the bodies, real as well as non-existent (imagined), of a difficult past are reclaimed.

Thus, *Muse & Drudge* allows the voices of both the damaging and the curative to be released on the page in a complex *train-wheels-over-track-juncture* of subjugating narratives and ideologies. To those who say racism is a thing of the past and class is the issue at hand, a text such as Mullen's shows that ideological subjugation continues to wreak damage in our society, as seen in our consumer culture, our music industry, our politics, and our media outlets.[9] Mullen's text reminds us that race, racism, and prejudice are pressing issues deeply embedded in our market-driven society; indeed, it is impossible to analyze class in the absence of race given the insidious media-driven messages that infiltrate our lives. Mullen's dialogic poem invites us to recognize such issues and, moreover, to begin to produce the necessary changes in individual and societal thought. As Sandoval reminds us, through Fredric Jameson and Roland Barthes, we are all trapped in ideological and linguistic structures from which we are not easily freed. Any freedom that is found, however elusive, necessarily resides in the places where one's speech is released from the limitations of role-playing in social and linguistic spheres. Dialogic poems such as Mullen's can therefore help us move closer to a fuller awareness of the deep and far-reaching subjugation and racism that continue to exist in our culture and in the very language we use, the programs we watch, and the music we listen to. Moreover, gaining deeper-level access to and a concomitant awareness of the damaging but often invisible power of these images can directly affect our very thought patterns, and thus the behavior and actions of both individuals and communities. In other words, dialogic poems created by such practitioners of emancipatory methodology can help us to better understand the complex racial divisions and subjugating social structures that persist in our world today and which must be confronted head on. *Muse & Drudge* is just such a poem. When told by Calvin Bedient that her "work seems . . . essentially sassy and jubilant," which, in turn, "has a political implication," Mullen answers, through her words to Bedient, but even more so through the multi-voiced subjectivities recreated in the emancipatory dialogic tableau of her poem, "We shall overcome" (657).

Notes

1. See, most recently, Ira Sadoff's *History Matters: Contemporary Poetry on the Margins of American Culture* (Iowa City: U of Iowa P, 2010) and the collection of essays edited by Jacob Blevins, *Dialogism and Lyric Self-fashioning: Bakhtin and the Voices of a Genre* (Selinsgrove, PA: Susquehanna UP, 2008).
2. In her book *Lyric Interventions: Feminism, Experimental Poetry, and Contemporary Discourse* (Iowa City: U of Iowa P, 2004), Linda A. Kinnahan says that "the issue increasingly addressed is not whether lyric subjectivity (or variant traces of voice, interiority, self-history, etc.) is evident but how it is deployed and what that deployment assumes about poetry's function" (13).
3. See my dissertation, "Reclaiming the Dialogic, Reframing the Topics: Culture, Violence, and Eros in Contemporary American Women's Lyric Poetry," University of Texas at Dallas, 2008, in which I propose that the lyric poem embraces four specific modes that allow for rich (and endless) dialogic possibilities; these are musicality, ambivalence, nonlinearity, and, above all, subjectivity.
4. Critics have various and interrelated takes on what the muse and drudge might represent. Frost, for example, believes the fattened animal might represent the slave body and its "denied subjectivity," while the "slender Muse" is "an ideal of *dis*embodiment, a deified feminine 'soul' that supplies the traditionally male poet with the means of androgynous creativity" (467). Deborah Mix, adding to this while using similar terminology, writes that "[o]n the one hand, the figure of the muse suggests a kind of disembodied perfection with no desires or needs of her own; on the other, the figure of the drudge suggests a kind of dis-intellected laborer, again one without desires or needs of her own" (4).
5. See Umberto Eco's *A Theory of Semiotics* (Bloomington: Indiana UP, 1978).
6. Michael Holquist argues that the Janus figure that plays into Bakhtin's work is a trope for three people and that "Janus, then, is the deity who presides over dialogue for many of the same reasons he is god of paronomasia, the generic word for word-play, more especially of punning" ("Why" 55).

7. See Mitchum Huehls's insightful essay "Spun Puns (And Anagrams): Exchange Economies, Subjectivity, and History in Harryette Mullen's 'Muse & Drudge,'" which looks specifically at the reflexive nature of puns and how they function in the text's heteroglossic elements.

8. Significantly, Baker's theories on train junctures, like Huehl's work on the pun and Mix's work on the "impudent" strategies of resistance in the text (and almost every other major critical text on Mullen's poetry), eventually lead to explications of how the poem exposes and confronts a historical past in which bodies were mere commodities.

9. Dialogism can also be a model for confronting class subjugation in conversation with race, which I address in my essay "'Between The Scylla and the Charybdis': Navigating the Dialogic Waters in Julia Alvarez's 'The Other Side/ El Otro Lado'" (in *Inhabiting "La Patria": Identity, Agency, And "Antojo" in the Work of Julia Alvarez*, ed. Rebecca Harrison and Emily Hipchen, SUNY P, 2013).

Works cited

Arnold, Matthew. "The Study of Poetry." *Essays: English and American.* Vol. XXVIII. The Harvard Classics. New York: P. F. Collier & Son, 1909–14; Bartleby. com, 2001. Web.

Bakhtin, M. M. "Discourse in the Novel." *The Dialogic Imagination: Four Essays.* Ed. Michael Holquist. Trans. Caryl Emerson and Michael Holquist. Moscow, 1975. Austin: U of Texas P, 1981. 259–422.

Bedient, Calvin. "The Solo Mysterioso Blues: An Interview with Harryette Mullen." *Callaloo* 19 (1996): 651–69.

Frost, Elisabeth. "'Ruses of the lunatic muse': Harryette Mullen and Lyric Hybridity." *Women's Studies* 27 (1998): 465–81.

Holquist, Michael. *Dialogism: Bakhtin and his World.* 2nd ed. New York: Routledge, 1990.

——. "Why is God's Name a Pun? Bakhtin's Theory of the Novel in Light of Theophilology." *The Novelness of Bakhtin: Perspective and Possibilities.* Ed. Joren Bruhn and Jan Lundquist. Museum Tusculanum Press: 2001. 53–70.

Huehls, Mitchum. "Spun Puns (And Anagrams): Exchange Economies, Subjectivity, and History in Harryette Mullen's 'Muse & Drudge.'" *Contemporary Literature* 44.1 (Spring 2004): 19–46.

Isaksen, Judy L. "Resistive Radio: African Americans' Evolving Portrayal and Participation from Broadcasting to Narrowcasting." *Journal of Popular Culture* 45.4 (2012): 749–68. *Academic Search Premier.* Web. 9 Oct. 2013.

Mill, John Stuart. *Essays on Poetry.* Ed. F. Parvin Sharpless. Columbia, SC: U of South Carolina P, 1976.

Mix, Deborah. "Inspiration, Perspiration, and Impudence in Harryette Mullen's *Muse & Drudge.*" *Contemporary Women's Writing* 8.1 (2014): 53–70.

Mullen, Harryette. *Recyclopedia (Muse & Drudge): Trimmings, S*PeRM**K*T, Muse & Drudge.* Saint Paul: Graywolf Press, 2006.

10
Zehra Çirak and the Aporia of Dialogism

Erin Trapp

> Whether the passage from otherness to the recognition of the other, the passage, in other words, from dialogism to dialogue, can be said to take place in Bakhtin as more than a desire, remains a question for Bakhtin interpretation to consider in the proper critical spirit.
>
> (Paul de Man, "Dialogism and Dialogue")

In her 1999 article, "'Innere Unruhe'? Zehra Çirak and Minority Literature Today," Marilya Veteto-Conrad describes how Çirak, like many other writers in Germany of Turkish origin, rejects the label "Turkish German" and the idea of multicultural dialogue that presupposes not only the existence of two relatively fixed identities but the correspondence of text and context. In "Ethnic Irony: The Poetic Parabasis of the Promiscuous Personal Pronoun in Yoko Tawada's 'Eine leere Flasche,'" John Kim argues that the practice of reading figures of ethnicity assumes a continuity between social context and poetic text to the extent that "wherever an ethnic appears *writing*, its writing appears *ethnic*" (334). Kim's insights into the relationship between the literary element of irony, which is "played out between two opposed figures that are in fact one" (348), and the problem of *reading* ethnicity build on the de Man-influenced work of Leslie Adelson and her understanding of the problem of referentiality, or what she calls the "riddle of referentiality," in reference to the aporetic relation between social context and literary text.

Kim's recovery of irony to the ethnic subject is premised, however, upon a dialogic moment in which dialogue that initially appears to be taking place between individuals turns out to be taking place *within* an individual. In this paper, I explore the phenomenon of internal dialogue, along with the psychical reality of "being two in one," which entails the nonintegration rather than the integration of social context and poetic text. Internal dialogue is premised upon there being dialogic instances that do not quite manage to *become* dialogue, but register this resistance as a form of searching or desiring that is purposeless in contrast to integration and disintegration, which are inherently meaningful and purposive.

In her poetry, Çirak often depicts figures whose component parts are appropriated to create new entities. These figures explain processes of inclusion and exclusion in a way that does not merely reproduce the other as the constitutive but excluded exception of Europe. For example, despite rather prevalent readings of the poem "Cultural Identity [*Kulturidentität*]" as an autobiographical confession of how Çirak "lives and longs for a mixed culture [*Mischkultur*]," the neologism *Mischkultur* models her refusal of dialogue as a kind of resistance of integration. This is because, although it seems to be formed in the way that many neologisms are in German, by compounding terms, *Mischkultur* is an antiquated term that refers not to the mixing of culture, but to a pre-capitalist form of agriculture known as "strip farming." While the neologism points from literary text to social context and toward Europe's role in providing an environment in which multicultural dialogue takes place, the word also refers, whether knowingly or not, to an archaic social formation. The presence of this additional meaning of *Mischkultur* points outside of the easily assumed idea that hybridity in discourse can be formed through the unity of two component parts. It literally reminds us that contemporary dialogue effaces, by proposing to integrate, these sedimented layers of historical meaning.

In their titles alone, both of the collections of poetry that I discuss here—*Bird on the Back of an Elephant* (*Vogel auf dem Rücken eines Elefanten*) and *Foreign Wing on Familiar Shoulder* (*Fremde Flügel auf eigener Schulter*)—challenge dialogue's presumption about the figures it takes place between. Both titles contain figures that entail relations of appropriation and attachment instead of exchange. Here "foreign (*fremd*)" and "familiar (*eigen*)" are brought into relation through the objects "wing" and "shoulder," yet what is depicted is neither their mutual exchange nor their integration into a larger entity, but rather the way that the "foreign wing" remains unintegrated even when in contact with this body. The figure of the "bird on the back on an elephant" proposes a similar relationship; here, the bird, like the wing, is attached to a body. In psychoanalysis, the notion of "nonintegration" or the "unintegrated state" provides us with a way of thinking about the continued presence of regressive formations, or about the way that the psyche exists as an object (a wing, a bird) instead of becoming integrated within a body. In particular, I will turn to ideas about psychoanalytic dialogue introduced by British psychoanalyst D. W. Winnicott in his somewhat scattered observations about the function of nonintegration, which entails a formless or non-purposive process of "searching for the self" from which a "me" can be postulated, in the therapeutic environment.[1]

Poetry, I argue, functions as the supportive environment required for accessing an object world that is designated not through the unifying activity of the psyche and soma, as in the process of integration and in the transformation of dialogism to dialogue, but in the opposite way, as a form of nonintegration in which the psyche does not dwell in the soma but is encountered as an object, as a "me," and must be reflected back to itself (as in the process of searching for the self) in order to be apprehended. This mode of apprehending a "me" from what poetry reflects back presupposes a backdrop of the failure of dialogism to complete its transition to dialogue (or for the disintegrated self to become integrated) for one or another social or psychological reason. In this essay, I'll describe how Çirak proposes a logic of understanding dialogue not as a process between two individuals based on the adequation of text and context, but as an internal dialogue between an "I" and a "me" that develops the inadequacy—or aporia—of text and context. This approach leads to questions about how the other is reproduced as a correlate of European identity.

The refusal of dialogue

In returning dialogue to dialogism, as she does by constantly returning to language its nonverbal aspects, Çirak also makes a pronounced critique of the way that dialogue serves to produce others and reproduce European values and civilization. In the poem "Aporue," Çirak depicts the failure of dialogism to complete its transformation into dialogue:

> This is not a street in France
> it is only quietly spoken
> something heard from behind
> europA somewhat a little too loud
> so that for one
> the national ears are burst
> foreignly to learn a language

is good
yet specifically (one's own) to understand something
is still much better
so much is on the one hand said in it
and on the other hand heard from it
that on the way from ear to ear
only the interchangers
remain hanging, from boxing the ears

(33)

Çirak's titular wordplay with the invented word "Aporue" invokes, through aural association, the idea of "aporia" (*Aporie* in German). The title points in several directions at once, but no single idea completely explains or accounts for the substantive "Aporue"; the complete meaning of this term, in other words, breaks down into constitutive parts (Apo + rue) that do not add up to it. The associative "aporia" of *Aporue* also signals a logic by which the poem operates, its logic of expression, the "state of loss" from which the utterance of its name emerges. As Çirak writes, "this Aporue" (*Europa* spelled backward) is "not a street in France." The first utterance of its identity is determined negatively, as a predicate that refers to the inclusion of the word *rue* (street) in *Aporue* and implies the formulation *Aporue* = not-France. This instance of a not-me—not-France—seems to propose, as a condition of its reversibility, that if *Aporue* is not a street in France, perhaps Europa *is* a street in France, a place that can be located geographically and called into being through its being uttered. But this transformation takes place on the basis of a negation—of a negative operator in this logical chain that serves to demonstrate how *Aporue* refurls to *europA*. Indeed, the poem registers a transformation from intralinguistic wordplay to an utterance (dialogue), a thing that exists only in being spoken, in the second line. As an instance of utterance, then, *Aporue* references the geographic street but only by signaling an alternative dialogism, in which dialogue itself is not about those static entities it might take place between, but about the way that, as an instance of utterance, dialogue creates static, produces "the street in France" as an instance of what Europe is not.

The poem describes a dialogue; it challenges the idea that learning a foreign language ("foreignly to learn a language"), learning to speak with "others" is a good idea. The poem's pronouncement that it is "good" to do this is undermined by the use of "foreignly" [*fremderlei*], which is an invented term that plays with other words that are formed by adding *"lei"*. But the play with *fremd*, or "foreign" in relation to *eigens*, meaning "specifically" or "one's own," here—which echoes the book title's pairing of *fremd* and *eigene*—points to how these choices, the good and the better, provide the somewhat faulty terms of dialogue. The poem sets up the possibility of there being an *eigene* entity (like a street in France) that is referenced in the idea of Europe. Indeed, there is no subject for the verbs "said in it [*hineingesagt*]" and "heard from it [*herausgehört*]." The model of dialogue that is presented emphasizes the presence of static between the ears, the fact that between the ears, those who are mediators or interchangers, exchangers, get stuck. Others, who pass from ear to ear, complete or bring to an end a dialogue; they make it from ear to ear. *Fremderlei*, those who get caught, or get stuck, between the ears, do not complete the transformation from dialogism to dialogue.

As Çirak indicates, dialogue may consist of this inequivalence, of the disjuncture of saying and hearing; this point requires the context of transnationalism in relation to national language to gain its emphasis. One of the points of reference for thinking about Çirak, then, is the critical discourse of the literature of migration in Germany, a discourse, as Leslie Adelson claims, that challenges common understandings of dialogic communication "as a process in which readers and characters engage as representatives of discrete worlds" (26). Adelson proposes that such dialogism be understood instead through the "riddle of referentiality," a phrase that she uses to indicate the chiasmic relation between figuration and referential meaning. She describes how this relation takes place as a dialogic encounter "between an object of analysis and its interpreter, one that seeks to bridge a gap inherent in the initial relationship" (24), and she usefully describes how this gap is usually (and problematically) bridged by the figure of an "I" that appears to represent the object. That Turkish German texts extend beyond the facile "intercultural dialogue" has been well established in scholarship of German literature since the turn of the century (Gramling, Fachinger, Adelson). Here, the idea of dialogue as the interaction between a European self and its other is framed as both the predominant model and as the thing to get beyond. Such a notion of dialogue, one that is posited as the interaction between two fixed identities and wherein resides the question of whether these—like reader and author—are interchangeable, can be interrogated in various ways. Çirak's poetry points not so much to the poverty of the sociological figure of the Turk or of the "I," but to an aporia between the "I" and the "me," between the subject and its utterance, in which the "I" posits itself as object.[2] This internal dialogue takes form in poetry because poetry—perhaps more than other genres—falls prey to the facile assumption of the speaker, the "I," as the "me" of the poet.

Dialogism and unintegrated poetry

As I've been arguing, Çirak's poetry develops an idea of poetic dialogism within the speaker in contrast to models of dialogue that conventionally describe the relation between Europe and its "others," and in this regard, it is necessary to develop some further thoughts about the relation between dialogism and poetry. Poetic dialogism departs from an aporia of Bakhtinian Dialogism (which I designate with a capital *D* throughout, in contrast to the mode of poetic dialogism that I propose) that Paul de Man gestures toward in his essay, "Dialogue and Dialogism." For Bakhtin, Dialogism refers to "an image of language," to the inevitable fact of language's status as a living word, and he finds that even what he calls the "internal dialogism of the word," "which does not assume any external compositional forms of dialogue," repeatedly completes the transformation from Dialogism to dialogue (Bakhtin 279). Looking critically at Bakhtin's assumption of how this transformation from Dialogism to dialogue happens as a fact of language, de Man describes how the referentiality of tropes, what he calls the "tropological polysemy of poetry," points instead to the aporia of Dialogism and dialogue. In looking at Bakhtin's writings, it is evident that the designation of "poetry" as that which *is not* dialogue functions as an exception to vouchsafe this transformation. This transformation—which, as de Man describes, entails a shift from the *intralinguistic* aspect of Dialogism as that which "says something about language rather than about the world" to the *intercultural*, which says something about the world—relies on a principle of radical alterity that identifies otherness with reality. It's this principle that discounts poetry as a form of Dialogism, since, for Bakhtin, poetry "directly and unmediatedly express[es] the semantic and expressive intentions of the author" (Bakhtin 299) and is thus not capable of presenting alterity within itself. For Bakhtin, poetry is only textual, not worldly: the "reflective" shortcoming of poetry (in contrast to the refractive principle of Dialogism) and the implied distinction between prose and poetry prevents the transformation from Dialogism to dialogue, from text to world.

The desire to move between text and world—to make these entities correspond to one another, to establish a system of referentiality, to figure and figure out the relation between poetry and society—has been as much the task of dialogue as it has been of lyric theory in the last half century. In his 1953 essay "Lyric Poetry and Society," Theodor Adorno highlights an aspect of the ambivalence of Dialogism that Julia Kristeva also identifies in "Word, Dialogue, and Novel" when she notes that any dialogic mode includes both monologic and dialogic forms.[3] This "ambivalence" refers to the way that the lyric speaker is regarded *at the same time* as an individual (monologic) moral subject and as a collective (dialogic) social force. Adorno finds that the relation between poetry and society contains a similar ambivalence, based upon the reflective and refractive figure of the "I"—its capacity as subject to register the object world as a form of "a subjectivity that turns into an objectivity." This is a key phrase in Adorno's argument about how lyric poetry is able to say more about society than "communicative discourse," which reifies language to produce a "liberated subject" whose "shadow-side" is "its degradation to something exchangeable" (42).

Following the critique of dialogue implicit in this discussion, poetic dialogism develops these concerns about the relation between the subject, the poetic "I," and its status as an "object," which Adorno describes as a "precipitate" formed "in the medium of a subjective spirit thrown back upon itself" (42). This formulation contrasts with readings of poetry that establish a priority for reading the "I" as a subject addressing either an implied or explicit "you." But as Çirak's refusal to identify as Turkish German demonstrates, the problem of inclusion and exclusion is no longer just about how the European subject is constituted in relation to its "others," but about how the very notion of dialogue produces the non-European subject as an "object." Çirak's poetry highlights this reflexive relationship between the subject and its object, frequently presenting a "dialogue" between the "I" and the "me" as a way of articulating the dialogism of poetry.

Highlighting an aporia not between the "I" and an other, but between the "I" and the "me," Çirak enters into figures that are no longer primarily sociological but instead psychoanalytic. In my understanding, the aporia of dialogism initially addressed by de Man in his essay "Dialogue and Dialogism" leads to an argument about the referentiality of figurative language, but it also indicates a gap in thinking about the way that psychodynamic models are employed as correlates of the sociological. Thus, an important part of thinking about how the processes of internalization and externalization constitute the subject has to do with addressing how psychodynamic models enter into descriptions of sociological otherness.

This movement toward the psychical can be traced in the poem "Duden Ichden," in which Çirak is critical of the issue of *Einheitsduden*

(Unified Duden), the unification of the East German and West German branches of the national dictionary, Duden, as a part of the process of unifying Germany in 1991.[4] The poem also plays more generally with the relation between the "I" and the "you," those figures posited by the very notion of dialogue itself:

> I [*ich*] say me [*mich*] little
> you [*du*] loud and big
> the commas between us [*uns*] are not supposed to be a
> dividing wall

Noting the difference between the enunciation of "you" and the enunciation of "me," Çirak registers, by way of their ironic unity as "us," that when there is the desire to be unified in dialogue, this desire can uncritically supersede the dimension of poetic dialogism in which there is also a difference between "I" and "me."

The terms that comprise the title, *Duden* and *Ichden*, are, like *Aporue*, compound terms that represent the ironic polysemy of language that Çirak highlights in the poem, the way that the correct form of the Duden dictionary [*Rechtschreibungduden*] permits paradox and "mistakes" to be made while presupposing that correctness assures the unity of referent and reference as well. *Duden* and *Ichden* highlight exactly the kind of language mistakes that help us to think about the aporia of the unintegrated state. Juxtaposing these terms emphasizes the false sameness and difference of both: the difference figured in the opposition between the correlative terms "you [*du*]" and "I [*ich*]" and the sameness figured through the identical "root" *den* ["the" or "it," accusative article, pronoun, or object]. This identical "root" is not, of course, a root at all, since *Duden* is a proper name, the family name of Konrad Duden, the 1880 founder of the dictionary. Next to the compound *Ichden*, however, we are compelled to separate *Duden* into its component parts, as we would with *Ichden*, and to then wonder about how *den* could be functioning similarly in each term. Considering the terms in this way, *den* is an accusative object, and thus it signals the interruption and annexation of these subjects by their objects. It's possible to see from this that one's status as a subject is always qualified by its also being an object and that this is a case in which the dialogism of the I-me-you can call into question the inherent value of our conversion into dialogue.

In thinking, then, about the transformation of (intralinguistic) textual heteroglossia into (intercultural) voiced otherness, I've maintained that this conversion is performed as a fantasy, one that powerfully informs not only Bahktin's work, but also the problem of how we understand or access the agency of the "subaltern."[5] In psychoanalytic literature, integration is seen as part of the developmental process, but there is present, in the work of D. W. Winnicott, the sense that outside the Freudian logic of integration/disintegration (in which civilization is constantly threatened by disintegration), nonintegration involves the toleration of a "non-purposive state," a state of relaxation or formless-ness that is as much a part of the healthy personality as it is a devel-opmental stage or a characteristic of the schizoid personality.[6] In "The Concept of a Healthy Individual," Winnicott describes how tolerating nonintegration "in resting and in relaxation and in dreaming" (29) allows what he calls in *Playing and Reality* a "sort of ticking over of the unintegrated personality" (78). He describes how encouraging the patient to yield to this state of nonintegration involves letting down one's defense against disintegration: "Organized defense against disinte-gration robs the individual of the precondition for the creative impulse and therefore prevents creative living" (29). My interest in Winnicott's notion of nonintegration lies primarily, then, in how nonintegration is present as a part of normal emotional life and can therefore be used to think about how the dynamic of a positively valued integration and negatively valued disintegration can be reorganized.

In *Playing and Reality*, Winnicott develops his observations about how nonintegration is the condition for creativity by describing a relation-ship with a patient that allows him to see the value of this process of "searching for a self." He writes,

> After this she said the very words that I need in order to express my meaning. She said, slowly, with deep feeling: "Yes, I see, one could postulate the existence of a me from the question, as from the search-ing." She had now made the essential interpretation in that the ques-tion arose out of what can only be called her creativity, creativity that was coming together after relaxation, which is the opposite of integration. (86)

The "creativity" that Winnicott describes refers to the patient's ability to create her own image of herself by allowing her to tolerate a state of formlessness in which she is not defined or identified for or by others. This creative act yields the postulation of "the existence of a me"; it's this that can result from nonintegration but that does not result from the normative process of integration and the organization of defenses around disintegration. Winnicott describes how such a state requires the "reflecting back" of a statement or question on behalf of the analyst. Such a "reflection" is precisely what initially seems to be too intentional for dialogism, but as Winnicott describes, this reflection allows for the subject to regard the negativity that constitutes its coherence into an "I."

Çirak's use of false compounds extends to terms that directly represent the relation between the psyche and soma. The poem "City Borders [*Stadtgrenze*]," for example, makes use of the densely ambivalent word "head room [*Kopfzimmer*]," which helps to further my speculations about nonintegration. The poem reads:

> On the edges of the city the complaint:
> my city is full of houses
> my houses are full of people
> who arrange their head room
> with needs of every sort
> our people are enough
> ours are enough for us
> for the number of plates
> we spice only exotically
> however we eat alone and locally
>
> Salt knows no national dish
> who wants now to throw
> the borders
> in whose eyes?
>
> (51)

Kopfzimmer refers, on a literal level, to the arrangement of space in a room (that is in a house, that is in a city), moving from social space, to domestic space, to mental space. But if this condensation, through language, functions to highlight the ambivalence of inside/outside, it is only by challenging, in the first place, the way that the inside—the European nation, writ large, but also constituted by the imagination of nested interiority, a reasoned and ordered "next smallest"[7] unit, like Çirak describes—produces its outside. In ordering one's *Kopf*zimmer, one is integrated within the nesting dolls of people—city—nation, against which rests the border, at the city's edges: its threatening aspect emerges in its simultaneous instantiation as Kopf*zimmer*, the mind's subordination to its domestic space. The use of *Kopfzimmer* in this doubled sense resonates with the dimensions of figural language that I am trying to develop in thinking about how the exclusion of tropes from Dialogism has to do with the (threatening) power of tropes, "condensed," as de Man finds, "in the key metaphor of the *subject as mind*" (emphasis mine).[8] In this light, poetry is excluded from dialogue not because it's incapable of accessing "otherness," but because it threatens to transform all dialogue into poetic dialogism, into the problem of how the "I" calls itself and its others into being.

Every "I" is a not-me

Poetry's failure of the dialogic test is not, then, a shortcoming of form, based on poetry's inability to sublate intention, but rather it is the interruption of episteme, a way of "knowing" others that does not objectify the human or define (and thus attempt to control) the relationship between people and things, the way that objects relate to society. Poetry's *excessive* intention quickly lapses into its opposite—a world in which the self is an object like any other—when categories indicating ethnicity and race are introduced.[9]

These psychoanalytic considerations can help us to think about how the subject that refuses its transformation into dialogue registers dissatisfaction with sociological parameters for thinking about immigration and national cultures. I'd like to propose, as a way of investigating the tension between these models for thinking about the inclusion and exclusion of racial and ethnic minorities and Europe, to read Çirak's refusal as an index of the ambivalence of the production of the historical European and the global other of Europe.

In *Toward a Global Idea of Race*, Sandra Ferreira da Silva, challenging the paradigm of inclusion and exclusion, argues that theorizations of the mutual constitution of nation and race, such as that found in Etienne Balibar's writing, formulate race as an add-on and prevent us from understanding "the conditions of production of today's global subjects" (xxxvi). Instead, she argues that historicity (associated with the nation) and globality (associated with the racial) are distinct ontological contexts that constitute "modern representation." Silva does so in order to address and describe "how precisely the racial institutes the others of Europe as subaltern subjects" (3), and she proposes to think of "the racial" as a "scientific construct" (3). Here, the significant aspect of her work lies in wanting to think about how the racial produces "modern subjects," by which she means not *historical* "Europeans," but the *global* "others of Europe as subaltern subjects." This thinking derives from an understanding of the way that "the racial" is *not* "extraneous to modern thought" (2). Balibar's move to think about how "Europeans" are constituted by their others is thus revised by Silva's efforts to think about how the "others of Europe" are produced by the (European idea of the) racial.

As Silva argues, a contemporary account of race should not just explain how the European externalizes this hostility (his barbarism), but how "the racial"—as a scientific construct—produces the "global subaltern" as barbarian, as a figure for the fear of disintegration felt by European subjects. The problem Silva describes occupies a space prior to and potentially critical of representation. Silva's renunciation of all previous models (and so of the historical European) as reproductive of the very categories of modern representation ends up proscribing an ontological mode that opposes the interiorizing and exteriorizing aspects of the subject. Yet, I think that the shift she proposes in thinking about how the racial produces the global subaltern, not just how the global subaltern produces Europe, can productively re-inspire thinking about the constitution—the borders and limits—of Europe. These critical moves take as their point of departure the problem in subaltern studies of how to access the agency of the "other," or how to describe the agency of persons whose identity continues to be formulated through a foundational negativity. Like these thinkers, Çirak concentrates on what forms the limits and extensions of knowledge about the violence and aggression that inform relations across borders. She challenges this discourse not to rest upon any facile division between externally and internally constituted subjectivity; it is the vaunting of exteriority, like exotopy (the principle of radical alterity) that she challenges by playing with the way that psyche (*Kopf*) and soma (*Zimmer*), for example, constitute the false unity of the external sociological *Kopfzimmer*.

Çirak's poetic speaker is a figure that is reflected back from a state of nonintegration, the space out of which the not-me emerges as a question of discourse. The ambivalence of the "I"—of the monologic/dialogic "I"—accounts for the double move of reflecting back and being reflected back. This is a space apposite to dialogue; it occurs where the work of dialogue also takes place, where dialogue ostensibly mediates social and textual reality. In "Cultural Identity," Çirak asks whether cultural identity is something "with which I re-recognize (*wiedererkennen*) me, or is it something, with which others are able to integrate [*einordnen*] me?" (94). Following Çirak's logic, if we emphasize the "me [*mich*]" as an object, not just as a reflexive "myself," we can see her asserting this activity of recognition as a way of registering one's object status. In the middle of the poem, the line "I re-recognize me [*Ich erkenne mich wieder*]" emphasizes the sense in which the "recognition" is already doubled, a form of "re-recognition [*wiedererkennen*]." After this line, the oft-quoted prose stanza describes how the speaker would "most like to awake japanly . . . breakfast englishly" and so on. This stanza again functions to indicate the arbitrariness not just of the literary signifier, but of the cultural. With these lines, Çirak registers the tropological aspect of language: its function to entail ambivalence (as it entails difference), not to be ambivalent, and more specifically to entail the ambivalence of desire. The poem ends with an iteration of the initial question: "So do I want something [*Will ich also etwas*], with which I can re-recognize me, or something, with which others can integrate me?" The poem shows how the initial opposition between these choices, which was presented as a matter of how "cultural identity" was defined, becomes a question about *how* an "I" desires a "me." The real question here is not about this choice (it's obvious what's being favored), but about a desire: "So do I want something . . . ?" And the answer, following Çirak's logic, is *yes*— but the "something" she wants is a "not" ("So do I want a not . . . ?"), a negating particle to affix to her "me," so that refusal is always the first word that comes out of the aporia of self-searching and integration.

In one final poem, "No Sand in the Wheel of Time [*Kein Sand im Rad der Zeit*]," I'd like to consider the related aspect of Çirak's logic and the logic of nonintegration by looking specifically at how dialogue processes the "other" as an object of discourse. In this "thing poem," the speaker is a bicycle. However, it is not just any bicycle, but a bicycle circulating dialogically between the poem and the tradition of political lyric poetry in Cold War and post-Cold War Germany. Çirak's poem alludes to two others, Bertolt Brecht's "Wheel Change [*Der Radwechsel*]" (1953) and Günter Eich's "Sand in the Gears [*Sand im Getriebe*]" (1960). With Brecht and Eich as points of reference, Çirak's poem can be seen to raise questions about how ethnic literature speaks the language of a national literature, even as it takes place in the gap between the things and words of a national language.

The elevation of Brecht's poem as an example of the postwar paradigm of political art was achieved after Hans Magnus Enzensberger, who, along with Eich, became one of the most prominent "postwar poets" to write extensively about the relationship between art and politics, took this poem as an example of the political poem *par excellence* in his 1962 essay, "Poetry and Politics." There he described the political content of "Wheel Change" as its not being "at the disposal of politics" by identifying the feeling of "impatience" experienced by the speaker of the poem as one also experienced by "ideological carpers" (31). The problem, then, of not "being able to use the poem for their purposes" is derived by Enzensberger from the description of the speaker observing a bike that requires "change" in order to be used "for its purpose."

Even as it produces a favorable and somewhat benign interpretation, Enzensberger's reading enforces the identification of the speaker with the reader, the speaker's experience of being between states with the reader's desire that the poem resist being used as others might intend. If it does this, the poem also points to the speaker's discomfort with his own feeling of impatience and he wonders why he still feels this way—why he still feels a desire—even if the speaker doesn't care "where I come from [*herkomme*]" and "where I am going [*hinfahre*]." As an observer, the speaker inhabits the postwar position of a bystander who watches another person change a flat tire and feels—projects—impatience at this delay. He feels impatient for the rider to get going again, for gears to be put in motion that will carry along not only him but also that world that he is marginally ("on the curb" [*am Strassenhang*]) a part of. As is expressed by the absent speaker of "Aporue," the coming and going (of people and words) raises questions about the substitutability of these various roles: speaker and receiver, rider and observer, subject and object world. Çirak's speaker is thus not the first to inhabit a position of substitution in relation to the bike and the bike rider; the rider and the bike here are objects of another's observation. In Çirak's case, however, this observing other is not the "I"—like Brecht's subject of national history, the speaker—but is produced as an object.

In "No Sand in the Wheel of Time," the poetic speaker, the "I" of the poem, enacts identification and dis-identification with groups that have been racially or ethnically oppressed or marginalized in Germany.[10] The poem reads:

> I stand in the subway leaning on the wall
> silently I sway in the metro
> five boys and two girls approach me
> faltering because of the speed
> firm grins are fixated on me
> and sneering ever closer
> I try to ignore the seven
> the other passengers are all
> busy with themselves
> the seven now stand
> hardly a step before me
> one and the others wind up
> to hit

once again and another time
the others jeer excitedly
now I am a Negro—Jew—Foreigner—
Bum—or some other
no, they do not see what I really am
now just a beaten thing
I still hear a little kid
who anxiously calls mama
and the other passengers make themselves
ready to deboard
I collapse
I am a bicycle
my owner is
a Negro—a Jew—a Foreigner
who with premonitions
already deboarded a station earlier
from now on I am
no more—only a bicycle[11]

The "I" is figured both as and *not* as "some other." "They" are persecut-
ing others who objectify both the bike and its rider. In the first instance,
the speaker is identified socially as an "other" whose essence—"what
I really am"—is "a beaten thing." In referencing this objectification of
the other, Çirak points to how not being seen for what "one really is"
means not seeing the violence that constitutes identity. The moment of
misrecognition in which the speaker becomes an object coincides with
being beaten and the speaker *becomes* a "Negro, Jew, Foreigner, Bum."
Yet there is another level of misrecognition at play: the bicycle is the
substitute object for its owner, who *is* "a Negro, Jew, Foreigner."

The final line, which pronounces the speaker's death—"from now on
I am / no more—only a bicycle"—can also be read as a statement of its
afterlife as an object. The copula of the last line, in the form of the dash,
enforces the aporetic logic of the poem to suggest that the speaker's
identity rests upon the simultaneous disavowal and invocation of its
object status. The poem takes place from the perspective of the bike, the
perspective of an object that has been separated from its "I." From this
perspective, there is not dialogue between the "I" and others, only violence, but this interaction between the "I" and its "me" is what emerges
out of the failure of dialogue, out of the perception that dialogue entails
this violence toward the other. This is the dialogism that is made possible in the many situations in which dialogue—as a form of direct

engagement between a "you" and a "me"—would only be possible if the violence that constitutes this relation were rendered imperceptible. Çirak's poems stage the return from the intercultural to the intralinguistic, but it's through the thwarted possibility of dialogue that they pass, so that the return to language is "not but nothing other than" this process of so-called intercultural exchange.[12] What is derived from this form, however, is knowledge about how the other is produced as a fact (or a fiction, or a form, or a figure) of discourse. In this scheme, the bike as "other" does not reflect back to the subject its blindness or its internal otherness, the exception through which it is constituted, but the bike is, as a parsing of Silva's text reads, "produced as an other so that the transparent 'I' exists."[13] Using the bike as a substitute object, Çirak draws attention to how thwarting dialogue functions as a way of opening up the confines of this space in which the "I" appears compelled to be defined through its relation to an other. By showing how nonintegration, as the unintegrated state of the psyche and soma, allows for the "me" to take place, in more cases than not, as a "not-me," Çirak also imagines an object world parallel to the world-as-a-force-of-integration.[14] Çirak seems to propose that such an object world has the capacity to call into question those relations between text and social world that are based on a scheme of referentiality that proceeds from the idea that the text can tell us something about the world and vice versa. Imagining the "world" of Europe as nothing more than a desire, but one that is powerfully interpellated in the processes of individual and collective constitution, Çirak describes a scenario in which what is valued is neither dialogic communication between an "I" and a "you" nor the disintegration of referentiality and of the "I" through heteroglossia and language play. Instead, the model of psychoanalytic nonintegration makes it possible to see the concomitant presence of alternative desire and of a dialogic relation between the "I" and its objective status as a "me." This alternative potentially marks a distinct limit to European knowledge because Europe's interaction with its others still extends only as far as its own not-me.

Notes

1. In this essay, the idea of "nonintegreation" will be considered mainly in contrast to the normative process of integration through the terms proposed by the British psychoanalyst D. W. Winnicott in his writings on the emotional life of children and healthy individuals.

2. John Kim discusses Naoki Sakai's critique of Émile Benveniste's distinction between the subject of enunciation and the subject of the enunciated. Citing Jacques Lacan, Kim proceeds to describe how the foreclosed subject is divided as a "first person" subject and ethnicized as a "third person," and he uses the trope of "deixis" to think about this disjuncture (349). My discussion focuses on the reflexive moment in which the "I" posits itself as its own object—not as an "I" in utterance or as a third-person object, but as a first-person object, as a "me."

3. Kristeva describes how Dialogism differs from the logic of monolingualism, but she concludes that dialogue in a work is composed from both monologic and dialogic spaces. She claims that the work's "ambivalent space thus can be seen as regulated by two formative principles: monological (each follow-ing sequence is determined by the preceding one), and dialogical (transfinite sequences that are next-larger to the preceding causal series)" (42–3).

4. See Petra Fachinger's discussion of this poem in *Rewriting Germany from the Margins* (47–8).

5. Gayatri Spivak's "Can the Subaltern Speak?" has phrased the question of subaltern agency in this manner; see also Peter Hitchcock, *Dialogics of the Oppressed*.

6. See Winnicott's discussion of the unintegrated state in infant life, schiz-oid disorder, and in the healthy individual in "The Concept of a Healthy Individual" (28–9).

7. The idea of the "next larger" is Julia Kristeva's, in her parsing of the logic of dialogic ambivalence.

8. The central example of the way that the mind functions as a metaphor is given in "The Epistemology of Metaphor" (25).

9. There is a discussion in theories of afro-pessimism about a subjective state that seems related to the idea of nonintegration and the unintegrated state, although there are notable differences in the social realities of negativity that these states refer to. The negativity of the unintegrated state is foundational of identity, as Jack Halberstam writes in "The Wild Beyond," an introduc-tion to Fred Moten and Stefano Harney's *The Undercommons*: "Indeed, black-ness, for Moten and Harney by way of Fanon, is the willingness to be in the space that has been abandoned by colonialism, by rule, by order" (8). One of the more prominent psychoanalytic models of ego nonintegration and race is David Marriott's theorization of the "subject of redress": "This state of being at war forecloses upon the possession of elements constitu-tive of psychic integration . . . the black ego, far from being too immature or weak to integrate, is an absence haunted by its and others' negativity" (Marriott, cited in Wilderson 30). In the critical thought of afro-pessimism, the black subject is an absence qualified by the concept "dispossession," as Marriot finds, an "evacuated space." The evacuated space coincides with the internalized negative other, and yet, they are not the same thing. Marriott writes: "This evacuated space represents a place where whites care to—or dare—not go, a space that a type of x-ray might reveal as black alienation and psychic dispossession" (*Haunted Life* 207). Moving toward an approxi-mation of this psychoanalytic register, Jared Sexton writes: "what I take to be a certain aggression, or perhaps anxiety, in the deconstruction of the structure of vulnerability and the grammar of suffering that undergird afro-pessimism is not a sign of pathology in the moral register, but rather a

matter of the apprehension of psychic—and political—reality in a properly psychoanalytic sense: an effect of misrecognition, a problem of register and symbolization, an optical illusion or echo that dissimulates the course and force of its propagation" (36). Sexton describes how the affective response of "anxiety" or "aggression" registers psychic and political reality, the reality of misrecognition, the effect of being misrecognized that attends a subject who is thought through the scheme of dependency that constantly references identity's negativity.

10. See Jennifer Marston William's reading of the metaphors invoked in this title in "Cognitive Poetics and Common Ground in a Multicultural Context: The Poetry of Zehra Çirak" (184).
11. Marilya Veteto-Conrad translates this title "No Sand in the Gears of Time" in "Zehra Çirak: Foreign Wings on Familiar Shoulders" (356–7).
12. Fred Moten uses the formulation "not but nothing other than," which I find logically appealing as a formula for poetic dialogism, to phrase the relationship between blackness and Western civilization: "Blackness is not but nothing other than Western civilization" (1744).
13. This quotation is a summary by *profacero* of Silva's *Toward a Global Idea of Race* posted under the entry "Breakdown of Denise Ferreira da Silva: *Toward a Global Theory of Race*" (12 March 2009) on the blog *Seminario Permanente de Teoria y Critica*.
14. Like Çirak, Sexton seems to find that the "world" exists as a desire, as a desire for integration: "No, Blackness is not the pathogen in afro-pessimism, the world is. Not the earth, but the world, and maybe even the whole possibility of and desire for a world" (30).

Works cited

Adelson, Leslie. *The Turkish Turn in Contemporary German Literature*. London: Palgrave Macmillan, 2005.

Adorno, Theodor. "On Lyric Poetry and Society." *Notes to Literature I*. Trans. Shierry Weber Nicholson. New York: Columbia UP, 1991. 37–54.

Bakhtin, Mikhail. "Discourse in the Novel." *The Dialogic Imagination: Four Essays by M.M. Bakhtin*. Ed. Michael Holquist. Trans. Caryl Emerson and Michael Holquist. Austin: U of Texas P, 1981. 259–422.

Balibar, Etienne. "Europe as Borderland." Talk given for the Alexander von Humboldt Lecture in Human Geography, University of Nijmegen, November 10, 2004.

——. "The Geneological Scheme: Race or Culture." *Trans-Scripts* 1 (2011): 1–9.

——. *We, the People of Europe? Reflections on Transnational Citizenship*. Trans. James Swenson. Princeton: Princeton UP, 2004.

Çirak, Zehra. *Fremde Flügel auf Eigener Schulter*. Cologne: Kiepenheuer & Witsch, 1994.

——. *Vogel auf dem Rücken eines Elefanten*. Cologne: Kiepenheuer & Witsch, 1991.

De Man, Paul. "Dialogism and Dialogue." *Resistance to Theory*. Minneapolis: U of Minnesota P, 1986. 106–14.

——. "The Epistemology of Metaphor." *Critical Inquiry* 5.1 (Autumn 1978): 13–30.

Enzensberger, Hans Magnus. "Poetry and Politics." Trans. Michael Roloff. *Critical Essays*. Ed. Reinhold Grimm. New York: Continuum, 1982. 15–34.

Fachinger, Petra. "A New Kind of Creative Energy: Yadé Kara's *Selam Berlin* and Fatih Akin's *Kurz und Schmerzlos* and *Gegen die Wand*." *German Life and Letters* 60.2 (April 2007): 243–60.

——. *Re-writing Germany from the Margins*. Montreal: McGill-Queen's UP, 2001.

Freud, Sigmund. *Civilization and its Discontents*. Ed. and Trans. James Strachey. New York: W. W. Norton & Company, 1989.

Gramling, David. "On the Other Side of Monolingualism: Fatih Akin's Linguistic Turn(s)." *The German Quarterly* 83.3 (Summer 2010): 353–72.

Halberstam, Jack. "Introduction." *The Undercommons: Fugitive Planning & Black Study*. New York: Minor Compositions, 2013. 2–12.

Hitchcock, Peter. *Dialogics of the Oppressed*. Minneapolis: U of Minnesota P, 1993.

Kim, John Namjun. "Ethnic Irony: The Poetic Parabasis of the Promiscuous Personal Pronoun in Yoko Tawada's 'Eine leere Flasche' (A Vacuous Flask)." *The German Quarterly* 83.3 (Summer 2010): 333–52.

Kristeva, Julia. "Word, Dialogue and Novel." Trans. Alice Jardine, Thomas Gora, and Leon S. Roudiez. *The Kristeva Reader*. Ed. Toril Moi. New York: Columbia UP, 1986. 34–61.

Marriott, David. *Haunted Life: Visual Culture and Black Modernity*. New Brunswick: Rutgers UP, 2007.

Moten, Fred. "Black Op." *PMLA* 123.5 (2008): 1743–7.

——. and Stefano Harney. *The Undercommons: Fugitive Planning & Black Study*. New York: Minor Compositions, 2013.

Sexton, Jared. "The Social Life of Social Death." *InTensions Journal* 5 (Fall/Winter 2011). York University. Web.

Silva, Denise Ferreira da. *Toward a Global Idea of Race*. Minneapolis: U of Minnesota P, 2005.

Spivak, Gayatri Chakravorty. "Can the Subaltern Speak?" *Marxism and the Interpretation of Culture*. Ed. C. Nelson and L. Grossberg. Basingstoke: Macmillan Education, 1998. 271–313.

Veteto-Conrad, Marilya. "'Innere Unruhe'? Zehra Çirak and Minority Literature Today." *Rocky Mountain Review of Language and Literature* 53.2 (1999): 59–74.

——. "Zehra Çirak: Foreign Wings on Familiar Shoulders." *Homemaking: Women Writers and the Politics and Poetics of Home*. Ed. Catherine Wiley and Fiona R. Barnes. New York: Garland Publishing, 1996. 335–59.

Wilderson, Frank B. III. "The Vengeance of Vertigo: Aphasia and Abjection in the Political Trials of Black Insurgents." *InTensions Journal* 5 (Fall/Winter 2011). York University. Web.

William, Jennifer Marston. "Cognitive Poetics and Common Ground in a Multicultural Context: The Poetry of Zehra Çirak." *The German Quarterly* 85.2 (Spring 2012): 173–92.

Winnicott, D. W. "The Concept of a Healthy Individual." *Home is Where We Start From: Essays by a Psychoanalyst*. New York: W. W. Norton & Company, 1990. 21–34.

——. *Playing and Reality*. London: Routledge, 2005.

——. "Primitive Emotional Development." *Collected Papers: Through Paediatrics to Psycho-Analysis*. New York: Basic Books, 1958. 145–56.

Index

CPSIA information can be obtained at www.ICGtesting.com
Printed in the USA
LVOW10*1734120315

430312LV00008B/137/P